The Library of Liberal Arts

OSKAR PIEST, *General Editor*

[NUMBER SEVENTY-ONE]

John Stuart Mill

CONSIDERATIONS ON
REPRESENTATIVE GOVERNMENT

Works of Mill
in "The Library of Liberal Arts"

Autobiography
   With an Introduction by Currin V. Shields. (LLA 91)

On Liberty
   Edited, with an Introduction, by Currin V. Shields.
   (LLA 61)

Representative Government
   Edited, with an Introduction, by Currin V. Shields.
   (LLA 71)

Theism
   Edited, with an Introduction, by Richard Taylor.
   (LLA 64)

Utilitarianism
   With an Introduction by Oskar Piest. (LLA 1)

John Stuart Mill

CONSIDERATIONS ON
REPRESENTATIVE
GOVERNMENT

Edited with an Introduction by
CURRIN V. SHIELDS
Associate Professor of Political Science
University of California, Los Angeles

THE LIBERAL ARTS PRESS
NEW YORK

Published at 153 West 72nd Street, New York 23, N. Y.

———————————————

Printed in the United States of America

CONTENTS

THE POLITICAL THOUGHT OF
JOHN STUART MILL

I

The *Considerations on Representative Government* was
John Stuart Mill's most ambitious political treatise. It is without doubt the fullest statement we have of his mature political
thought.[1]

Representative Government was one of Mill's later works.
It was written years after both *A System of Logic* (1843) and
Principles of Political Economy (1848)—the writings which
made Mill a prominent figure in British intellectual life—had
become standard works in the library of every well-read gen-
tleman. Several years after his retirement from service with the
East India Company and the death of his wife—two major
events in Mill's life, both occurring in 1858—and several years
before his election as a member of the House of Commons
for Westminster, Mill wrote his treatise. He composed it for
the most part in 1860.

This was a year of great controversy in England, generally
over political principles and their philosophical foundations,

[1] This introduction is almost entirely devoted to an analysis and criticism of Mill's political thought. For other discussions about Mill, the
reader is referred to three other volumes in "The Library of Liberal Arts"
recently published by the Liberal Arts Press: for an account of the philosophical tradition which is the background for the younger Mill's thought,
see my introduction to James Mill, *An Essay on Government* (LLA 47;
1955); for information about Mill's life and work, see my introduction
to John Stuart Mill, *Autobiography* (LLA 91; 1957); for a sketch of
Mill as a political essayist and a brief critical analysis of his views about
liberty and authority, see my introduction to John Stuart Mill, *On
Liberty* (LLA 61; 1956).

and specifically over parliamentary reform. In America, where democratic principles had been carried to the most advanced point in political experience, the bitter conflict between the States was ready to break out in violent war. In England, where Liberal principles had been vested with the sanctity of law, the dominance of the middle class was in jeopardy. Spokesmen for the new industrial working class, which was rapidly increasing in importance in British life, were demanding a share of political privilege and were getting a hearing from the Tory Democrat, Benjamin Disraeli. The movement into which John Mill had been born—Utilitarianism—was, after a short history of glorious accomplishment, disintegrating into squabbling sects. New movements, stimulated by a congenial Darwinian climate, were just getting under way. During this year of intellectual ferment and social change—and political crisis—John Stuart Mill, son of a radical reformer but himself a reformed radical, summed up his thoughts about politics in his major treatise.[2]

In *Representative Government* we find no really new ideas. This Mill himself concedes in his preface. Mill's friend and first biographer, Alexander Bain, states that even Mill's earliest political essays pointed in the direction of *Representative Government*.[3] This statement perhaps says too much. However, the main themes developed in *Representative Government* were initially advanced in works written years before. In his review of Tocqueville's two volume *Democracy in America* (1835, 1840) Mill set the pattern of his argument against majority rule. In a pamphlet published in 1859, *Thoughts on Parliamentary Reform*, he stated his distinctive views about minority representation, plural voting, and the secret ballot. Neither the principle of representation nor Mill's use of it in his theory was novel. The concept of representation which Mill elaborated in *Representative Government*

[2] The *Considerations on Representative Government* was first published in April, 1861, at London. Many other editions have since appeared.

[3] Alexander Bain, *John Stuart Mill: A Criticism; with Personal Recollections* (London, 1882), p. 40.

bears a close family resemblance to the doctrine his father advanced in the famous *Essay on Government* (1820). That essay, the finest statement we have of Benthamite political teachings, was (by John Stuart's own testimony) regarded by the "Philosophical Radicals" as "a masterpiece of political wisdom."

For the most part, then, *Representative Government* is a systematic summation of political views already expressed by Mill in one way or another. This summation takes the form of an extended discussion, divided into eighteen chapters, of a series of cognate political questions. Mill ostensibly discusses these questions in relation to representative government.

Mill's *Representative Government* has value today as a political treatise even though parts of it are definitely dated. Many questions which in Mill's time were highly controversial no longer agitate British opinion; in the course of almost a century of political change they have, for practical purposes, been satisfactorily settled. But in setting forth his views about those questions, Mill elucidated his distinctive political theory. Mill's beliefs were popular with an impressive body of Victorian opinion. They still find some adherents today.

First let us sketch the main line of argument Mill advances in his treatise, and then proceed to examine the major articles in John Stuart Mill's political creed.

II

Mill begins his treatise by considering a question suggested by Benthamite teachings: Are forms of government invented by men to suit their desires, or are they products of historical experience? Bentham held that men can deliberately design and adopt political institutions as they choose. Mill concedes that in this view there is some truth, but also, he says, there is some truth in the opposite view. He takes a middle position— political institutions are the work of men, but they must be adjusted to the capacities of the people who live under them. For a set of institutions to function properly, a people must be ready, willing, and able to work them. Though political institutions reflect the more fundamental conditions in a society, such as property and intelligence, they also reflect "moral influence"—the condition of opinion and will—at work in that society. So, Mill concludes, the form of government is a matter of rational choice, though choices must be made within very definite limits. Hence the question of the best form of government, both ideally and relative to a particular people, is a worthwhile one to consider.

Mill next turns to the question of the proper criterion for choosing political institutions. What form of government best promotes the interests of a society? To answer this question it is first necessary, says Mill, to determine the proper end of government, since government is merely a means. To say that "order" or "progress" are the objects of government is no help. The preservation of what exists is an indispensable condition of government but not the sole object. Moreover, the same human qualities—industry, integrity, justice, and prudence—contribute to the improvement as well as to the preservation of society; and the qualities which contribute to progress—mental activity, enterprise, courage, and inventiveness—are likewise required for order. Similarly with political institutions and policies, such as the police and taxation. However, though progress is not a requisite for order, order is a requisite for progress. Since order is a means, it follows that there is a sense in which "conduciveness to Progress . . . includes the whole excellence of a government."

But, Mill claims, another criterion is needed. It is as important to good government that a society not deteriorate as that it improve. So Mill poses the question: What are the causes and conditions of good government? The qualities of the citizens, he answers, the virtue and intelligence of the governed, is one element of good government. Hence a pertinent question to answer about political institutions is: To what extent do they foster the moral and intellectual qualities of the governed, individually and collectively? Another important element of good government is the quality of the machinery itself. To what extent do the political institutions utilize the moral and intellectual worth in the community? Mill thus concludes that the two proper criteria for evaluating forms of government are (1) the improvement in the character of the governed, and (2) the utilization of the community's virtue and talent.

Under any form of government, Mill claims, it is possible to utilize virtue and talent. But not so with the improvement of the governed. It is true that good government is relative; political institutions must be adapted to a society's stage of culture. For example, despotic rule might be best for a primitive tribe. At the same time, however, government is a principal means for cultural advancement. Hence the best form of government is always that which tends to advance a people to a higher level of social development. It follows that, to assure good government, political institutions must change as a people's culture advances.

After these preliminaries, Mill proceeds to consider the ideal form of government and the conditions necessary for its existence. Despotic rule, he says, may be a model of efficiency, and it may be temporarily necessary. But as a permanent arrangement despotism is unacceptable. Its main defect is the failure to exercise and improve the moral and intellectual faculties of the governed. The greatest benefits to a people are provided by a form of government where sovereignty is located in the entire community and every citizen performs a public function. This conclusion rests on two principles: first, that a person's interests are secure to the extent that he can actively promote them, and second, that the general interest of a community is best promoted by the maximum activity of individual members. The truth of the first principle is obvious. In regard to the second, active characters are intrinsically better than passive characters, since active characters are required for the cultivation of the three varieties of mental excellence—intellectual, practical, and moral. Passive characters are encouraged by government by one or a few, while government by the many encourages active characters. Thus popular government is superior to despotic rule in both advancing the welfare of a community and improving the characters of its citizens. Because of these advantages, popular participation in government should be as great as a community's stage of cultural development allows. The ultimate aim would be participation by all in the sovereign power. But as a practical matter, self-government is an impossible goal. Hence the ideally best form is representative government.

What are the social conditions necessary for representative government? Representative government cannot permanently exist unless the three afore-mentioned conditions—that the people are ready, willing, and able to participate in public affairs—are fulfilled. At the earliest stage of a community's development, when the people have yet to learn the first lesson of civilization—obedience—royal rule is most suitable. Other shortcomings in a people can disqualify them for representative government, though rule by one or a few might not be any improvement over popular rule. In some cases, where the people lack capacity and a really superior class exists, some form of aristocratic rule may be the best possible. The critical test of a people's fitness for popular rule is the relative strength of two conflicting desires which varies among different peoples—the desire to exercise power over others, and the desire not to have power exercised over themselves. A people in whom the second desire is predominant is fit for representative government.

After considering the best form of government and the conditions necessary for its existence, Mill turns to questions about the functioning of representative government. Representative government, he says, is where the whole people exercise the sovereign power through their elected deputies. What are the proper functions of a representative assembly? It is important to distinguish, says Mill, between actually performing the business of government and controlling the performance. A representative assembly should do only that which it can best perform and control the rest. An assembly can deliberate better than an individual, but it cannot act nearly as well. Hence a representative assembly should not try to administer governmental affairs directly. Administration is a highly skilled business which depends on special information and rules of conduct. A representative assembly is not fit even to determine the special qualifications of administrators. What it can do is to select the ministers by passing on nominees (as in the British cabinet system). Further, a representative assembly is not competent to enact laws. Legislation, too, is a "work of skilled labor and special study and experience" which calls for professional talent. The representative assembly should determine who should draft the laws. The technical job of drafting legislation would be best done, Mill contends, by a nonpolitical legislative commission composed of experts. The representative assembly should merely pass on the proposals submitted, by approving, rejecting, or referring them back to the commission. In general, then, the proper function of a representative assembly is to "watch and control" the conduct of governmental affairs entrusted to "a specially trained and experienced Few." Another sort of function a representative assembly can perform is to serve as "an arena of public opinion" where conflicting views can be expressed and explored in public debate.

What are the infirmities and dangers to which representative government is liable? In any form of government, the defects may be negative or positive. A negative defect is insufficient power in the offices of government to do the job of governing. In a representative system, the danger is that the power to govern will not be properly concentrated because of legislative interference in the work of administration. Another negative defect is insufficient exercise of the citizens' capabilities; this results when public functions are not widely enough diffused among the people. Of the positive defects, one is the low level of competence in the "controlling body"; representative government is specially liable to this defect. Bureaucratic rule, though it fails to exercise the citizens' capabilities, tends to be efficient because technical skill and ability are utilized. The opposite is true with representative government; there the tendency is toward inefficiency because the need for professional talent is not fully appreciated. The danger is that the citizens and their representatives attempt more than they are competent to do. Another positive defect is the tendency of special interests to influence the representative assembly at the expense of the general interest. In a monarchy or an aristocracy, a common weakness is the continuing conflict between the interests of the rulers and those of the community. The same weakness exists in popular government, where the tendency is for the special interest of a numerical majority to displace the interest of all. The result is class legislation. We must recognize that in practice rulers often neglect their real interest in the pursuit of their apparent interest. It is true that persons differ in character, but power encourages everyone to prefer his selfish and immediate interest to his indirect and remote interest. Since governments must be made for men as they are or can soon become, how can this evil tendency be prevented in a representative government? The two great sets of interests in modern society are those of capital and labor. These two classes should be equally balanced in the government so neither can dominate the other. Since a minority of each class tends to pursue the general interest, the aim should be to balance the conflicting interests in such a way that each part of one class is dependent on a part of the other class to obtain a majority.

Mill next considers the question of how the dangers inherent in representative government—incompetence and class legislation—can be minimized without impairing the benefits of popular government. The government of all by a majority, exclusively represented, is, says Mill, a false idea of democracy. "False democracy" is actually a government of privilege, for minorities are in effect disfranchised. A majority should be able to outvote a minority in a representative assembly, but minorities should have their representatives too. In a "true democracy" minorities would be adequately represented in the assembly. Hence the true idea of democracy is a government of all by all, equally represented. The best way to assure adequate representation of minorities is the scheme proposed by Thomas Hare for parliamentary elections. By Hare's plan for proportional representation: (1) all representatives would be elected "at large" in one national constituency; (2) to be elected, a candidate must secure the number of votes equal to the quotient of the number of voters divided by the number of seats in the assembly; (3) voters could list several candidates on their ballots in order of preference; (4) any candidate who received the necessary quota of first-choice votes would immediately be elected; (5) alternate choices would then be counted until the prescribed number of representatives was elected. This scheme, Mill claims, has some real advantages. Minorities could elect representatives in proportion to their voting strength; virtually every elector would be represented in the assembly. The elected representatives would possess the highest possible qualifications—they would be a true elite. Why? The natural tendency in popular government, Mill argues, is toward collective mediocrity, a tendency encouraged by extending the franchise. Hare's plan offers an effective antidote to this tendency. Minorities would of course vote for exceptionally able candidates; thus the majority would have to run candidates of similar caliber in order to win votes. Also, opposition by an "instructed minority"—which after all is the best check on a majority in a representative assembly—would be guaranteed. While Hare's plan has these advantages, Mill says, there is no valid argument against adopting it. America already suffers from "collective despotism," but England still can, through Hare's plan, avoid such a fate. The main arguments offered against the plan are that it would permit sects and cliques to obtain undue power, and that it would be abused to augment the influence of parties. Actually, by Hare's plan, party influences would be curbed and minorities would simply obtain the representation they deserve. The real obstacle to adoption is a mistaken notion about the plan's complexity. That it is not in practice so complex could be shown by giving it a fair trial.

Mill then considers whether the franchise should be restricted. The real issue in representative government, says Mill, is how to prevent the abuse of power by a numerical majority. Restricting the suffrage is not a satisfactory solution to this problem. Moreover, a restricted franchise does some harm. Voting has educational value for the citizen. Also, a person who is denied the vote is apt to become malcontent. To deny a person the vote unless the purpose is to prevent an evil is unjust. Though the franchise should be extended as much as possible, certain qualifications for voting are imperative. A voter should be able to read, write, and "calculate," and should be a payer of direct taxes. A person who is on parish relief, hence financially dependent on the community, should be disqualified from voting.

But even when only really qualified persons have the vote, Mill says, the danger of ignorant, class legislation remains. The solution to this problem is to give persons whose opinions are entitled to greater weight two or more votes—"plural voting." Though everyone should have a voice, it should not be an equal voice. Political equality as practiced in America is a false creed, detrimental to moral and intellectual excellence since those who have strength can rely on will rather than reason. Voting should be weighted in favor of knowledge and intelligence. The basis for weighting should be, not property, but "mental superiority." How can such superiority be ascertained, as a practical matter? Occupation is an adequate test; for example, a banker is likely to be more intelligent than a shopkeeper, an employer more intelligent than an employee. Educational attainment is another test. Plural voting should be limited only so that no single class would be able to outvote the rest of the community. Mill adds that sex should not be a disqualification for voting.

Mill next discusses the merits of direct and indirect elections. Indirect elections, where voters choose electors who in turn select the representatives, have been advocated as a means to curb the popular influence. This view is plausible, but the practice lessens the benefits of popular government since public spirit and political intelligence are thereby cultivated less than with direct election. Indirect election may also, as in the case of the American presidency, encourage partisanship. The best form of election in America is the system of indirect election of United States senators.[4] But this system requires a federal constitution with the electors (state legislators) performing other public functions as well. The conclusion: the advantages of indirect election can actually be obtained by direct election, and indirect election has certain disadvantages. So although indirect election might have a temporary use, it is undesirable as a permanent arrangement.

Should voting be in public, or by secret ballot? The secret ballot, Mill says, is undesirable; it encourages the pursuit of selfish interests. The vote is a public trust, and the voter's duty is to give his best opinion of the public good. This duty should be performed in the public eye and subject to criticism, because a person's need to justify his act conduces to more responsible conduct. The claim that public voting allows the voter to be subjected to sinister influences is unfounded. The secret ballot is no longer necessary; the power of the few over the many is so declining in western Europe that there is now no need to fear class dictation. At the same time, persons who may not be fit to be electors (such as members of the working class) may still be fit to exert influence on electors; this they can do best if voting is public.

Mill then turns to some related issues of parliamentary reform. He argues that campaign expenditures of candidates should be strictly limited so voters are not influenced by extraneous considerations in casting their ballots. Also, that members of Parliament should not be paid because a salaried post would attract self-seeking, vulgar persons and demagogues; a qualified person without independent income should be subsidized by the subscription of his affluent constituents.

How long should the term of a representative be? It should not be so long that he forgets his reponsibility to the public good, or so short that he is unable to pursue a course of action.

[4] Abolished in 1913 by the Seventeenth Amendment to the United States Constitution.

Depending on whether the prevailing tendency is toward aristocratic or democratic domination, the term should be from three to five years. But even the seven-year term, though rather long, is not so long as to warrant much effort to reduce it. In regard to the question of whether representatives should be eligible for re-election, Mill contends that there are no advantages in banning re-election and some serious disadvantages.

Should a representative be bound by instructions from his constituents? No. A representative should be responsible to the voters, but he is naturally wiser than they. Superior minds, which conclude differently from ordinary minds, should not be restrained by pledges sought by ordinary minds. The voters should respect differences from their opinions and should judge their representative's ability by such signs as proven public service, leadership, and experience. With untried men whose characters are as yet unknown, it is necessary to rely on the judgments of those who know them best. Generally, then, a representative should not make pledges to his constituents; he should insist on following his better judgment of the public good. It is even more important in a "false democracy" than in a "true democracy" that a representative be a free agent.

The institution of the second chamber as a means of curbing the popular influence is, says Mill, of secondary importance. If there are two chambers, they can be similar or dissimilar in composition. If the upper chamber is similar to the popular house, no special advantage is achieved. And with two houses there is always the disadvantage of inconvenient delay in the proceedings. In a representative government a second chamber would be useful only if it tended to oppose the class interests of the majority. The strongest argument in favor of a second chamber is that, generally, when power is diffused despotism is discouraged and compromise is encouraged; this of course is desirable. If the second chamber is intended to restrain the popular house, it must be composed differently. But its effectiveness would depend on its public support; the House of Lords restrains the Commons only to the extent that British society is aristocratic in character. It is true that in every well-ordered polity there should be a center of resistance to the predominant power—in a representative government, to the democratic assembly. But the best way to curb the popular influence is to diffuse power, not between two chambers, but within the democratic assembly itself through proportional representation and plural voting. The finest example of a second chamber is the Roman Senate, which was composed of elder statesmen of proven merit and virtue. In England, the best form of second chamber would be an assembly of life peers selected on the basis of merit from among the most distinguished figures in British public life.

Next Mill turns to the question of the executive in a representative government. As a general rule, says Mill, the authority and responsibility to act should not be divided; instead, they should be concentrated and clearly fixed in one individual. Plural bodies are not suited for administrative work, though an administrator should use a "council" of competent professionals as advisors. No executive official should be elected by the people or their representatives. Administering government business is skilled employment for which special qualifications are required. Executive officials should be appointed by their administrative superiors, who should also have the power to remove them. The "chief executive" should be selected by the legislature. Popular election of the chief executive means that eminent men will not be selected and that the chief executive must cater to the public for approval. The principle of dissolution of the House of Commons is sound because it forestalls a serious deadlock between the executive and the legislature. The judiciary above all must be completely free from popular influence. The people are not competent to assess judicial qualifications; voters are partial, while impartiality is the essential quality of justice. The jury is one of the very few cases, however, where it is better for the people to act directly rather than through their representatives; it is "almost the only case in which the errors that a person exercising authority may commit can be better borne than the consequences of making him responsible for them." Of course professional civil servants should be completely divorced from politics. Appointments should be made on a merit basis, by competitive examinations. Such recruitment has an added advantage of exerting a salutary influence on the educational system. Promotion generally should depend on seniority, but in special circumstances on record of performance.

Mill moves next to some questions of local government. Central governments, he says, try to do too much; local representative bodies should handle strictly local affairs. Moreover, the educational value of participation in local government for the citizens is so great that local authority should be as extensive as possible. How should local representative bodies be composed? Generally on the same principles as for the national legislature, except that in local affairs property should be allowed a larger voice. Every municipality should have one central council. Most difficulties in local government result from the poor caliber of the persons who participate; one council would attract into public service the highest quality of mind available in the community. The same principles apply to the administration of local governmental affairs as to the national. Should a local government have full authority to perform its functions or should its activities be supervised by central authorities? Local officials are inferior in ability to national officials, and local opinion, both public and press, is likewise inferior. On the other hand, interest in a community and the opportunity to observe the conduct of public business is greater in a locality. Knowledge is centralized, though power is localized. Generally, the central authority should restrict its function to that of instructing in principles, which should then be applied by the local officials. However, the central authority should interfere in local affairs if a majority attempts to oppress a minority.

Then Mill considers the relation between "nationality" and representative government. Nationality, he says, exists when a people share common sympathies not shared with other people.

Nationality is based more on common experiences than on a common race, language, or religion. As a general principle, the boundaries of a government should coincide with those of nationality, though geography sometimes hinders the application of this principle. In a country of different nationalities, where antipathies are strong, joint resistance to government ineffective, and sympathy between the army and the public lacking, popular government is not possible. The mixing of nationalities in one country, where the inferior are improved by the influence of a superior nationality, is beneficial, though sometimes this intermingling is not practical.

Mill next discusses the subject of "federalism." In a country where national union is not possible, a federal system, wherein power is divided between a central and state governments, is sometimes desirable. For a stable federation, several conditions must be fulfilled. The population of the country must have mutual sympathies, the separate states must not be so strong that they can rely on their own strength in dealing with foreign countries, and the several states must be roughly equal—no one or a few can be predominant within the federation. The two modes of federal government are (1) where the central government acts on the component states only, and (2) where it acts directly on the citizens. The second is the only satisfactory principle, since otherwise local majorities can with impunity act contrary to the central government. In a federal system a supreme court is the best means to determine questions of state-federal jurisdictions. A federation is beneficial to the extent that the practice of co-operation is extended. But if conditions permit, union is much more desirable than federation.

In the final chapter Mill discusses the government of dependencies by a "free state." Dependencies, he says, are of two types: one, where the peoples are backward and inferior; the other where they are equal in advancement to the governing state. With the second type of dependency, the only wise policy is that of self-determination within the empire. Imperial federation is not practical, since in an empire the requisite conditions for federation are lacking. Yet an empire has value in that international peace and co-operation are encouraged. With a backward people, the dependency is in a state of tutelage. What is the best mode of governing such peoples? The dangers are twofold: that the natives will be forced to conform to the customs and practices of the ruling state, and that the special interests of colonists from the mother country will be favored over the interests of the native peoples. The general principle is that a free state should not directly rule backward peoples (like the East Indians); instead, it should provide able rulers through an intermediate governing body (like the East India Company). This intermediate body should have a vested interest in good government of the dependency, and as little interest as possible in poor government. Experience shows that by keeping the government of dependencies out of domestic politics and in the hands of professional, career administrators, the most effective rule of backward peoples is possible. The only colonial official who should be selected from outside the career service is a governor-general.

Thus ends Mill's argument in *Representative Government.*

III

What exactly is John Stuart Mill trying to accomplish in this treatise? Aside from the final chapter appended to the rest of the work where he is obviously attempting to vindicate his former employer, the East India Company, Mill is occupied not so much with considerations on representative government as with criticisms of self-government. The theme he elaborates throughout his argument is that the common people are not competent to govern themselves; they should be ruled by "a specially trained and experienced Few." Though he starts out by praising the virtues of popular government, he ends by repudiating the essential principles of democratic rule. In this treatise Mill is evidently trying to discredit democracy as a form of government.

Why does Mill, in his principal treatise on politics, set this task for himself? When Mill was thirty years of age, he read the first volume of Alexis de Tocqueville's remarkable work, *Democracy in America*, and wrote a lengthy, laudatory review of it. Five years later, when the second volume was published, Mill wrote another review, again praising Tocqueville's book. In this review Mill termed *Democracy in America* "the first philosophical book ever written on Democracy, as it manifests itself in modern society." [5] This book, Mill concedes in his *Autobiography,* exerted a profound influence on his thinking about politics.

By "democracy" Tocqueville, and Mill, meant self-government, direct participation by the governed in the exercise of governmental authority. Democratic rule depended on two principles widely accepted in America: that in exercising authority each member of a community should count for one and no more than one, and that the exercise of authority over a community should be determined by the vote of a majority. Such a mode of government, founded on these principles of political equality and majority rule, was, Mill realized, a novel phenomenon in political experience. For many centuries a few had ruled the many; now in the American experiment the many were governing themselves, without benefit of an elite. Mill believed, as did Tocqueville, that as time passed the principles of democracy practiced in America would gain wider favor and more adherents in Europe. Democracy, for good or ill, was "on the march." In fact, it was the agitation for democratic reforms in Britain which largely inspired Mill to write *Representative Government.*

To his study of *Democracy in America* Mill attributed his "growing reservations" about the desirability of popular government. The book gave him, he said, a keener awareness of the "dangers" of democratic rule. Over the years, in company with Harriet Taylor, Mill's reservations continued to grow. It was Harriet's influence, Mill records, which first led him to doubt the desirability of "pure democracy"; Tocque-

5 *Edinburgh Review,* LXXII (Oct., 1840), 3.

ville's book merely confirmed their suspicions. By the time
Mill began writing his major political treatise, he had abandoned the principles of democratic rule.[6]

What Tocqueville portrayed with accuracy as democracy in
America, Mill feared and despised. Mill takes pains to define
the form of popular rule practiced in this country as "false
democracy." In *Representative Government* as in his other
writings Mill often points to American practice to illustrate a
political principle to which he was opposed. It is true that
Mill did accept, after a fashion and within limits, the principle of popular sovereignty—that the authority binding on
the members of a community should be located in the
governed. Historical circumstances allowed him no feasible
alternative. With the religious convictions of one born into
the British Liberal tradition, he could not accept a doctrine
of divine right, either of one or a few, to rule. If authority
has no supernatural origins, it must be located, naturally
somehow, among men. For several centuries British Liberals
had contended that authority should be located in the
governed. Mill concurred. But he refused to accept the democratic corollaries of popular sovereignty exemplified in American experience—political equality and majority rule.

In 1840 Mill wrote: "Now, as ever, the great problem in
government is to prevent the strongest from becoming the
only power." [7] In 1860 this problem, as Mill posed it in his
treatise, took this form: In view of the trend toward democracy, how can rule by the many be restrained so that rule by a
qualified few can be preserved? The people are not competent
to govern themselves, yet they insist on playing a role in
government. This problem Mill was anxious to solve for his
time so that what had happened in America would not be repeated in Britain. In his treatise he stresses the "defects,"

6 In a letter written in 1865 to the American editor, E. L. Godkin,
Mill expressed grave fears about the leveling influence of democracy on
civilization. See *Letters of John Stuart Mill*, 2 vols., edited by Hugh
Elliott (London, 1910), II, 35-36. Mill expresses similar fears in several
passages in his *Autobiography*.

7 *Edinburgh Review*, LXXII (Oct., 1840), 47.

"infirmities," "inadequacies," "dangers" of democratic rule revealed by the American experience. *Representative Government* is mainly an appeal to British Liberals to stand firm in opposing those democratic reforms which would allow the "untutored masses" to participate in exercising governmental authority.

For this problem of how to stem the democratic tide, Mill proposes a solution which is ingenious, if not original, with him, and which has been a favorite scheme of elitist thinkers for generations. It is a rather intricate formula by which the people are supreme in theory but in practice are permitted to play no important role in exercising authority. The formula is evident in Mill's commendation of the theory of democracy. The virtue of popular government, he says, is its educational value; the moral and intellectual capacities of the governed are cultivated by participation in political affairs. But this is a backhanded denunciation of the practice of democracy. The education has value only because the people are not competent to exercise authority. Ruling is a skilled business for which ordinary people lack the requisite qualifications.

The key to Mill's formula for elite rule is the principle of representation. The people should not rule directly; they should rule through their "representatives." This principle is in Mill's theory an essential device for perpetuating elite rule. His formula includes in addition the following principles: (1) The vote should be restricted, by literacy and property qualifications, to the "better sort" of people. (2) The voters should be discouraged, by the casting of ballots in public, from voting in accord with their "sinister interests and discreditable feelings." (3) The elections should be weighted, by the practice of plural voting, in favor of the prosperous and educated minority. (4) The only officials popularly elected should be the members of the representative assembly. (5) Elections should guarantee, through proportional representation, that minorities elect representatives of their choice. (6) The representatives should be chosen from among the wealthy who have independent incomes. (7) The representative should not be bound by any commitment to his constituents. (8) The assembly should be limited in its function to that of ratifying proposals determined by professional rulers. (9) The professional rulers should be selected on a merit basis, free from political influence.

By this formula Mill would take the business of government out of politics. Plato's *Republic,* it has been said, is not a treatise on politics at all, but rather a scheme for a utopia wherein politics could not exist. The philosopher-kings would be responsible, in all their wisdom, only to themselves. In *Representative Government* Mill compromises his desires to admit the existence of politics. But then he systematically restricts popular participation in government to a point where "ordinary minds" have no chance to interfere with "superior minds" in the serious business of ruling. "Mere politicians" as well as ordinary citizens Mill denies any significant role in the governing process. The only role he allows any nonprofessional to play is in connection with deciding *who* should rule. Yet even here, Mill doubts the ability of ordinary voters to select "representatives," and of ordinary representatives to select the professional rulers. Mill insists that exercising authority is a skilled function which only technically trained specialists are competent to perform. Popular participation, beneficial as it may be in theory, is a luxury no well-ordered polity can afford in practice. Hence Mill's intricate formula for "the ideally best form of representative government"—by which the function of ruling would be a monopoly of an elite of "merit."

IV

Mill's attack on democratic rule and his defense of elite rule go hand in hand. The substance of his argument in *Representative Government* is that democracy may be desirable in theory but is impossible in practice and hence is not a suitable form of government. Rule by an elite of "merit" is both possible and desirable.

This thesis raises two fundamental political questions: Who should exercise authority? How should it be exercised? Mill's answer to the first question is that authority should be exercised by a "mentally superior" few; to the second, that authority should be exercised according to "true principles." Mill's belief that his answers to these questions are correct was not at all tempered by modesty. He was less sure about how to persuade the multitude of unenlightened disbelievers that his were the really true answers. Most passages in *Representative Government* Mill devoted to this effort, diligently and doggedly offering argument after argument.

Mill's contention that authority should in practice be exercised by an elite of "merit" appears to depend on a doctrine of cultural evolution according to which a people progresses from one stage of advancement to another. This doctrine supplies Mill with plausible grounds for denying the "lower classes" of his day any opportunity to participate meaningfully in political life. But by stressing the educational value of political participation, Mill certainly is saying that "in theory" popular rule is desirable, and he seems to be leaving the door open for the practice of democracy at some future date when society has progressed to a more advanced point in civilization.

This doctrine of cultural evolution, however, is not what it appears to be. In a naturalistic theory like Mill's, such a doctrine serves the same function that the doctrine of immortality does in the theory of a standpat religionist. Paradise cannot be entered yet, but perhaps it can be later, provided supplicants obtain redemption from their sins. Because salvation is never a sure thing, the endless search for redemption is all-important in this life. But paradise is not for this dreary world we live in, and such a doctrine adds nothing significant to Mill's theory.

Mill's actual case against democratic rule is quite differently founded. The governed would not rule themselves even in the ideally best form of representative government. Why? The answer turns on the second criterion of "good government" Mill stipulates. Certainly it is *desirable* that government cultivate the worth of the governed. But it is *necessary* that government call into the public service the finest "virtue and talent" available in the community. Otherwise the government would be inefficient. Relying on this criterion of "efficiency," Mill develops his case against the practice of democracy.

Mill predicates his political theory on some underlying beliefs about the nature of man and the world he lives in. Mill assumes that these beliefs provide firm theoretical grounds for his contention that a "mentally superior" few should exercise authority according to the "true principles" of politics. This assumption no doubt seemed more plausible to a nineteenth-century British rationalist like Mill than it does to a present-day thinker.

Mill believed that men are naturally endowed with a capacity for "reason." By using reason, they can obtain "knowledge" about the world. Men can do this by studying the lessons of "experience." Thus rational men can perceive in experience the "true principles" of nature. But in order for men to obtain knowledge, their natural capacity for reason must be duly cultivated; the mental faculties must be trained and exercised to understand the principles of things. The capacity for reason is not cultivated to the same extent in every individual. Because they differ in training and experience, individuals differ in their ability to obtain knowledge. Mill also believed—in any elitist theory this is crucial—that a higher degree of "intellectual and moral excellence" is always found in relatively few individuals. And because the differences among men individually result in differences among them collectively, some classes of individuals are superior to other classes. A select minority is always superior in quality to a great majority.

Related to these beliefs are Mill's views about human conduct. An individual should act to promote his interests in order to obtain what he desires. This he can do only when he acts rationally, guided by experience. Mental ability is thus a requisite for moral conduct. Though individuals should act to promote their interests, many actually do not. Ordinary individuals whose mental capacities are insufficiently cultivated cannot understand what their interests are or how to promote them. Out of passion and ignorance, they act contrary to their true interests, pursuing false ones. Hence they are incapable of moral conduct. Since a few "mentally superior" individuals know better than the rest what should and should not be done, individuals are not equal in their competence for moral conduct. Nor, of course, are classes of individuals.

From these beliefs Mill derives his arguments against democratic rule and in favor of elite rule: In every field of human experience there are "true principles" which can be known. In the field of politics there is a body of knowledge composed of the most enlightened doctrines and the principles they justify. These principles are better understood by those who are specially trained and experienced than by others. By use of their practiced reason and acquired knowledge, they can determine the real interests of individuals and classes. The majority of individuals, who are incapable of moral conduct, are of course not qualified to decide how authority should be exercised. Just as lack of ability disqualifies the majority from ruling, exceptional ability entitles a minority to direct political conduct. Hence Mill's conclusion that a "mentally superior" minority should exercise authority according to the true principles of politics.

Apparently Mill was convinced that by these arguments he had successfully rebutted the case for democratic rule. But Mill's claims for elite rule leave more than a few difficulties unresolved. His theory entails many assumptions of value which he is obliged somehow to justify. For Mill does not claim that a superior few in fact exercise authority or that authority is in fact exercised according to true principles. His claims are normative, not empirical: a superior few *should* exercise authority and it *should* be exercised according to true principles. It is from Mill's conception—or lack of conception

—of the role of value in political conduct that most of the unresolved difficulties in his theory result, in one way or another.

Mill is disposed to treat questions of value as if they were questions of fact. He mistakenly assumes that normative principles for guiding political conduct can be derived by an elite from their special knowledge or experience. A moral principle is, for Mill, a rule to be observed in conduct. Actual conduct may not be guided by Mill-type reason and knowledge, but moral conduct can be. By acting in accord with moral principles, an individual *can* promote his interests. Since an individual *should* desire to promote his interests, he *should* act morally. These assumptions of value, not fact, present real difficulties in Mill's theory.

We can perhaps most readily identify the difficulties in Mill's use of the terms "end" and "means" of conduct. Moral conduct, says Mill, results from the use of a desirable means to achieve a desired end. By examining the end sought and the means used to attain it, the morality of conduct can be determined. A desirable means is the best possible way to attain the end sought. This test of means poses some difficulty for Mill's theory, but the significant difficulty centers on his test for the "ends" of conduct.

Mill distinguishes between "instrumental" and "ultimate" ends. An instrumental end is desired not for itself but as a means to another end. Mill concedes that no proof can be offered for accepting an ultimate end; it is simply "given," so to speak. But Mill then argues that, given an end, the proper means can be determined by use of reason and knowledge, and that those competent to judge the desirability of means are qualified to prescribe moral conduct. In so arguing Mill in effect claims that competence to determine the desirability of the means carries with it competence to determine the desirability of the end of conduct. For this claim there is no basis in fact. In practice the value of a means cannot be determined apart from the value of the end in view. Before an individual can act "morally," a choice of an end as well as a means is required. The relation between an end and a means, hence a choice of means, may or may not turn on answers to questions of fact. And by reason and knowledge perhaps the relation between a "lower" and a "higher" end can be determined; the relation may be, as Mill assumes, a question of fact. However, the choice of an end of conduct, no matter its relation to another end, still turns on answers to questions of value. For an act to be moral, the end as well as the means must be judged desirable. Hence Mill's claim—that a superior few who know which means is best to attain an end are competent to prescribe moral conduct in practice—does not stand up.

Between what is desired by an individual and what is desirable for an individual there is a difference, obvious even to Mill. One is a question of fact, the other a question of value. Why should an individual act, not the way he desires, but the way Mill believes is desirable? The question suggests the problem of moral sanction. Why should a moral principle be practiced? In a theory of conduct founded on religious tenets, the ultimate sanction for moral principles is usually supernatural in character. In Christian teachings, for example, God punishes sinners: come the day of judgment, the damned enter eternal hell. Any sort of supernatural sanction is out of the question for Mill; the sanction for moral principles in his theory must be natural to this world. What Mill offers is the contention that experience shows conduct contrary to moral principles to have undesirable consequences: it is self-defeating for an individual, and it is detrimental to a society's progress. Supposedly, then, reason and knowledge conduce men to act morally. But this concept of moral sanction is meaningless even in Mill's own terms. He admits that experience shows nothing to ordinary individuals; only a select few ever see the light of true principles. Hence an ordinary individual cannot act morally if he acts in accord with his own desires. But he can act morally if he faithfully accepts as desirable whatever Mill believes is desirable. In Mill's theory, moral conduct for the majority of individuals depends on their unreasoned and uninformed acceptance of Mill's standards of value. A curious theory of morals indeed.

What Mill desires is a question of fact, but what Mill believes is desirable is a question of value. Why should anyone accept Mill's standards of value? Of course he assumed that his value standards were a harvest of reason and knowledge; the principles Mill embraced could be discerned in experience by any intelligent and informed person. So Mill believed, wrongly. Mill's principles are in fact the "discoveries" of such "scientists" as Adam Smith and David Ricardo, Jeremy Bentham and James Mill. The principles were revealed, to be sure, not by true experience but by true prophets—the preachers of the "most enlightened doctrines" of nineteenth-century British Liberalism.

Some difficulties in Mill's theory which result from his inadequate conception of the role of value in political conduct are evident in the argument he advances against majority rule. Majority rule, Mill contends, means the domination of society by one class. For the general interest to be promoted, authority must be exercised according to the true principles of politics. The special interest of a majority conflicts with the general interest of all. A majority of ordinary individuals would, from passion and ignorance, exercise authority for their class benefit at the expense of the rest of the community. A select minority who understand how the interests of individuals and classes can be achieved are best qualified to rule.

The theoretical issue which Mill attempts to settle by this argument is indeed a serious one for any thinker who, like Mill, accepts the principle of popular sovereignty. For him the legitimacy of authority depends on the consent of the governed; without consent, rule rests on force rather than authority. Unless authority is in some sense exercised to advance a good common to the governed, there is no basis for consent. The practical issue is: How can authority be exercised so that the governed will consent to it? The form in which Mill poses the issue is: How can authority be exercised to promote the general interest of all the governed? This is not only a serious issue, but it is as well a difficult one to resolve satisfactorily. Many other political thinkers have tried, without success, to work out a practical resolution. Mill apparently appreciated the seriousness of the issue but not the difficulty in resolving it. His answer does not in practice dispose of the problem of the consent of the governed.

Mill says that a qualified elite can determine better than the governed themselves how authority should be exercised, and it should be exercised not as a majority of the governed desire but as the general interest requires. This claim implies that standards of political value exist external to and independent from the governed; by consulting these objective principles, an elite can determine how authority should be exercised to promote the general interest. That such value standards exist is not evident in practice. It is evident, however, that what Mill regarded as objective principles were in fact the value standards of a minor part of the British community. Lacking objective principles for determining political conduct, the principles observed must be those of the governed. Why should authority be exercised the way a minority believes it should rather than the way a majority desires it? This is not a question of fact. And because Mill argues that an elite *must* exercise authority contrary to the actual desires of ordinary individuals, he eliminates any practical basis for consent by a majority of the governed.

By the democratic principles Mill attacks, on the other hand, this problem of consent is to a greater extent resolved. If the governed are to determine how authority should be exercised, the principle of majority rule is indispensable. According to this principle, the exercise of authority over the members of a community should be determined by the vote of a majority. The only practical way to find out what people desire is to ask them. Put the question to a vote. Otherwise what they desire is merely a matter for conjecture, not fact. Since the vote of the larger part shall be binding on the entire community, the exercise of authority conforms to a majority's desires. This principle at least assures that the larger part of a community will consent to the exercise of authority. Contrary to Mill's thesis, elite rule may or may not be desirable in theory, but in practice it is not desirable—for a person who believes in the consent of the governed.

Mill's theory, we find, is less firmly established in political experience than it is rooted in Mill's prejudices. The actual value of his Liberal principles Mill failed to appreciate. Consequently his effort to present a persuasive case for the practice of elite rule was largely unavailing.

V

John Stuart Mill was pre-eminently the middle-class philosopher of nineteenth-century British Liberalism. His political thought, like the Liberal creed itself, suffers from defects. Some are merely indicative of the time in which Mill lived and wrote: his thought necessarily bears the mark of a pre-Darwinian age. Others are reflective of the man's peculiar character, his odd personality and bent of mind. The most serious defects in Mill's political theory result from the role it was his destiny to play in British thought as the latter-day apologist for middle-class Liberalism.

Mill was not a broad-gauged philosopher who probed the profound problems of the modern era. In considering politics, Mill's frame of reference was almost limited to nineteenth-century British experience.

For a person who maintained that experience is the source of truth, Mill was surprisingly parochial in outlook. He wrote on a vast variety of subjects—Hungarian refugees in Turkey, sugar plantations in the West Indies, spring flowers in southern Europe, landholding in Australia, and even the new constitution of California. But about such subjects Mill wrote without benefit of firsthand experience. He did have some direct contact with French life, having from his youth spent much time in France. He did have, too, as a consequence of his professional work, some understanding of British India—the understanding of a career administrator in London who had never set foot on Indian soil. Mill's understanding of American life was superficial as well as secondhand. His writings reveal scant appreciation of American or, for that matter, of any other foreign experience. Mill's political writings are particularly narrow in perspective. In many passages of *Representative Government,* Mill does not seem to be considering representative government at all but rather to be commenting on the British parliamentary system.

Despite his parochial outlook, Mill was never reticent about expounding political principles. From his limited British experience, he boldly inferred sweeping generalizations about the nature of political life. Some had little correspondence with facts. For example, Mill declares: "Free institutions are next to impossible in a country made up of different nationalities." What about Canada? The United States? Switzerland? Though Mill talks much about experience, he was not, to put it mildly, rigorously empirical in his thinking. Often his political views are so directly observations about British experience that they have no relevance for any other political system. Mill was essentially a commentator on British politics who reacted to the passing events of his time.

And how did he react? Though Mill explored varied regions of intellectual inquiry—he certainly was a versatile writer—he produced no coherent system of political thought. In part this can be explained by his peculiar affiliation with Utilitarianism.

John Stuart Mill was born into the Utilitarian movement. His father was the chief prophet of the Benthamite gospel, and the master himself selected young John as a protégé. In his youth Mill was a leader of the Benthamite coterie called the "Philosophical Radicals," champions of Utilitarian reform. But following a nervous breakdown and his intimate association with Harriet Taylor, Mill rebelled against the teachings of those who had so meticulously fashioned his mind. He no longer uncritically accepted the doctrines he had inherited from his father, yet he was unable to repudiate them completely. This dilemma in Mill's thinking is evident throughout his political writings.

The characteristic format of a discussion of a political question by Mill is as follows. First he declares the Benthamite belief, and then examines the views of Bentham's critics. Next Mill concedes the partial inadequacy of Bentham's teachings and the partial validity of his critic's charges. Mill then adopts a third position, a "higher synthesis," where he neither fully accepts nor rejects the Benthamite beliefs—or those to the contrary. This is the format. But usually when Mill has concluded a discussion, little remains intact of the beliefs which distinguish a genuine Benthamite.

The remark that John Stuart Mill was a Utilitarian only by accident of birth is, then, essentially correct. Though Mill professed the Utilitarian creed to the end of his days, he did not permit his views to be dictated by Utilitarian principles. For example, Mill insisted on a qualitative test for pleasure; in fact he insisted on qualitative tests for everything, contrary to the egalitarian tendency in Benthamite teachings. However, though abandoning the Benthamite system of beliefs, Mill failed to devise in its stead a coherent system of thought of his own.

Mill's lifelong inability to choose between accepting or rejecting the Utilitarian system does not entirely account for the lack of coherence in his political thought. In many instances Mill changed his views about political questions as his thinking matured; this is to his credit. But not all contradictions in Mill's views span the space of years. Some are separated by only a few sentences.

An argument Mill advances against majority rule illustrates this. Majority rule is undesirable in practice, Mill says, because a majority would rule for the benefit of the many at the expense of the minority, contrary to the general interest of all. Only a "mentally superior" few who know the interest of all are qualified to rule. This argument can, in Mill's own terms, be turned with equal force against minority rule. For Mill

also contends that power over others corrupts those who possess it. A ruler always tends to pursue his self-interest to the
neglect of the general interest. It is not that the ruler may not
know what the general interest is; the defect is one of will,
not reason. The ruler knows what is right yet does wrong.
But granted this moral depravity coincident with power as
a fact of human nature, it is just as likely that a "mentally
superior" elite would rule contrary to the general interest as
that a majority would. What Mill's argument amounts to
is the claim that any ruler, if he can, will use his power to
benefit a part of the community. If this is so, elite rule actually
is, on the Utilitarian terms Mill sometimes employs, a less
desirable form of rule in practice than democracy. When a
majority rules, it is the interest of a few rather than the many
which is adversely affected. Of course Mill does not intend
this at all. But the contradiction in his argument is indicative of a logical weakness which pervades Mill's political
thought.

The distinctive character of Mill's political thought cannot
be explained, however, apart from his relation to British
Liberalism. Mill was a product, not simply of Great Britain
and the nineteenth century, but also of a definite social class.
His lot was to serve as an apologist for the interests of the new
middle class which had prospered from trade and industry. It
was his fate to champion the Liberal cause at a time when the
movement, having achieved its reform mission for the middle
class, had outlived its historic purpose. Both the strength and
the weaknesses of nineteenth-century British Liberalism are
reflected in Mill's political thought.

The traditional task of the British Liberal ideologist was
to discredit rule by an aristocracy of birth and land. With
the rise of industrial capitalism, the new class, drawn from the
skilled trades and crafts, neither noble rich nor common poor,
acquired great wealth, profiting from the manufacture and
sale of commodities. But wealth—in money, not land—gave
the middle-class merchants and manufacturers no social status or political privilege; such the law of the land guaranteed

to be a monopoly of the aristocracy. In its origins Liberalism was understandably a radical reform movement, bent on changes in the status quo. The Liberal demanded an end to government-sponsored privilege for the upper class. He demanded the repeal of legislation which favored a few at the expense of many. The Liberal agitated for reforms by which prosperous merchants and manufacturers could enjoy the status and privilege long the prerogative of the landed nobility. The triumph of the movement was symbolized by the Act of 1832; by that victory the door was opened for the middle class to achieve the social esteem and political influence which accorded with the wealth and talent they exhibited. Middle-class leaders rapidly rose to prominence in British life. By mid-century and the reign of Queen Victoria, the devotees of Liberalism had come to dominate British politics.

But for the middle class, industrial capitalism was a mixed blessing. Along with prosperity for merchants and manufacturers, it brought forth another social class: the wage-earning employees. Displaced from farms and shops, gathered in commercial and manufacturing centers, these industrial workers were, as earlier their employers had been, without status or privilege in British society. And they were as well without wealth or education. As the working class grew in size and strength, their leaders demanded an end to privilege for a middle-class few at the expense of the working-class many. In fact they used the same arguments the Liberal ideologists had a generation before used against the aristocracy. But they did not stop short of the goal in their demand that special privilege be abolished. The working-class ideologists agitated for reforms by which every member of British society would enjoy social and political equality. Their goal was democracy.

The task of the British Liberal ideologist in Mill's day had become, then, an exacting one. In the perspective of history, Liberalism was a half-way house between aristocratic and democratic rule. Passing time and changing circumstances compelled the Liberal propagandist first to discredit rule by an aristocratic elite and then to justify rule by a middle-class

elite. The refuge for the Liberal who feared and despised democracy was a scheme for rule by a few of supposed "virtue
and talent." Mill's formula for representative government,
we have seen, was such a scheme to perpetuate rule by an elite
of "merit." In his devotion to the middle-class cause, Mill was
remarkably consistent. Never did he waver in denying a claim
to exercise authority from the rich and the well-born, or from
the "untutored masses."

Rationalizing the interests of a middle-class minority in
his day, without doing violence to fact and logic, called for
greater philosophical ingenuity than Mill could muster. Many
times in the course of his lifetime Mill argued contrary positions on the same question. At one time he argued that judges
should be made responsible to the "people," [8] yet in *Representative Government* we find him arguing against popular
election of judges on the grounds that they should be immune
to political influence. At one time Mill argued in favor of
the secret ballot,[9] yet later we find him contending that the
vote should be cast in public because the secret ballot encourages the elector to neglect his public duty. At one time
Mill argued in favor of pledging candidates for public office,[10]
yet later we find him saying that a candidate should make no
pledges whatsoever to his constituents. These examples are not
of exceptions in Mill's writings. They are indicative of a
characteristic in his thought. Many views Mill entertained in
his youth he later abandoned when they no longer served
middle-class interests; many views he held late in life he had
roundly criticized as a young reformer.

Of course to convert a creed of reform into a catechism of
reaction is no slight philosophical feat. Though Mill's attempt
was unsuccessful, it was valiant. For his effort he earned a
reputation as the foremost nineteenth-century British Liberal
political thinker. The theory he concocted puts to severe test

[8] In a letter to the *Morning Chronicle,* Sept. 25, 1823.
[9] In a series of articles in the *Examiner,* Nov. 18, Dec. 5, and Dec.
12, 1830.
[10] In the *Examiner,* July 1, 1832.

the faith of a devout Liberal who still believes that fact and logic have some intellectual value. But this is as much a commentary on British Liberalism as it is on Mill's prowess as a philosopher.

John Stuart Mill's political thought, a fine sum of middle-class values set forth in *Representative Government*, is a fitting monument of nineteenth-century British Liberalism.

CURRIN V. SHIELDS

SELECTED BIBLIOGRAPHY

MILL'S MAJOR WORKS

A System of Logic. 2 vols. London, 1843; 9th ed., 1875.

Principles of Political Economy. 2 vols. London, 1848; 7th ed., 1871.

On Liberty. London, 1859.

Thoughts on Parliamentary Reform. London, 1859.

Dissertations and Discussions. 2 vols. London, 1859; 3 vols., 1867; 4 vols., 1875.

Considerations on Representative Government. London, 1861.

Utilitarianism. London, 1863.

An Examination of Sir William Hamilton's Philosophy. London, 1865; 3rd ed., 1867.

Auguste Comte and Positivism. London, 1865.

The Subjection of Women. London, 1869.

Posthumously published:

Autobiography. Edited by Helen Taylor. London, 1873.

Nature, the Utility of Religion, Theism; Being Three Essays on Religion. London, 1874.

Socialism. Edited by W. D. P. Bliss. New York, 1891.

On Social Freedom. New York, 1941. (Mill's authorship in doubt.)

Letters of John Stuart Mill. Edited by Hugh Elliott. 2 vols. London, 1910.

COLLATERAL READING

Albee, Ernest. *A History of English Utilitarianism.* New York, 1902.

Bain, Alexander. *John Stuart Mill: A Criticism; with Personal Recollections.* London, 1882.

Bosanquet, Bernard. *The Philosophical Theory of the State.* London, 1899.

Davidson, William L. *Political Thought in England: The Utilitarians from Bentham to J. S. Mill.* New York, 1916.

Grote, John. *Examination of the Utilitarian Philosophy.* Cambridge, 1870.

Halévy, Élie. *The Growth of Philosophical Radicalism.* London, 1949.

MacCunn, John. *Six Radical Thinkers.* London, 1910.

MacMinn, Ney, J. R. Hainds, and James McNab McCrimmon (eds). *Bibliography of the Published Writings of John Stuart Mill.* Evanston, Ill., 1945.

Morlan, G. *America's Heritage from John Stuart Mill.* New York, 1936.

Neff, Emery. *Carlyle and Mill, Mystic and Utilitarian.* New York, 1926.

Packe, Michael St. John. *The Life of John Stuart Mill.* London, 1954.

Plamenatz, John P. *The English Utilitarians.* Oxford, 1949.

Stephen, J. Fitzjames. *Liberty, Equality, and Fraternity.* London, 1873.

Stephen, Leslie. *The English Utilitarians,* Vol. III. London, 1900.

West, Julius. *J. S. Mill.* Fabian Society Tract No. 168. London, 1913.

JOHN STUART MILL: A CHRONOLOGY

1806	May 20, born at Pentonville, London
1809	Began study of Greek language and literature
1814	Began study of Latin, Euclid, and algebra
1818	Began study of Aristotle's logical works and Scholastic logic
1819	Began study of political economy under his father
1820-21	Sojourn in France with Sir Samuel Bentham
1822	Entered as clerk in examiner's office, East India Company
1822	Established the "Utilitarian Society"
1826-c. 30	Period of disillusionment and depression
1828	Promoted to assistant examiner of East India Company
1835	Became editor of new *London Review*
1836-40	Edited and owned the *London and Westminster Review*
1851	Married Mrs. Harriet Hardy Taylor
1856-58	Chief of examiner's office, East India Company
1858	Death of Mrs. Mill
1865	Elected to Parliament from Westminster
1868	Defeated in election, retired to Avignon
1873	May 8, died at Avignon

NOTE ON THE TEXT

The present edition of Mill's *Representative Government* is based upon the third edition (1865). Some slight modifications have been made in spelling and punctuation to conform to preferred current usage without significantly affecting Mill's style. Footnotes, within brackets, and a biographical index have been added by the publisher's editorial staff to aid the reader.

O.P.

CONSIDERATIONS ON
REPRESENTATIVE GOVERNMENT

PREFACE

THOSE who have done me the honor of reading my previous writings will probably receive no strong impression of novelty from the present volume; for the principles are those to which I have been working up during the greater part of my life, and most of the practical suggestions have been anticipated by others or by myself. There is novelty, however, in the fact of bringing them together and exhibiting them in their connection; and also, I believe, in much that is brought forward in their support. Several of the opinions at all events, if not new, are for the present as little likely to meet with general acceptance as if they were.

It seems to me, however, from various indications and from none more than the recent debates on Reform of Parliament, that both Conservatives and Liberals (if I may continue to call them what they still call themselves) have lost confidence in the political creeds which they nominally profess, while neither side appears to have made any progress in providing itself with a better. Yet such a better doctrine must be possible, not a mere compromise by splitting the difference between the two, but something wider than either, which in virtue of its superior comprehensiveness might be adopted by either Liberal or Conservative without renouncing anything which he really feels to be valuable in his own creed. When so many feel obscurely the want of such a doctrine, and so few even flatter themselves that they have attained it, anyone may without presumption offer what his own thoughts, and the best that he knows of those of others, are able to contribute toward its formation.

CHAPTER I

TO WHAT EXTENT FORMS OF GOVERN-
MENT ARE A MATTER OF CHOICE

ALL SPECULATIONS concerning forms of government bear the impress, more or less exclusive, of two conflicting theories respecting political institutions, or, to speak more properly, conflicting conceptions of what political institutions are.

By some minds government is conceived as strictly a practical art, giving rise to no questions but those of means and an end. Forms of government are assimilated to any other expedients for the attainment of human objects. They are regarded as wholly an affair of invention and contrivance. Being made by man, it is assumed that man has the choice either to make them or not, and how or on what pattern they shall be made. Government, according to this conception, is a problem, to be worked like any other question of business. The first step is to define the purposes which governments are required to promote. The next is to inquire what form of government is best fitted to fulfill those purposes. Having satisfied ourselves on these two points and ascertained the form of government which combines the greatest amount of good with the least of evil, what further remains is to obtain the concurrence of our countrymen, or those for whom the institutions are intended, in the opinion which we have privately arrived at. To find the best form of government, to persuade others that it is the best, and, having done so, to stir them up to insist on having it, is the order of ideas in the minds of those who adopt this view of political philosophy. They look upon a constitution in the same light (difference of scale being allowed for) as they would upon a steam plow or a threshing machine.

To these stand opposed another kind of political reasoners who are so far from assimilating a form of government to a machine that they regard it as a sort of spontaneous product, and the science of government as a branch (so to speak) of natural history. According to them, forms of government are not a matter of choice. We must take them, in the main, as we find them. Governments cannot be constructed by premeditated design. They "are not made, but grow." Our business with them, as with the other facts of the universe, is to acquaint ourselves with their natural properties and adapt ourselves to them. The fundamental political institutions of a people are considered by this school as a sort of organic growth from the nature and life of that people: a product of their habits, instincts, and unconscious wants and desires, scarcely at all of their deliberate purposes. Their will has had no part in the matter but that of meeting the necessities of the moment by the contrivances of the moment, which contrivances, if in sufficient conformity to the national feelings and character, commonly last and by successive aggregation constitute a polity suited to the people who possess it, but which it would be vain to attempt to superinduce upon any people whose nature and circumstances had not spontaneously evolved it.

It is difficult to decide which of these doctrines would be the most absurd, if we could suppose either of them held as an exclusive theory. But the principles which men profess on any controverted subject are usually a very incomplete exponent of the opinions they really hold. No one believes that every people is capable of working every sort of institutions. Carry the analogy of mechanical contrivances as far as we will, a man does not choose even an instrument of timber and iron on the sole ground that it is in itself the best. He considers whether he possesses the other requisites which must be combined with it to render its employment advantageous, and in particular whether those by whom it will have to be worked possess the knowledge and skill necessary for its management. On the other hand, neither are those who speak of institutions as if they were a kind of living organisms really the political fatalists they give themselves out to be. They do not pretend that mankind have absolutely no range of choice as to the government they will live under, or that a consideration of the consequences which flow from different forms of polity is no element at all in deciding which of them should be preferred. But though each side greatly exaggerates its own theory, out of opposition to the other, and no one holds without modification to either, the two doctrines correspond to a deep-seated difference between two modes of thought; and though it is evident that neither of these is entirely in the right, yet it being equally evident that neither is wholly in the wrong, we must endeavor to get down to what is at the root of each and avail ourselves of the amount of truth which exists in either.

Let us remember, then, in the first place, that political institutions (however the proposition may be at times ignored) are the work of men, owe their origin and their whole existence to human will. Men did not wake on a summer morning and find them sprung up. Neither do they resemble trees which, once planted, "are aye growing" while men "are sleeping." In every stage of their existence they are made what they are by human voluntary agency. Like all things, therefore, which are made by men, they may be either well or ill made; judgment and skill may have been exercised in their production, or the reverse of these. And again, if a people have omitted, or from outward pressure have not had it in their power, to give themselves a constitution by the tentative process of applying a corrective to each evil as it arose or as the sufferers gained strength to resist it, this retardation of political progress is no doubt a great disadvantage to them, but it does not prove that what has been found good for others would not have been good also for them, and will not be so still when they think fit to adopt it.

On the other hand, it is also to be borne in mind that political machinery does not act of itself. As it is first made, so it has to be worked, by men, and even by ordinary men. It needs not their simple acquiescence, but their active participation and must be adjusted to the capacities and qualities of such men as are available. This implies three conditions. The people for whom the form of government is intended must be willing to accept it, or at least not so unwilling as to oppose an insurmountable obstacle to its establishment. They must be willing and able to do what is necessary to keep it standing. And they must be willing and able to do what it requires of them to enable it to fulfill its purposes. The word "do" is to be understood as including forbearances as well as acts. They must be capable of fulfilling the conditions of action and the conditions of self-restraint, which are necessary either for keeping the established polity in existence or for enabling it to achieve the ends, its conduciveness to which forms its recommendation.

The failure of any of these conditions renders a form of government, whatever favorable promise it may otherwise hold out, unsuitable to the particular case.

The first obstacle, the repugnance of the people to the particular form of government, needs little illustration because it never can in theory have been overlooked. The case is of perpetual occurrence. Nothing but foreign force would induce a tribe of North American Indians to submit to the restraints of a regular and civilized government. The same might have been said, though somewhat less absolutely, of the barbarians who overran the Roman Empire. It required centuries of time, and an entire change of circumstances, to discipline them into regular obedience even to their own leaders when not actually serving under their banner. There are nations who will not voluntarily submit to any government but that of certain families which have from time immemorial had the privilege of supplying them with chiefs. Some nations could not, except by foreign conquest, be made to endure a monarchy; others are equally averse to a republic. The hindrance often amounts, for the time being, to impracticability.

But there are also cases in which, though not averse to a

form of government—possibly even desiring it—a people may be unwilling or unable to fulfill its conditions. They may be incapable of fulfilling such of them as are necessary to keep the government even in nominal existence. Thus a people may prefer a free government, but if from indolence or carelessness or cowardice or want of public spirit they are unequal to the exertions necessary for preserving it; if they will not fight for it when it is directly attacked; if they can be deluded by the artifices used to cheat them out of it; if by momentary discouragement or temporary panic or a fit of enthusiasm for an individual they can be induced to lay their liberties at the feet even of a great man or trust him with powers which enable him to subvert their institutions—in all these cases they are more or less unfit for liberty; and though it may be for their good to have had it even for a short time, they are unlikely long to enjoy it. Again, a people may be unwilling or unable to fulfill the duties which a particular form of government requires of them. A rude people, though in some degree alive to the benefits of civilized society, may be unable to practice the forbearance which it demands: their passions may be too violent or their personal pride too exacting to forego private conflict and leave to the laws the avenging of their real or supposed wrongs. In such a case a civilized government, to be really advantageous to them, will require to be in a considerable degree despotic: to be one over which they do not themselves exercise control, and which imposes a great amount of forcible restraint upon their actions. Again, a people must be considered unfit for more than a limited and qualified freedom who will not co-operate actively with the law and the public authorities in the repression of evildoers. A people who are more disposed to shelter a criminal than to apprehend him; who, like the Hindus, will perjure themselves to screen the man who has robbed them rather than take trouble or expose themselves to vindictiveness by giving evidence against him; who, like some nations of Europe down to a recent date, if a man poniards another in the public street, pass by on the other side because it is the business of the police to look to the matter and it is safer not to interfere in what does not concern them; a people who are revolted by an execution, but not shocked at an assassination—require that the public authorities should be armed with much sterner powers of repression than elsewhere, since the first indispensable requisites of civilized life have nothing else to rest on. These deplorable states of feeling, in any people who have emerged from savage life, are, no doubt, usually the consequence of previous bad government, which has taught them to regard the law as made for other ends than their good and its administrators as worse enemies than those who openly violate it. But however little blame may be due to those in whom these mental habits have grown up, and however the habits may be ultimately conquerable by better government, yet while they exist a people so disposed cannot be governed with as little power exercised over them as a people whose sympathies are on the side of the law, and who are willing to give active assistance in its enforcement. Again, representative institutions are of little value and may be a mere instrument of tyranny or intrigue when the generality of electors are not sufficiently interested in their own government to give their vote or, if they vote at all, do not bestow their suffrages on public grounds but sell them for money or vote at the beck of someone who has control over them, or whom for private reasons they desire to propitiate. Popular election thus practiced, instead of a security against misgovernment, is but an additional wheel in its machinery. Besides these moral hindrances, mechanical difficulties are often an insuperable impediment to forms of government. In the ancient world, though there might be, and often was, great individual or local independence, there could be nothing like a regulated popular government beyond the bounds of a single city-community; because there did not exist the physical conditions for the formation and propagation of a public opinion except among those who could be brought together to discuss public matters in the same agora. This obstacle is generally thought to have ceased by the adoption of the representative system.

But to surmount it completely required the press, and even the newspaper press, the real equivalent, though not in all respects an adequate one, of the Pnyx and the Forum.[1] There have been states of society in which even a monarchy of any great territorial extent could not subsist but unavoidably broke up into petty principalities, either mutually independent, or held together by a loose tie like the feudal, because the machinery of authority was not perfect enough to carry orders into effect at a great distance from the person of the ruler. He depended mainly upon voluntary fidelity for the obedience even of his army, nor did there exist the means of making the people pay an amount of taxes sufficient for keeping up the force necessary to compel obedience throughout a large territory. In these and all similar cases it must be understood that the amount of the hindrance may be either greater or less. It may be so great as to make the form of government work very ill, without absolutely precluding its existence or hindering it from being practically preferable to any other which can be had. This last question mainly depends upon a consideration which we have not yet arrived at—the tendencies of different forms of government to promote progress.

We have now examined the three fundamental conditions of the adaptation of forms of government to the people who are to be governed by them. If the supporters of what may be termed the naturalistic theory of politics mean but to insist on the necessity of these three conditions, if they only mean that no government can permanently exist which does not fulfill the first and second conditions and in some considerable measure the third, their doctrine thus limited is incontestable. Whatever they mean more than this appears to me untenable. All that we are told about the necessity of a historical basis for institutions, of their being in harmony with the national usages and character, and the like, means either this or nothing to the purpose. There is a great quantity of mere sentimentality connected with these and similar phrases,

[1] [Pnyx, the meeting place of the Athenian assembly; Forum, the chief public square in ancient Rome.]

over and above the amount of rational meaning contained in them. But, considered practically, these alleged requisites of political institutions are merely so many facilities for realizing the three conditions. When an institution, or a set of institutions, has the way prepared for it by the opinions, tastes, and habits of the people, they are not only more easily induced to accept it, but will more easily learn, and will be, from the beginning, better disposed to do what is required of them both for the preservation of the institutions and for bringing them into such action as enables them to produce their best results. It would be a great mistake in any legislator not to shape his measures so as to take advantage of such pre-existing habits and feelings when available. On the other hand, it is an exaggeration to elevate these mere aids and facilities into necessary conditions. People are more easily induced to do, and do more easily, what they are already used to; but people also learn to do things new to them. Familiarity is a great help, but much dwelling on an idea will make it familiar, even when strange at first. There are abundant instances in which a whole people have been eager for untried things. The amount of capacity which a people possess for doing new things and adapting themselves to new circumstances is itself one of the elements of the question. It is a quality in which different nations, and different stages of civilization, differ much from one another. The capability of any given people for fulfilling the conditions of a given form of government cannot be pronounced on by any sweeping rule. Knowledge of the particular people and general practical judgment and sagacity must be the guides. There is also another consideration not to be lost sight of. A people may be unprepared for good institutions; but to kindle a desire for them is a necessary part of the preparation. To recommend and advocate a particular institution or form of government and set its advantages in the strongest light is one of the modes, often the only mode within reach, of educating the mind of the nation not only for accepting or claiming, but also for working, the institution. What means had Italian

patriots, during the last and present generation, of preparing
the Italian people for freedom in unity but by inciting them
to demand it? [2] Those, however, who undertake such a task
need to be duly impressed, not solely with the benefits of the
institution or polity which they recommend, but also with
the capacities, moral, intellectual, and active, required for
working it—that they may avoid, if possible, stirring up a desire too much in advance of the capacity.

The result of what has been said is that, within the limits
set by the three conditions so often adverted to, institutions
and forms of government are a matter of choice. To inquire
into the best form of government in the abstract (as it is called)
is not a chimerical but a highly practical employment of
scientific intellect; and to introduce into any country the best
institutions which, in the existing state of that country, are
capable of, in any tolerable degree, fulfilling the conditions
is one of the most rational objects to which practical effort
can address itself. Everything which can be said by way of dis-
paraging the efficacy of human will and purpose in matters of
government might be said of it in every other of its appli-
cations. In all things there are very strict limits to human
power. It can only act by wielding some one or more of the
forces of nature. Forces, therefore, that can be applied to the
desired use must exist, and will only act according to their own
laws. We cannot make the river run backwards, but we do
not therefore say that watermills "are not made, but grow."
In politics, as in mechanics, the power which is to keep the
engine going must be sought for outside the machinery; and
if it is not forthcoming, or is insufficient to surmount the obstacles which may reasonably be expected, the contrivance will

2 [Mill wrote shortly after the north Italian kingdom of Piedmont had
finally succeeded (1859-61), by military and diplomatic means, in imposing unity on most of the Italian peninsula—something which the revolu-
tionary nationalism of Italian patriots since the French Revolution had
signally failed to accomplish. Unification was completed with the occupation of Venetia in 1866, of Rome in 1870, and of the Trentino in 1918.]

fail. This is no peculiarity of the political art, and amounts only to saying that it is subject to the same limitations and conditions as all other arts.

At this point we are met by another objection, or the same objection in a different form. The forces, it is contended, on which the greater political phenomena depend are not amenable to the direction of politicians or philosophers. The government of a country, it is affirmed, is, in all substantial respects, fixed and determined beforehand by the state of the country in regard to the distribution of the elements of social power. Whatever is the strongest power in society will obtain the governing authority, and a change in the political constitution cannot be durable unless preceded or accompanied by an altered distribution of power in society itself. A nation, therefore, cannot choose its form of government. The mere details and practical organization it may choose, but the essence of the whole, the seat of the supreme power, is determined for it by social circumstances.

That there is a portion of truth in this doctrine I at once admit; but to make it of any use, it must be reduced to a distinct expression and proper limits. When it is said that the strongest power in society will make itself strongest in the government, what is meant by power? Not thews and sinews, otherwise pure democracy would be the only form of polity that could exist. To mere muscular strength add two other elements, property and intelligence, and we are nearer the truth but far from having yet reached it. Not only is a greater number often kept down by a less, but the greater number may have a preponderance in property, and individually in intelligence, and may yet be held in subjection, forcibly or otherwise, by a minority in both respects inferior to it. To make these various elements of power politically influential they must be organized; and the advantage in organization is necessarily with those who are in possession of the government. A much weaker party in all other elements of power may greatly preponderate when the powers of government are thrown into the scale, and may long retain its predominance through this alone, though, no doubt, a government so situated is in the condition called in mechanics unstable equilibrium, like a thing balanced on its smaller end which, if once disturbed, tends more and more to depart from, instead of reverting to, its previous state.

But there are still stronger objections to this theory of government in the terms in which it is usually stated. The power in society which has any tendency to convert itself into political power is not power quiescent, power merely passive, but active power—in other words, power actually exerted; that is to say, a very small portion of all the power in existence. Politically speaking, a great part of all power consists in will. How is it possible, then, to compute the elements of political power, while we omit from the computation anything which acts on the will? To think that because those who wield the power in society wield in the end that of government, therefore it is of no use to attempt to influence the constitution of the government by acting on opinion, is to forget that opinion is itself one of the greatest active social forces. One person with a belief is a social power equal to ninety-nine who have only interests. They who can succeed in creating a general persuasion that a certain form of government, or social fact of any kind, deserves to be preferred have made nearly the most important step which can possibly be taken toward ranging the powers of society on its side. On the day when the protomartyr was stoned to death at Jerusalem, while he who was to be the Apostle of the Gentiles stood by "consenting unto his death," would anyone have supposed that the party of that stoned man were then and there the strongest power in society? [3] And has not the event proved that they were so? Because theirs was the most powerful of then existing beliefs. The same element made a monk of Wittenberg,[4] at

[3] [Reference is to St. Stephen, the first Christian martyr, and to St. Paul who, as Saul, supervised the execution of Stephen (Acts 7: 54-60).]

[4] [Martin Luther (1483-1546), who at Worms (1521) defied the Emperor and the German princes by refusing to recant his teachings. The meeting marks the beginning of the Reformation in Germany.]

the meeting of the Diet of Worms, a more powerful social force than the Emperor Charles the Fifth and all the princes there assembled. But these, it may be said, are cases in which religion was concerned, and religious convictions are something peculiar in their strength. Then let us take a case purely political, where religion, so far as concerned at all, was chiefly on the losing side. If anyone requires to be convinced that speculative thought is one of the chief elements of social power, let him bethink himself of the age in which there was scarcely a throne in Europe which was not filled by a liberal and reforming king, a liberal and reforming emperor, or, strangest of all, a liberal and reforming pope: the age of Frederick the Great, of Catherine the Second, of Joseph the Second, of Peter Leopold, of Benedict XIV, of Ganganelli, of Pombal, of Aranda; [5] when the very Bourbons of Naples were liberals and reformers, and all the active minds among the noblesse of France were filled with the ideas which were soon after to cost them so dear.[6] Surely a conclusive example how far mere physical and economic power is from being the whole of social power. It was not by any change in the distribution of material interests, but by the spread of moral convictions, that Negro slavery has been put an end to in the British Empire and elsewhere. The serfs in Russia owe their emancipation, if not to a sentiment of duty, at least to the growth of a more enlightened opinion respecting the true interest of the State. It is what men think that determines how they act; and though the persuasions and convictions of average men are in a much greater degree determined by their personal position than by reason, no little power is exercised over them by the persuasions and convictions of those whose personal position is different and by the united authority of

5 [The group enumerated were statesmen more or less under the influence of the Enlightenment. They all instituted social reforms and strengthened secular authority with a markedly adverse attitude toward the Jesuit order. (See also biographical index.)]

6 [Mill implies that the ideas of the Enlightenment helped prepare the way to the French revolution (1789-1793).]

the instructed. When, therefore, the instructed in general can be brought to recognize one social arrangement, or political or other institution, as good, and another as bad, one as desirable, another as condemnable, very much has been done toward giving to the one, or withdrawing from the other, that preponderance of social force which enables it to subsist. And the maxim that the government of a country is what the social forces in existence compel it to be is true only in the sense in which it favors, instead of discouraging, the attempt to exercise, among all forms of government practicable in the existing condition of society, a rational choice.

CHAPTER II

THE CRITERION OF A GOOD FORM OF GOVERNMENT

THE FORM of government for any given country being (within certain definite conditions) amenable to choice, it is now to be considered by what test the choice should be directed: what are the distinctive characteristics of the form of government best fitted to promote the interests of any given society.

Before entering into this inquiry, it may seem necessary to decide what are the proper functions of government; for, government altogether being only a means, the eligibility of the means must depend on their adaptation to the end. But this mode of stating the problem gives less aid to its investigation than might be supposed, and does not even bring the whole of the question into view. For, in the first place, the proper functions of a government are not a fixed thing but different in different states of society—much more extensive in a backward than in an advanced state. And, secondly, the character of a government or set of political institutions cannot be sufficiently estimated while we confine our attention to the legitimate sphere of governmental functions. For though the goodness of a government is necessarily circumscribed within that sphere, its badness unhappily is not. Every kind and degree of evil of which mankind are susceptible may be inflicted on them by their government; and none of the good which social existence is capable of can be any further realized than as the constitution of the government is compatible with, and allows scope for, its attainment. Not to speak of indirect effects, the direct meddling of the public authorities has no necessary limits but those of human existence; and the influence of government on the well-being of society can be considered or estimated in reference to nothing less than the whole of the interests of humanity.

Being thus obliged to place before ourselves as the test of good and bad government so complex an object as the aggregate interests of society, we would willingly attempt some kind of classification of those interests which, bringing them before the mind in definite groups, might give indication of the qualities by which a form of government is fitted to promote those various interests respectively. It would be a great facility if we could say the good of society consists of such and such elements; one of these elements requires such conditions, another such others; the government, then, which unites in the greatest degree all these conditions must be the best. The theory of government would thus be built up from the separate theorems of the elements which compose a good state of society.

Unfortunately, to enumerate and classify the constituents of social well-being so as to admit of the formation of such theorems is no easy task. Most of those who, in the last or present generation, have applied themselves to the philosophy of politics in any comprehensive spirit have felt the importance of such a classification, but the attempts which have been made toward it are as yet limited, so far as I am aware, to a single step. The classification begins and ends with a partition of the exigencies of society between the two heads of

Order and Progress (in the phraseology of French thinkers); Permanence and Progression in the words of Coleridge. This division is plausible and seductive from the apparently clean-cut opposition between its two members and the remarkable difference between the sentiments to which they appeal. But I apprehend that (however admissible for purposes of popular discourse) the distinction between Order, or Permanence, and Progress, employed to define the qualities necessary in a government, is unscientific and incorrect.

For, first, what are Order and Progress? Concerning Progress there is no difficulty, or none which is apparent at first sight. When Progress is spoken of as one of the wants of human society, it may be supposed to mean Improvement. That is a tolerably distinct idea. But what is Order? Sometimes it means more, sometimes less, but hardly ever the whole of what human society needs except improvement.

In its narrowest acceptation Order means obedience. A government is said to preserve order if it succeeds in getting itself obeyed. But there are different degrees of obedience, and it is not every degree that is commendable. Only an unmitigated despotism demands that the individual citizen shall obey unconditionally every mandate of persons in authority. We must at least limit the definition to such mandates as are general and issued in the deliberate form of laws. Order thus understood expresses, doubtless, an indispensable attribute of government. Those who are unable to make their ordinances obeyed cannot be said to govern. But though a necessary condition, this is not the object of government. That it should make itself obeyed is requisite in order that it may accomplish some other purpose. We are still to seek what is this other purpose which government ought to fulfill, abstractedly from the idea of improvement, and which has to be fulfilled in every society, whether stationary or progressive.

In a sense somewhat more enlarged, Order means the preservation of peace by the cessation of private violence. Order is said to exist where the people of the country have, as a general rule, ceased to prosecute their quarrels by private force and acquired the habit of referring the decision of their disputes and the redress of their injuries to the public authorities. But in this larger use of the term, as well as in the former narrow one, Order expresses rather one of the conditions of government than either its purpose or the criterion of its excellence. For the habit may be well established of submitting to the government, and referring all disputed matters to its authority, and yet the manner in which the government deals with those disputed matters, and with the other things about which it concerns itself, may differ by the whole interval which divides the best from the worst possible.

If we intend to comprise in the idea of Order all that society requires from its government which is not included in the idea of Progress, we must define Order as the preservation of all kinds and amounts of good which already exist, and Progress as consisting in the increase of them. This distinction does comprehend in one or the other section everything which a government can be required to promote. But, thus understood, it affords no basis for a philosophy of government. We cannot say that, in constituting a polity, certain provisions ought to be made for Order and certain others for Progress; since the conditions of Order, in the sense now indicated, and those of Progress are not opposite but the same. The agencies which tend to preserve the social good which already exists are the very same which promote the increase of it, and vice versa, the sole difference being that a greater degree of those agencies is required for the latter purpose than for the former.

What, for example, are the qualities in the citizens individually which conduce most to keep up the amount of good conduct, of good management, of success and prosperity which already exist in society? Everybody will agree that those qualities are industry, integrity, justice, and prudence. But are not these, of all qualities, the most conducive to improvement, and is not any growth of these virtues in the community in itself the greatest of improvements? If so, whatever qualities in the government are promotive of industry, integrity, justice, and prudence conduce alike to permanence and to progression; only there is needed more of those qualities to make the society decidedly progressive than merely to keep it permanent.

What, again, are the particular attributes in human beings which seem to have a more especial reference to Progress and do not so directly suggest the ideas of Order and Preservation? They are chiefly the qualities of mental activity, enterprise, and courage. But are not all these qualities fully as much required for preserving the good we have, as for adding to it? If there is anything certain in human affairs, it is that valuable acquisitions are only to be retained by the continuation of the same energies which gained them. Things left to take care of themselves inevitably decay. Those whom success induces to relax their habits of care and thoughtfulness, and their willingness to encounter disagreeables, seldom long retain their good fortune at its height. The mental attribute which seems exclusively dedicated to Progress and is the culmination of the tendencies to it, is originality, or invention. Yet this is no longer necessary for Permanence since, in the inevitable changes of human affairs, new inconveniences and dangers continually grow up, which must be encountered by new resources and contrivances in order to keep things going on even only as well as they did before. Whatever qualities, therefore, in a government tend to encourage activity, energy, courage, originality are requisites of Permanence as well as of Progress; only a somewhat less degree of them will on the average suffice for the former purpose than for the latter.

To pass now from the mental to the outward and objective requisites of society, it is impossible to point out any contrivance in politics, or arrangement of social affairs, which conduces to Order only or to Progress only; whatever tends to either promotes both. Take, for instance, the common institution of a police. Order is the object which seems most immediately interested in the efficiency of this part of the social organization. Yet if it is effectual to promote Order, that is, if it represses crime and enables everyone to feel his person and property secure, can any state of things be more conducive to Progress? The greater security of property is one of the main conditions and causes of greater production, which is Progress in its most familiar and vulgarest aspect. The better repression of crime represses the dispositions which tend to crime, and this is Progress in a somewhat higher sense. The release of the individual from the cares and anxieties of a state of imperfect protection sets his faculties free to be employed in any new effort for improving his own state and that of others, while the same cause, by attaching him to social existence and making him no longer see present or prospective enemies in his fellow creatures, fosters all those feelings of kindness and fellowship toward others and interest in the general well-being of the community which are such important parts of social improvement.

Take, again, such a familiar case as that of a good system of taxation and finance. This would generally be classed as belonging to the province of Order. Yet what can be more conducive to Progress? A financial system which promotes the one conduces, by the very same excellences, to the other. Economy, for example, equally preserves the existing stock of national wealth and favors the creation of more. A just distribution of burdens, by holding up to every citizen an example of morality and good conscience applied to difficult adjustments, and an evidence of the value which the highest authorities attach to them, tends in an eminent degree to educate the moral sentiments of the community both in respect of strength and of discrimination. Such a mode of levying the taxes as does not impede the industry, or unnecessarily interfere with the liberty, of the citizen promotes, not the preservation only, but the increase of the national wealth and encourages a more active use of the individual faculties. And vice versa, all errors in finance and taxation which obstruct the improvement of the people in wealth and morals tend also, if of sufficiently serious amount, positively to impoverish and demoralize them. It holds, in short, universally that when Order and Permanence are taken in their widest sense, for the stability of existing advantages, the requisites of Progress are but the requisites of

Order in a greater degree; those of Permanence merely those of Progress in a somewhat smaller measure.

In support of the position that Order is intrinsically different from Progress, and that preservation of existing and acquisition of additional good are sufficiently distinct to afford the basis of a fundamental classification, we shall perhaps be reminded that Progress may be at the expense of Order—that, while we are acquiring, or striving to acquire, good of one kind, we may be losing ground in respect to others; thus there may be progress in wealth, while there is deterioration in virtue. Granting this, what it proves is not that Progress is generically a different thing from Permanence, but that wealth is a different thing from virtue. Progress is Permanence and something more; and it is no answer to this to say that Progress in one thing does not imply Permanence in everything. No more does Progress in one thing imply Progress in everything. Progress of any kind includes Permanence in that same kind; whenever Permanence is sacrificed to some particular kind of Progress, other Progress is still more sacrificed to it; and if it be not worth the sacrifice, not the interest of Permanence alone has been disregarded, but the general interest of Progress has been mistaken.

If these improperly contrasted ideas are to be used at all in the attempt to give a first commencement of scientific precision to the notion of good government, it would be more philosophically correct to leave out of the definition the word "Order," and to say that the best government is that which is most conducive to Progress. For Progress includes Order, but Order does not include Progress. Progress is a greater degree of that of which Order is a less. Order in any other sense stands only for a part of the prerequisites of good government, not for its idea and essence. Order would find a more suitable place among the conditions of Progress, since, if we would increase our sum of good, nothing is more indispensable than to take due care of what we already have. If we are endeavoring after more riches, our very first rule should be not to squander uselessly our existing means. Order, thus considered, is not an additional end to be reconciled with Progress, but a part and means of Progress itself. If a gain in one respect is purchased by a more than equivalent loss in the same or in any other, there is not Progress. Conduciveness to Progress, thus understood, includes the whole excellence of a government.

But, though metaphysically defensible, this definition of the criterion of good government is not appropriate because, though it contains the whole of the truth, it recalls only a part. What is suggested by the term "Progress" is the idea of moving onward, whereas the meaning of it here is quite as much the prevention of falling back. The very same social causes—the same beliefs, feelings, institutions, and practices— are as much required to prevent society from retrograding as to produce a further advance. Were there no improvement to be hoped for, life would not be the less an unceasing struggle against causes of deterioration; as it even now is. Politics, as conceived by the ancients, consisted wholly in this. The natural tendency of men and their works was to degenerate, which tendency, however, by good institutions virtuously administered, it might be possible for an indefinite length of time to counteract. Though we no longer hold this opinion, though most men in the present age profess the contrary creed, believing that the tendency of things, on the whole, is toward improvement, we ought not to forget that there is an incessant and ever-flowing current of human affairs toward the worse, consisting of all the follies, all the vices, all the negligences, indolences, and supinenesses of mankind; which is only controlled and kept from sweeping all before it by the exertions which some persons constantly, and others by fits, put forth in the direction of good and worthy objects. It gives a very insufficient idea of the importance of the strivings which take place to improve and elevate human nature and life to suppose that their chief value consists in the amount of actual improvement realized by their means, and that the consequence of their cessation would merely be that we should remain as we are. A very small diminution of those exertions would not only put a stop to improvement, but would turn the general tendency of things toward deterioration which, once begun, would proceed with increasing rapidity and become more and more difficult to check, until it reached a state often seen in history, and in which many large portions of mankind even now grovel—when hardly anything short of superhuman power seems sufficient to turn the tide and give a fresh commencement to the upward movement.

These reasons make the word Progress as unapt as the terms Order and Permanence to become the basis for a classification of the requisites of a form of government. The fundamental antithesis which these words express does not lie in the things themselves so much as in the types of human character which answer to them. There are, we know, some minds in which caution, and others in which boldness, predominates: in some, the desire to avoid imperiling what is already possessed is a stronger sentiment than that which prompts to improve the old and acquire new advantages; while there are others who lean the contrary way and are more eager for future than careful of present good. The road to the ends of both is the same, but they are liable to wander from it in opposite directions. This consideration is of importance in composing the *personnel* of any political body: persons of both types ought to be included in it, that the tendencies of each may be tempered, in so far as they are excessive, by a due proportion of the other. There needs no express provision to ensure this object, provided care is taken to admit nothing inconsistent with it. The natural and spontaneous admixture of the old and the young, of those whose position and reputation are made and those who have them still to make, will in general sufficiently answer the purpose, if only this natural balance is not disturbed by artificial regulation.

Since the distinction most commonly adopted for the classification of social exigencies does not possess the properties needful for that use, we have to seek for some other leading distinction better adapted to the purpose. Such a distinction

would seem to be indicated by the considerations to which I
now proceed.

If we ask ourselves on what causes and conditions good
government in all its senses, from the humblest to the most
exalted, depends, we find that the principal of them, the one
which transcends all others, is the qualities of the human beings composing the society over which the government is exercised.

We may take, as a first instance, the administration of justice; with the more propriety, since there is no part of public
business in which the mere machinery, the rules and contrivances for conducting the details of the operation, are of such
vital consequence. Yet even these yield in importance to the
qualities of the human agents employed. Of what efficacy are
rules of procedure in securing the ends of justice if the moral
condition of the people is such that the witnesses generally
lie and the judges and their subordinates take bribes? Again,
how can institutions provide a good municipal administration if there exists such indifference to the subject that those
who would administer honestly and capably cannot be induced to serve, and the duties are left to those who undertake
them because they have some private interest to be promoted?
Of what avail is the most broadly popular representative system if the electors do not care to choose the best member of
parliament, but choose him who will spend most money to be
elected? How can a representative assembly work for good if its
members can be bought, or if their excitability of tempera-
ment, uncorrected by public discipline or private self-control,
makes them incapable of calm deliberation, and they resort to
manual violence on the floor of the House or shoot at one another with rifles? How, again, can government, or any joint
concern, be carried on in a tolerable manner by a people so
envious that, if one among them seems likely to succeed in
anything, those who ought to co-operate with him form a tacit
combination to make him fail? Whenever the general disposition of the people is such that each individual regards those
only of his interests which are selfish, and does not dwell on,

or concern himself for, his share of the general interest, in such a state of things good government is impossible. The influence of defects of intelligence in obstructing all the elements of good government requires no illustration. Government consists of acts done by human beings; and if the agents, or those who choose the agents, or those to whom the agents are responsible, or the lookers-on whose opinion ought to influence and check all these are mere masses of ignorance, stupidity, and baleful prejudice, every operation of government will go wrong, while in proportion as the men rise above this standard, so will the government improve in quality, up to the point of excellence attainable, but nowhere attained where the officers of government, themselves persons of superior virtue and intellect, are surrounded by the atmosphere of a virtuous and enlightened public opinion.

The first element of good government, therefore, being the virtue and intelligence of the human beings composing the community, the most important point of excellence which any form of government can possess is to promote the virtue and intelligence of the people themselves. The first question in respect to any political institutions is how far they tend to foster in the members of the community the various desirable qualities, moral and intellectual; or rather (following Bentham's more complete classification) moral, intellectual, and active. The government which does this the best has every likelihood of being the best in all other respects, since it is on these qualities, so far as they exist in the people, that all possibility of goodness in the practical operations of the government depends.

We may consider, then, as one criterion of the goodness of a government the degree in which it tends to increase the sum of good qualities in the governed, collectively and individually; since, besides that their well-being is the sole object of government, their good qualities supply the moving force which works the machinery. This leaves, as the other constituent element of the merit of a government, the quality of the machinery itself; that is, the degree in which it is adapted to take advantage of the amount of good qualities which may at any time exist and make them instrumental to the right purposes. Let us again take the subject of judicature as an example and illustration. The judicial system being given, the goodness of the administration of justice is in the compound ratio of the worth of the men composing the tribunals, and the worth of the public opinion which influences or controls them. But all the difference between a good and a bad system of judicature lies in the contrivances adopted for bringing whatever moral and intellectual worth exists in the community to bear upon the administration of justice and making it duly operative on the result. The arrangements for rendering the choice of the judges such as to obtain the highest average of virtue and intelligence; the salutary forms of procedure; the publicity which allows observation and criticism of whatever is amiss; the liberty of discussion and censure through the press; the mode of taking evidence, according as it is well or ill adapted to elicit truth; the facilities, whatever be their amount, for obtaining access to the tribunals; the arrangements for detecting crimes and apprehending offenders—all these things are not the power, but the machinery for bringing the power into contact with the obstacle; and the machinery has no action of itself, but without it the power, let it be ever so ample, would be wasted and of no effect. A similar distinction exists in regard to the constitution of the executive departments of administration. Their machinery is good when the proper tests are prescribed for the qualifications of officers, the proper rules for their promotion; when the business is conveniently distributed among those who are to transact it, a convenient and methodical order established for its transaction, a correct and intelligible record kept of it after being transacted; when each individual knows for what he is responsible, and is known to others as responsible for it; when the best-contrived checks are provided against negligence, favoritism, or jobbery in any of the acts of the department. But political checks will no more act of themselves than a bridle will direct a horse without a rider. If the checking functionaries are as corrupt or as negligent as those whom they ought to check, and if the public, the mainspring of the whole checking machinery, are too ignorant, too passive, or too careless and inattentive to do their part, little benefit will be derived from the best administrative apparatus. Yet a good apparatus is always preferable to a bad. It enables such insufficient moving or checking power as exists to act at the greatest advantage; and without it no amount of moving or checking power would be sufficient. Publicity, for instance, is no impediment to evil nor stimulus to good if the public will not look at what is done; but without publicity, how could they either check or encourage what they were not permitted to see? The ideally perfect constitution of a public office is that in which the interest of the functionary is entirely coincident with his duty. No mere system will make it so, but still less can it be made so without a system, aptly devised for the purpose.

What we have said of the arrangements for the detailed administration of the government is still more evidently true of its general constitution. All government which aims at being good is an organization of some part of the good qualities existing in the individual members of the community for the conduct of its collective affairs. A representative constitution is a means of bringing the general standard of intelligence and honesty existing in the community, and the individual intellect and virtue of its wisest members, more directly to bear upon the government, and investing them with greater influence in it than they would in general have under any other mode of organization, though under any such influence as they do have is the source of all good that there is in the government, and the hindrance of every evil that there is not. The greater the amount of these good qualities which the institutions of a country succeed in organizing, and the better the mode of organization, the better will be the government.

We have now, therefore, obtained a foundation for a two-fold division of the merit which any set of political institutions can possess. It consists partly of the degree in which

they promote the general mental advancement of the community, including under that phrase advancement in intellect,
in virtue, and in practical activity and efficiency; and partly
of the degree of perfection with which they organize the
moral, intellectual, and active worth already existing, so as to
operate with the greatest effect on public affairs. A government
is to be judged by its action upon men, and by its action upon
things; by what it makes of the citizens, and what it does with
them; its tendency to improve or deteriorate the people themselves, and the goodness or badness of the work it performs
for them, and by means of them. Government is at once a
great influence acting on the human mind and a set of organized arrangements for public business: in the first capacity its
beneficial action is chiefly indirect, but not therefore less vital,
while its mischievous action may be direct.

The difference between these two functions of a government
is not, like that between Order and Progress, a difference
merely in degree, but in kind. We must not, however, suppose
that they have no intimate connection with one another. The
institutions which ensure the best management of public affairs practicable in the existing state of cultivation tend by
this alone to the further improvement of that state. A people
which had the most just laws, the purest and most efficient
judicature, the most enlightened administration, the most
equitable and least onerous system of finance, compatible with
the stage it had attained in moral and intellectual advancement, would be in a fair way to pass rapidly into a higher
stage. Nor is there any mode in which political institutions
can contribute more effectually to the improvement of the
people than by doing their more direct work well. And, re-
versely, if their machinery is so badly constructed that they do
their own particular business ill, the effect is felt in a thousand ways in lowering the morality and deadening the intelligence and activity of the people. But the distinction is nevertheless real, because this is only one of the means by which
political institutions improve or deteriorate the human mind,
and the causes and modes of that beneficial or injurious influ-

ence remain a distinct and much wider subject of study.

Of the two modes of operation by which a form of government or set of political institutions affects the welfare of the community—its operation as an agency of national education, and its arrangements for conducting the collective affairs of the community in the state of education in which they already are; the last evidently varies much less, from difference of country and state of civilization, than the first. It has also much less to do with the fundamental constitution of the government. The mode of conducting the practical business of government which is best under a free constitution would generally be best also in an absolute monarchy: only an absolute monarchy is not so likely to practice it. The laws of property, for example, the principles of evidence and judicial procedure, the system of taxation and of financial administration need not necessarily be different in different forms of government. Each of these matters has principles and rules of its own, which are a subject of separate study. General jurisprudence, civil and penal legislation, financial and commercial policy are sciences in themselves or, rather, separate members of the comprehensive science or art of government; and the most enlightened doctrines on all these subjects, though not equally likely to be understood or acted on under all forms of government, yet, if understood and acted on, would in general be equally beneficial under them all. It is true that these doctrines could not be applied without some modifications to all states of society and of the human mind; nevertheless, by far the greater number of them would require modifications solely of details to adapt them to any state of society sufficiently advanced to possess rulers capable of understanding them. A government to which they would be wholly unsuitable must be one so bad in itself, or so opposed to public feeling, as to be unable to maintain itself in existence by honest means.

It is otherwise with that portion of the interests of the community which relate to the better or worse training of the people themselves. Considered as instrumental to this, institutions need to be radically different, according to the stage of advancement already reached. The recognition of this truth, though for the most part empirically rather than philosophically, may be regarded as the main point of superiority in the political theories of the present above those of the last age; in which it was customary to claim representative democracy for England or France by arguments which would equally have proved it the only fit form of government for Bedouins or Malays. The state of different communities, in point of culture and development, ranges downward to a condition very little above the highest of the beasts. The upward range, too, is considerable, and the future possible extension vastly greater. A community can only be developed out of one of these states into a higher by a concourse of influences among the principal of which is the government to which they are subject. In all states of human improvement ever yet attained, the nature and degree of authority exercised over individuals, the distribution of power, and the conditions of command and obedience are the most powerful of the influences, except their religious belief, which make them what they are, and enable them to become what they can be. They may be stopped short at any point in their progress by defective adaptation of their government to that particular stage of advancement. And the one indispensable merit of a government, in favor of which it may be forgiven almost any amount of other demerit compatible with progress, is that its operation on the people is favorable, or not unfavorable, to the next step which it is necessary for them to take in order to raise themselves to a higher level.

Thus (to repeat a former example) a people in a state of savage independence, in which everyone lives for himself, exempt, unless by fits, from any external control, is practically incapable of making any progress in civilization until it has learned to obey. The indispensable virtue, therefore, in a government which establishes itself over a people of this sort is that it make itself obeyed. To enable it to do this, the constitution of the government must be nearly, or quite, despotic. A constitution in any degree popular, dependent on the voluntary surrender by the different members of the community of

their individual freedom of action, would fail to enforce the
first lesson which the pupils, in this stage of their progress, require. Accordingly, the civilization of such tribes, when not
the result of juxtaposition with others already civilized, is
almost always the work of an absolute ruler deriving his power
either from religion or military prowess; very often from foreign arms.

Again, uncivilized races, and the bravest and most energetic
still more than the rest, are averse to continuous labor of an
unexciting kind. Yet all real civilization is at this price; without such labor neither can the mind be disciplined into the
habits required by civilized society, nor the material world
prepared to receive it. There needs a rare concurrence of circumstances, and for that reason often a vast length of time,
to reconcile such a people to industry, unless they are for a
while compelled to it. Hence even personal slavery, by giving
a commencement to industrial life and enforcing it as the exclusive occupation of the most numerous portion of the community, may accelerate the transition to a better freedom than
that of fighting and rapine. It is almost needless to say that
this excuse for slavery is only available in a very early state of
society. A civilized people have far other means of imparting
civilization to those under their influence; and slavery is, in all
its details, so repugnant to that government of law which is
the foundation of all modern life, and so corrupting to the
master-class when they have once come under civilized influences, that its adoption under any circumstances whatever in
modern society is a relapse into worse than barbarism.

At some period, however, of their history almost every people, now civilized, have consisted, in majority, of slaves. A
people in that condition require to raise them out of it a very
different polity from a nation of savages. If they are energetic
by nature, and especially if there be associated with them in
the same community an industrious class who are neither
slaves nor slave owners (as was the case in Greece), they need
probably no more to ensure their improvement than to make
them free; when freed, they may often be fit, like Roman

freedmen, to be admitted at once to the full rights of citizenship. This, however, is not the normal condition of slavery
and is generally a sign that it is becoming obsolete. A slave,
properly so called, is a being who has not learned to help himself. He is, no doubt, one step in advance of a savage. He has
not the first lesson of political society still to acquire. He has
learned to obey. But what he obeys is only a direct command.
It is the characteristic of *born* slaves to be incapable of con-
forming their conduct to a rule or law. They can only do what
they are ordered, and only when they are ordered to do it. If
a man whom they fear is standing over them and threatening
them with punishment, they obey; but when his back is
turned, the work remains undone. The motive determining
them must appeal not to their interests, but to their instincts;
immediate hope or immediate terror. A despotism, which may
tame the savage, will, in so far as it is a despotism, only confirm the slaves in their incapacities. Yet a government under
their own control would be entirely unmanageable by them.
Their improvement cannot come from themselves, but must
be superinduced from without. The step which they have to
take, and their only path to improvement, is to be raised from
a government of will to one of law. They have to be taught
self-government, and this, in its initial stage, means the capacity to act on general instructions. What they require is not
a government of force, but one of guidance. Being, however,
in too low a state to yield to the guidance of any but those to
whom they look up as the possessors of force, the sort of government fittest for them is one which possesses force but seldom uses it: a parental despotism or aristocracy resembling
the St. Simonian form of Socialism: [1] maintaining a general
superintendence over all the operations of society so as to keep
before each the sense of a present force sufficient to compel his
obedience to the rule laid down, but which, owing to the impossibility of descending to regulate all the minutiae of indus-

---

1 [Mill here refers to St. Simon's plan of a society controlled by industrial
leaders and men of science, in which every member should be employed
according to his abilities and rewarded in proportion to his achievements.]

try and life, necessarily leaves and induces individuals to do much of themselves. This, which may be termed the government of leading-strings, seems to be the one required to carry such a people the most rapidly through the next necessary step in social progress. Such appears to have been the idea of the government of the Incas of Peru, and such was that of the Jesuits of Paraguay. I need scarcely remark that leading-strings are only admissible as a means of gradually training the people to walk alone.

It would be out of place to carry the illustration further. To attempt to investigate what kind of government is suited to every known state of society would be to compose a treatise, not on representative government, but on political science at large. For our more limited purpose we borrow from political philosophy only its general principles. To determine the form of government most suited to any particular people, we must be able, among the defects and shortcomings which belong to that people, to distinguish those that are the immediate impediment to progress, to discover what it is which (as it were) stops the way. The best government for them is the one which tends most to give them that for want of which they cannot advance or advance only in a lame and lopsided manner. We must not, however, forget the reservation necessary in all things which have for their object improvement, or Progress—namely, that in seeking the good which is needed, no damage, or as little as possible, be done to that already possessed. A people of savages should be taught obedience, but not in such a manner as to convert them into a people of slaves. And (to give the observation a higher generality) the form of government which is most effectual for carrying a people through the next stage of progress will still be very improper for them if it does this in such a manner as to obstruct, or positively unfit them for, the step next beyond. Such cases are frequent and are among the most melancholy facts in history. The Egyptian hierarchy, the paternal despotism of China were very fit instruments for carrying those nations up to the point of civilization which they attained. But having reached that point,

they were brought to a permanent halt for want of mental
liberty and individuality—requisites of improvement which the
institutions that had carried them thus far entirely incapaci-
tated them from acquiring; and as the institutions did not
break down and give place to others, further improvement
stopped. In contrast with these nations, let us consider the
example of an opposite character afforded by another and a
comparatively insignificant Oriental people—the Jews. They,
too, had an absolute monarchy and a hierarchy, and their organized institutions were as obviously of sacerdotal origin as
those of the Hindus. These did for them what was done for
other Oriental races by their institutions—subdued them to
industry and order and gave them a national life. But neither
their kings nor their priests ever obtained, as in those other
countries, the exclusive molding of their character. Their
religion, which enabled persons of genius and a high religious
tone to be regarded and to regard themselves as inspired from
heaven, gave existence to an inestimably precious unorganized
institution—the Order (if it may be so termed) of Prophets.
Under the protection, generally though not always effectual,
of their sacred character, the Prophets were a power in the
nation, often more than a match for kings and priests, and
kept up, in that little corner of the earth, the antagonism of
influences which is the only real security for continued progress. Religion, consequently, was not there what it has been in
so many other places—a consecration of all that was once established, and a barrier against further improvement. The
remark of a distinguished Hebrew, M. Salvador, that the
prophets were, in Church and State, the equivalent of the
modern liberty of the press, gives a just but not an adequate
conception of the part fulfilled in national and universal history by this great element of Jewish life; by means of which,
the canon of inspiration never being complete, the persons
most eminent in genius and moral feeling could not only de-
nounce and reprobate, with the direct authority of the Al-
mighty, whatever appeared to them deserving of such treatment, but could give forth better and higher interpretations

of the national religion, which thenceforth became part of the religion. Accordingly, whoever can divest himself of the habit of reading the Bible as if it was one book, which until lately was equally inveterate in Christians and in unbelievers, sees with admiration the vast interval between the morality and religion of the Pentateuch, or even of the historical books (the unmistakable work of Hebrew Conservatives of the sacerdotal order), and the morality and religion of the Prophecies—a distance as wide as between these last and the Gospels. Conditions more favorable to Progress could not easily exist: accordingly the Jews, instead of being stationary like other Asiatics, were, next to the Greeks, the most progressive people of antiquity, and, jointly with them, have been the starting point and main propelling agency of modern cultivation.

It is, then, impossible to understand the question of the adaptation of forms of government to states of society without taking into account not only the next step, but all the steps which society has yet to make—both those which can be foreseen, and the far wider indefinite range which is at present out of sight. It follows that to judge of the merits of forms of government, an ideal must be constructed of the form of government most eligible in itself, that is, which, if the necessary conditions existed for giving effect to its beneficial tendencies, would, more than all others, favor and promote not some one improvement, but all forms and degrees of it. This having been done, we must consider what are the mental conditions of all sorts necessary to enable this government to realize its tendencies, and what, therefore, are the various defects by which a people is made incapable of reaping its benefits. It would then be possible to construct a theorem of the circumstances in which that form of government may wisely be introduced; and also to judge, in cases in which it had better not be introduced, what inferior forms of polity will best carry those communities through the intermediate stages which they must traverse before they can become fit for the best form of government.

Of these inquiries, the last does not concern us here; but the first is an essential part of our subject, for we may, without rashness, at once enunciate a proposition the proofs and illustrations of which will present themselves in the ensuing pages—that this ideally best form of government will be found in some one or other variety of the Representative System.

CHAPTER III

THAT THE IDEALLY BEST FORM OF GOVERNMENT IS REPRESENTATIVE GOVERNMENT

IT HAS long (perhaps throughout the entire duration of British freedom) been a common saying that, if a good despot could be ensured, despotic monarchy would be the best form of government. I look upon this as a radical and most pernicious misconception of what good government is; which, until it can be got rid of, will fatally vitiate all our speculations on government.

The supposition is that absolute power, in the hands of an eminent individual, would ensure a virtuous and intelligent performance of all the duties of government. Good laws would be established and enforced, bad laws would be reformed; the best men would be placed in all situations of trust; justice would be as well administered, the public burdens would be as light and as judiciously imposed, every branch of administration would be as purely and as intelligently conducted as the circumstances of the country and its degree of intellectual and moral cultivation would admit. I am willing, for the sake of the argument, to concede all this; but I must point out how great the concession is, how much more is needed to produce even an approximation to these results than is conveyed in the simple expression "a good despot." Their realization would in fact imply, not merely a good monarch, but an all-seeing one. He must be at all times informed correctly, in considerable detail, of the conduct and working of every branch of administration, in every district of the country, and must be able, in the twenty-four hours per day which are all that is granted to a king as to the humblest laborer, to give an effective share of attention and superintendence to all parts of this vast field; or he must at least be capable of discerning and choosing out, from among the mass of his subjects, not only a large abundance of honest and able men, fit to conduct every branch of public administration under supervision and control, but also the small number of men of eminent virtues and talents who can be trusted not only to do without that supervision, but to exercise it themselves over others. So extraordinary are the faculties and energies required for performing this task in any supportable manner that the good despot whom we are supposing can hardly be imagined as consenting to undertake it, unless as a refuge from intolerable evils and a transitional preparation for something beyond. But the argument can do without even this immense item in the account. Suppose the difficulty vanquished. What should we then have? One man of superhuman mental activity managing the entire affairs of a mentally passive people. Their passivity is implied in the very idea of absolute power. The nation as a whole and every individual composing it are without any potential voice in their own destiny. They exercise no will in respect to their collective interests. All is decided for them by a will not their own, which it is legally a crime for them to disobey. What sort of human beings can be formed under such a regimen? What development can either their thinking or their active faculties attain under it? On matters of pure theory they might perhaps be allowed to speculate, so long as their speculations either did not approach politics or had not the remotest connection with its practice. On practical affairs they could at most be only suffered to suggest; and even under the most moderate of despots, none but persons of already admitted or reputed superiority could hope that their suggestions would be known to, much less regarded by, those who had the management of affairs. A person must have a very unusual taste for intellectual exercise in and for itself, who will put himself to the trouble of thought when it is to have no outward effect, or qualify himself for functions which he has no chance of being allowed to exercise. The only sufficient incitement to mental exertion, in any but a few minds in a generation, is the prospect of some practical use to be made of its results. It does not follow that the nation will be wholly destitute of intellectual power. The common business of life, which must necessarily be performed by each individual or family for themselves, will call forth some amount of intelligence and practical ability, within a certain narrow range of ideas. There may be a select class of *savants* who cultivate science with a view to its physical uses or for the pleasure of the pursuit. There will be a bureaucracy, and persons in training for the bureaucracy, who will be taught at least some empirical maxims of government and public administration. There may be, and often has been, a systematic organization of the best mental power in the country in some special direction (commonly military) to promote the grandeur of the despot. But the public at large remains without information and without interest on all the greater matters of practice; or, if they have any knowledge of them, it is but a *dilettante* knowledge, like that which people have of the mechanical arts who have never handled a tool. Nor is it only in their intelligence that they suffer. Their moral capacities are equally stunted. Wherever the sphere of action of human beings is artificially circumscribed, their sentiments are narrowed and dwarfed in the same proportion. The food of feeling is action: even domestic affection lives upon voluntary good offices. Let a person have nothing to do for his country, and he will not care for it. It has been said of old that in a despotism there is at most but one patriot, the despot himself; and the saying rests on a just appreciation of the effects of absolute subjection, even to a good and wise master. Religion remains: and here at least, it may be thought, is an agency that may be relied on for lifting men's eyes and minds above the dust at their feet. But religion, even supposing it to escape perversion for the purposes of despotism, ceases in these circumstances to be a social concern and narrows into a personal affair between an individual and his Maker in which the issue at stake is but his private salvation. Religion in this shape is quite consistent with the most selfish and contracted egoism and identifies the votary as little in feeling with the rest of his kind as sensuality itself.

A good despotism means a government in which, so far as depends on the despot, there is no positive oppression by officers of state, but in which all the collective interests of the people are managed for them, all the thinking that has relation to collective interests done for them, and in which their minds are formed by, and consenting to, this abdication of their own energies. Leaving things to the Government, like leaving them to Providence, is synonymous with caring nothing about them and accepting their results, when disagreeable, as visitations of Nature. With the exception, therefore, of a few studious men who take an intellectual interest in speculation for its own sake, the intelligence and sentiments of the whole people are given up to the material interests and, when these are provided for, to the amusement and ornamentation of private life. But to say this is to say, if the whole testimony of history is worth anything, that the era of national decline has arrived; that is, if the nation had ever attained anything to decline from. If it has never risen above the condition of an Oriental people, in that condition it continues to stagnate. But if, like Greece or Rome, it had realized anything higher, through the energy, patriotism, and enlargement of mind, which as national qualities are the fruits solely of freedom, it relapses in a few generations into the Oriental state. And that state does not mean stupid tranquillity, with security against change for the worse; it often means being overrun, conquered, and reduced to domestic slavery, either by a stronger despot or by the nearest barbarous people who retain along with their savage rudeness the energies of freedom.

Such are not merely the natural tendencies, but the inherent necessities of despotic government; from which there is no outlet unless in so far as the despotism consents not to be despotism; in so far as the supposed good despot abstains from exercising his power and, though holding it in reserve, allows the general business of government to go on as if the people really governed themselves. However little probable it may be, we may imagine a despot observing many of the rules and restraints of constitutional government. He might allow such freedom of the press and of discussion as would enable a public opinion to form and express itself on national affairs. He might suffer local interests to be managed, without the interference of authority, by the people themselves. He might even surround himself with a council or councils of government, freely chosen by the whole or some portion of the nation, retaining in his own hands the power of taxation and the supreme legislative as well as executive authority. Were he to act thus, and so far abdicate as a despot, he would do away with a considerable part of the evils characteristic of despotism. Political activity and capacity for public affairs would no longer be prevented from growing up in the body of the nation, and a public opinion would form itself not the mere echo of the government. But such improvement would be the beginning of new difficulties. This public opinion, independent of the monarch's dictation, must be either with him or against him; if not the one, it will be the other. All governments must displease many persons, and these having now regular organs and being able to express their sentiments, opinions adverse to the measures of government would often be expressed. What is the monarch to do when these unfavorable opinions happen to be in the majority? Is he to alter his course? Is he to defer to the nation? If so, he is no longer a despot, but a constitutional king—an organ or first minister of the people, distinguished only by being irremovable. If not, he must either put down opposition by his despotic power, or there will arise a permanent antagonism between the people and one man, which can have but one possible ending. Not even a religious principle of passive obedience and "right divine" would long ward off the natural consequences of such a position. The monarch would have to succumb and conform to the conditions of constitutional royalty, or give place to someone who would. The despotism, being thus chiefly nominal, would possess few of the advantages supposed to belong to absolute monarchy, while it would realize in a very imperfect degree those of a free government; since, however great an amount of liberty the citizens might practically enjoy, they could never forget that they held it on sufferance and by a concession which under the existing constitution of the state might at any moment be resumed; that they were legally slaves, though of a prudent, or indulgent, master.

It is not much to be wondered at if impatient or disappointed reformers, groaning under the impediments opposed to the most salutary public improvements by the ignorance, the indifference, the intractableness, the perverse obstinacy of a people, and the corrupt combinations of selfish private interests armed with the powerful weapons afforded by free institutions, should at times sigh for a strong hand to bear down all these obstacles and compel a recalcitrant people to be better governed. But (setting aside the fact that for one despot who now and then reforms an abuse, there are ninety-nine who do nothing but create them) those who look in any such direction for the realization of their hopes leave out of the idea of good government its principal element, the improvement of the people themselves. One of the benefits of freedom is that under it the ruler cannot pass by the people's minds and amend their affairs for them without amending them. If it were possible for the people to be well governed in spite of themselves, their good government would last no longer than the freedom of a people usually lasts who have been liberated by foreign arms without their own co-operation. It is true, a despot may educate the people; and to do so really would be the best apology for his despotism. But any education which aims at making human beings other than machines in the long run makes them claim to have the control of their own actions. The leaders of French philosophy in the eighteenth century had been educated by the Jesuits. Even Jesuit education, it seems, was sufficiently real to call forth the appetite for freedom. Whatever invigorates the faculties, in however small a measure, creates an increased desire for their more unimpeded exercise; and a popular education is a failure if it educates the people for any state but that which it will certainly induce them to desire, and most probably to demand.

I am far from condemning, in cases of extreme exigency, the assumption of absolute power in the form of a temporary dictatorship. Free nations have, in times of old, conferred such power by their own choice, as a necessary medicine for diseases of the body politic which could not be got rid of by less violent means. But its acceptance, even for a time strictly limited, can only be excused if, like Solon or Pittacus, the dictator employs the whole power he assumes in removing the obstacles which debar the nation from the enjoyment of freedom. A good despotism is an altogether false ideal, which practically (except as a means to some temporary purpose) becomes the most senseless and dangerous of chimeras. Evil for evil, a good despotism in a country at all advanced in civilization is more noxious than a bad one; for it is far more relaxing and enervating to the thoughts, feelings, and energies of the people. The despotism of Augustus prepared the Romans for Tiberius. If the whole tone of their character had not first been prostrated by nearly two generations of that mild slavery, they would probably have had spirit enough left to rebel against the more odious one.

There is no difficulty in showing that the ideally best form of government is that in which the sovereignty, or supreme controlling power in the last resort, is vested in the entire aggregate of the community, every citizen not only having a voice in the exercise of that ultimate sovereignty, but being, at least occasionally, called on to take an actual part in the government by the personal discharge of some public function, local or general.

To test this proposition, it has to be examined in reference to the two branches into which, as pointed out in the
last chapter, the inquiry into the goodness of a government
conveniently divides itself—namely, how far it promotes the
good management of the affairs of society by means of the
existing faculties, moral, intellectual, and active, of its various
members, and what is its effect in improving or deteriorating
those faculties.

The ideally best form of government, it is scarcely necessary
to say, does not mean one which is practicable or eligible in
all states of civilization, but the one which, in the circumstances in which it is practicable and eligible, is attended with
the greatest amount of beneficial consequences, immediate and
prospective. A completely popular government is the only
polity which can make out any claim to this character. It is
pre-eminent in both the departments between which the excellence of a political constitution is divided. It is both more
favorable to present good government and promotes a better
and higher form of national character than any other polity
whatsoever.

Its superiority in reference to present well-being rests upon
two principles of as universal truth and applicability as any
general propositions which can be laid down respecting human affairs. The first is that the rights and interests of every
or any person are only secure from being disregarded when
the person interested is himself able, and habitually disposed,
to stand up for them. The second is that the general prosperity attains a greater height and is more widely diffused in
proportion to the amount and variety of the personal energies
enlisted in promoting it.

Putting these two propositions into a shape more special
to their present application: human beings are only secure
from evil at the hands of others in proportion as they have
the power of being, and are, self-*protecting;* and they only
achieve a high degree of success in their struggle with nature
in proportion as they are self-*dependent,* relying on what they

themselves can do, either separately or in concert, rather than on what others do for them.

The former proposition—that each is the only safe guardian of his own rights and interests—is one of those elementary maxims of prudence which every person capable of conducting his own affairs implicitly acts upon wherever he himself is interested. Many, indeed, have a great dislike to it as a political doctrine and are fond of holding it up to obloquy as a doctrine of universal selfishness. To which we may answer that whenever it ceases to be true that mankind, as a rule, prefer themselves to others, and those nearest to them to those more remote, from that moment Communism is not only practicable but the only defensible form of society, and will, when that time arrives, be assuredly carried into effect. For my own part, not believing in universal selfishness, I have no difficulty in admitting that Communism [1] would even now be practicable among the *élite* of mankind, and may become so among the rest. But as this opinion is anything but popular with those defenders of existing institutions who find fault with the doctrine of the general predominance of self-interest, I am inclined to think they do in reality believe that most men consider themselves before other people. It is not, however, necessary to affirm even thus much in order to support the claim of all to participate in the sovereign power. We need not suppose that when power resides in an exclusive class, that class will knowingly and deliberately sacrifice the other classes to themselves; it suffices that, in the absence of its natural defenders, the interest of the excluded is always in dan-

[1] [By Communism, Mill means pre-Marxian socialism. Nowhere in his writings does Mill indicate any awareness of Marxian socialism, which was formulated during his lifetime. (The first volume of Marx's *Das Kapital* appeared in 1867.) He often speaks sympathetically of the various pre-Marxian schools of socialism represented by Claude Henri de Rouvroy, Comte de Saint-Simon (1760-1825; see also note 1 on p. 32), François Marie Charles Fourier (1772-1837), Robert Owen (1771-1858), Pierre Joseph Proudhon (1809-1865), and others whom the Marxians dismissed as unscientific and utopian.]

ger of being overlooked, and, when looked at, is seen with
very different eyes from those of the persons whom it directly
concerns. In this country, for example, what are called the
working classes may be considered as excluded from all direct
participation in the government. I do not believe that the
classes who do participate in it have in general any intention
of sacrificing the working classes to themselves. They once
had that intention—witness the persevering attempts so long
made to keep down wages by law. But in the present day
their ordinary disposition is the very opposite: they willingly
make considerable sacrifices, especially of their pecuniary interest, for the benefit of the working classes, and err rather by
too lavish and indiscriminating beneficence; nor do I believe
that any rulers in history have been actuated by a more sincere desire to do their duty toward the poorer portion of their
countrymen. Yet does Parliament, or almost any of the members composing it, ever for an instant look at any question
with the eyes of a workingman? When a subject arises in
which the laborers as such have an interest, is it regarded from
any point of view but that of the employers of labor? I do not
say that the workingmen's view of these questions is in general nearer to the truth than the other, but it is sometimes
quite as near; and in any case it ought to be respectfully
listened to instead of being, as it is, not merely turned away
from, but ignored. On the question of strikes, for instance,
it is doubtful if there is so much as one among the leading
members of either House who is not firmly convinced that
the reason of the matter is unqualifiedly on the side of the
masters, and that the men's view of it is simply absurd. Those
who have studied the question know well how far this is from
being the case, and in how different and how infinitely less
superficial a manner the point would have to be argued if the
classes who strike were able to make themselves heard in Parliament.

It is an adherent condition of human affairs that no intention, however sincere, of protecting the interests of others can
make it safe or salutary to tie up their own hands. Still more

obviously true is it that by their own hands only can any positive and durable improvement of their circumstances in life
be worked out. Through the joint influence of these two principles, all free communities have both been more exempt
from social injustice and crime, and have attained more brilliant prosperity, than any others, or than they themselves
after they lost their freedom. Contrast the free states of the
world, while their freedom lasted, with the contemporary
subjects of monarchical or oligarchical despotism: the Greek
cities with the Persian satrapies; the Italian republics and the
free towns of Flanders and Germany with the feudal mon-
archies of Europe; Switzerland, Holland, and England with
Austria or ante-revolutionary France. Their superior prosperity was too obvious ever to have been gainsaid, while their
superiority in good government and social relations is proved
by the prosperity, and is manifest besides in every page of history. If we compare, not one age with another, but the different governments which coexisted in the same age, no
amount of disorder which exaggeration itself can pretend to
have existed amidst the publicity of the free states can be compared for a moment with the contemptuous trampling upon
the mass of the people which pervaded the whole life of the
monarchical countries, or the disgusting individual tyranny
which was of more than daily occurrence under the systems
of plunder which they called fiscal arrangements and in the
secrecy of their frightful courts of justice.

It must be acknowledged that the benefits of freedom, so far
as they have hitherto been enjoyed, were obtained by the extension of its privileges to a part only of the community; and
that a government in which they are extended impartially to
all is a desideratum still unrealized. But though every approach to this has an independent value, and in many cases
more than an approach could not, in the existing state of general improvement, be made, the participation of all in these
benefits is the ideally perfect conception of free government.

In proportion as any, no matter who, are excluded from it, the interests of the excluded are left without the guaranty accorded to the rest, and they themselves have less scope and encouragement than they might otherwise have to that exertion of their energies for the good of themselves and of the community, to which the general prosperity is always proportioned.

Thus stands the case as regards present well-being; the good management of the affairs of the existing generation. If we now pass to the influence of the form of government upon character, we shall find the superiority of popular government over every other to be, if possible, still more decided and indisputable.

This question really depends upon a still more fundamental one, viz., which of two common types of character, for the general good of humanity, it is most desirable should predominate—the active or the passive type: that which struggles against evils or that which endures them; that which bends to circumstances or that which endeavors to make circumstances bend to itself.

The commonplaces of moralists, and the general sympathies of mankind, are in favor of the passive type. Energetic characters may be admired, but the acquiescent and submissive are those which most men personally prefer. The passiveness of our neighbors increases our own sense of security and plays into the hands of our willfulness. Passive characters, if we do not happen to need their activity, seem an obstruction the less in our own path. A contented character is not a dangerous rival. Yet nothing is more certain than that improvement in human affairs is wholly the work of the uncontented characters, and, moreover, that it is much easier for an active mind to acquire the virtues of patience than for a passive one to assume those of energy.

Of the three varieties of mental excellence, intellectual, practical, and moral, there never could be any doubt in regard to the first two which side had the advantage. All intellectual superiority is the fruit of active effort. Enterprise, the desire to keep moving, to be trying and accomplishing new things for

our own benefit or that of others, is the parent even of speculative, and much more of practical, talent. The intellectual
culture compatible with the other type is of that feeble and
vague description which belongs to a mind that stops at amusement or at simple contemplation. The test of real and vigorous thinking, the thinking which ascertains truths instead of
dreaming dreams, is successful application to practice. Where
that purpose does not exist to give definiteness, precision, and
an intelligible meaning to thought, it generates nothing better
than the mystical metaphysics of the Pythagoreans or the
Vedas.[2] With respect to practical improvement, the case is
still more evident. The character which improves human life
is that which struggles with natural powers and tendencies,
not that which gives way to them. The self-benefiting qualities are all on the side of the active and energetic character;
and the habits and conduct which promote the advantage of
each individual member of the community must be at least
a part of those which conduce most in the end to the advancement of the community as a whole.

But on the point of moral preferability there seems at
first sight to be room for doubt. I am not referring to the
religious feeling which has so generally existed in favor of the
inactive character, as being more in harmony with the submission due to the divine will. Christianity, as well as other
religions, has fostered this sentiment; but it is the prerogative
of Christianity, as regards this and many other perversions,
that it is able to throw them off. Abstractedly from religious
considerations, a passive character which yields to obstacles
instead of striving to overcome them may not indeed be very
useful to others, no more than to itself, but it might be expected to be at least inoffensive. Contentment is always
counted among the moral virtues. But it is a complete error
to suppose that contentment is necessarily or naturally attend-

2 [The followers of Pythagoras, a Greek philosopher and mathematician
of the 6th century B.C., practiced a mystical religion derived in part from
a belief that the universe could be interpreted numerically. The Vedas,
or Vedanta, is an Indian religion which flourished from 1500-600 B.C.]

ant on passivity of character; and unless it is, the moral consequences are mischievous. Where there exists a desire for advantages not possessed, the mind which does not potentially
possess them by means of its own energies is apt to look with
hatred and malice on those who do. The person bestirring
himself with hopeful prospects to improve his circumstances
is the one who feels good will toward others engaged in, or
who have succeeded in, the same pursuit. And where the majority are so engaged, those who do not attain the object have
had the tone given to their feelings by the general habit of
the country, and ascribe their failure to want of effort or opportunity or to their personal ill luck. But those who, while
desiring what others possess, put no energy into striving for
it, are either incessantly grumbling that fortune does not do
for them what they do not attempt to do for themselves or
overflowing with envy and ill will toward those who possess
what they would like to have.

In proportion as success in life is seen or believed to be the
fruit of fatality or accident, and not of exertion, in that same
ratio does envy develop itself as a point of national character.
The most envious of all mankind are the Orientals. In Oriental moralists, in Oriental tales, the envious man is remarkably prominent. In real life, he is the terror of all who possess
anything desirable, be it a palace, a handsome child, or even
good health and spirits: the supposed effect of his mere look
constitutes the all pervading superstition of the evil eye. Next
to Orientals in envy, as in activity, are some of the Southern
Europeans. The Spaniards pursued all their great men with
it, embittered their lives, and generally succeeded in putting
an early stop to their successes.[3] With the French, who are
essentially a southern people, the double education of despot-

---

[3] I limit the expression to past time, because I would say nothing de-
rogatory of a great, and now at last a free, people, who are entering into
the general movement of European progress with a vigor which bids fair
to make up rapidly the ground they have lost. No one can doubt what
Spanish intellect and energy are capable of; and their faults as a people
are chiefly those for which freedom and industrial ardor are a real specific.

ism and Catholicism has, in spite of their impulsive tempera-
ment, made submission and endurance the common character
of the people, and their most received notion of wisdom and
excellence; and if envy of one another, and of all superiority,
is not more rife among them than it is, the circumstance
must be ascribed to the many valuable counteracting elements
in the French character, and most of all to the great individual
energy which, though less persistent and more intermittent
than in the self-helping and struggling Anglo-Saxons, has
nevertheless manifested itself among the French in nearly
every direction in which the operation of their institutions
has been favorable to it.

There are, no doubt, in all countries really contented characters who not merely do not seek, but do not desire, what they
do not already possess, and these naturally bear no ill will
toward such as have apparently a more favored lot. But the
great mass of seeming contentment is real discontent combined with indolence or self-indulgence, which, while taking
no legitimate means of raising itself, delights in bringing
others down to its own level. And if we look narrowly even
at the cases of innocent contentment, we perceive that they
only win our admiration when the indifference is solely to
improvement in outward circumstances, and there is a striving
for perpetual advancement in spiritual worth or at least a
disinterested zeal to benefit others. The contented man, or
the contented family, who have no ambition to make anyone
else happier, to promote the good of their country or their
neighborhood, or to improve themselves in moral excellence,
excite in us neither admiration nor approval. We rightly
ascribe this sort of contentment to mere unmanliness and want
of spirit. The content which we approve is an ability to do
cheerfully without what cannot be had: a just appreciation of
the comparative value of different objects of desire and a
willing renunciation of the less when incompatible with the
greater. These, however, are excellences more natural to the
character, in proportion as it is actively engaged in the attempt
to improve its own or some other lot. He who is continually

measuring his energy against difficulties learns what are the difficulties insuperable to him, and what are those which, though he might overcome, the success is not worth the cost. He whose thoughts and activities are all needed for, and habitually employed in, practicable and useful enterprises is the person of all others least likely to let his mind dwell with brooding discontent upon things either not worth attaining, or which are not so to him. Thus the active, self-helping character is not only intrinsically the best, but is the likeliest to acquire all that is really excellent or desirable in the opposite type.

The striving, go-ahead character of England and the United States is only a fit subject of disapproving criticism on account of the very secondary objects on which it commonly expends its strength. In itself it is the foundation of the best hopes for the general improvement of mankind. It has been acutely remarked that whenever anything goes amiss the habitual impulse of French people is to say, "Il faut de la patience"; [4] and of English people, "What a shame." The people who think it a shame when anything goes wrong—who rush to the conclusion that the evil could and ought to have been prevented are those who, in the long run, do most to make the world better. If the desires are low placed, if they extend to little beyond physical comfort, and the show of riches, the immediate results of the energy will not be much more than the continual extension of man's power over material objects; but even this makes room, and prepares the mechanical appliances, for the greatest intellectual and social achievements; and while the energy is there, some persons will apply it, and it will be applied more and more, to the perfecting not of outward circumstances alone, but of man's inward nature. Inactivity, unaspiringness, absence of desire are a more fatal hindrance to improvement than any misdirection of energy, and are that through which alone, when existing in the mass, any very formidable misdirection by an energetic few becomes possible. It is this, mainly, which retains in a savage or semi-

4 ["Be patient."]

savage state the great majority of the human race.

Now there can be no kind of doubt that the passive type of character is favored by the government of one or a few, and the active self-helping type by that of the many. Irresponsible rulers need the quiescence of the ruled more than they need any activity but that which they can compel. Submissiveness to the prescriptions of men as necessities of nature is the lesson inculcated by all governments upon those who are wholly without participation in them. The will of superiors, and the law as the will of superiors, must be passively yielded to. But no men are mere instruments or materials in the hands of their rulers who have will or spirit or a spring of internal activity in the rest of their proceedings; and any manifestation of these qualities, instead of receiving encouragement from despots, has to get itself forgiven by them. Even when irresponsible rulers are not sufficiently conscious of danger from the mental activity of their subjects to be desirous of repressing it, the position itself is a repression. Endeavor is even more effectually restrained by the certainty of its impotence than by any positive discouragement. Between subjection to the will of others and the virtues of self-help and self-government, there is a natural incompatibility. This is more or less complete, according as the bondage is strained or relaxed. Rulers differ very much in the length to which they carry the control of the free agency of their subjects or the supersession of it by managing their business for them. But the difference is in degree, not in principle; and the best despots often go the greatest lengths in chaining up the free agency of their subjects. A bad despot, when his own personal indulgences have been provided for, may sometimes be willing to let the people alone; but a good despot insists on doing them good, by making them do their own business in a better way than they themselves know of. The regulations which restricted to fixed processes all the leading branches of French manufactures were the work of the great Colbert.

Very different is the state of the human faculties where a

human being feels himself under no other external restraint than the necessities of nature, or mandates of society which he has his share in imposing, and which it is open to him, if he thinks them wrong, publicly to dissent from and exert himself actively to get altered. No doubt, under a government partially popular, this freedom may be exercised even by those who are not partakers in the full privileges of citizenship. But it is a great additional stimulus to anyone's self-help and self-reliance when he starts from even ground and has not to feel that his success depends on the impression he can make upon the sentiments and dispositions of a body of whom he is not one. It is a great discouragement to an individual, and a still greater one to a class, to be left out of the constitution—to be reduced to plead from outside the door to the arbiters of their destiny, not taken into consultation within. The maximum of the invigorating effect of freedom upon the character is only obtained when the person acted on either is, or is looking forward to becoming, a citizen as fully privileged as any other. What is still more important than even this matter of feeling is the practical discipline which the character obtains from the occasional demand made upon the citizens to exercise, for a time and in their turn, some social function. It is not sufficiently considered how little there is in most men's ordinary life to give any largeness either to their conceptions or to their sentiments. Their work is a routine; not a labor of love, but of self-interest in the most elementary form, the satisfaction of daily wants; neither the thing done nor the process of doing it introduces the mind to thoughts or feelings extending beyond individuals; if instructive books are within their reach, there is no stimulus to read them; and in most cases the individual has no access to any person of cultivation much superior to his own. Giving him something to do for the public supplies, in a measure, all these deficiencies. If circumstances allow the amount of public duty assigned him to be considerable, it makes him an educated man. Notwithstanding the defects of the social system and moral ideas of antiquity, the practice of the dicastery and the ecclesia [5] raised the intellectual standard of an average Athenian citizen far beyond anything of which there is yet an example in any other mass of men, ancient or modern. The proofs of this are apparent in every page of our great historian of Greece; [6] but we need scarcely look further than to the high quality of the addresses which their great orators deemed best calculated to act with effect on their understanding and will. A benefit of the same kind, though far less in degree, is produced on Englishmen of the lower middle class by their liability to be placed on juries and to serve parish offices; which, though it does not occur to so many, nor is so continuous, nor introduces them to so great a variety of elevated considerations as to admit of comparison with the public education which every citizen of Athens obtained from her democratic institutions, must make them nevertheless very different beings, in range of ideas and development of faculties, from those who have done nothing in their lives but drive a quill or sell goods over a counter. Still more salutary is the moral part of the instruction afforded by the participation of the private citizen, if even rarely, in public functions. He is called upon, while so engaged, to weigh interests not his own; to be guided, in case of conflicting claims, by another rule than his private partialities; to apply, at every turn, principles and maxims which have for their reason of existence the common good; and he usually finds associated with him in the same work minds more familiarized than his own with these ideas and operations, whose study it will be to supply reason to his understanding, and stimulation to his feeling for the general interest. He is made to feel himself one of the public, and whatever is for their benefit to be for his benefit. Where this school of public spirit does not exist, scarcely any sense is entertained that private persons, in no eminent social situation, owe any duties to society, ex-

5 [The popular court and assembly, respectively, in which all Athenian citizens could participate.]

6 [George Grote (1794-1871), whose twelve-volume *History of Greece* appeared between 1846 and 1856.]

cept to obey the laws and submit to the government. There is no unselfish sentiment of identification with the public. Every thought or feeling, either of interest or of duty, is absorbed in the individual and in the family. The man never thinks of any collective interest, of any objects to be pursued jointly with others, but only in competition with them, and in some measure at their expense. A neighbor, not being an ally or an associate, since he is never engaged in any common undertaking for joint benefit, is therefore only a rival. Thus even private morality suffers, while public is actually extinct. Were this the universal and only possible state of things, the utmost aspirations of the lawgiver or the moralist could only stretch to make the bulk of the community a flock of sheep innocently nibbling the grass side by side.

From these accumulated considerations it is evident that the only government which can fully satisfy all the exigencies of the social state is one in which the whole people participate; that any participation, even in the smallest public function, is useful; that the participation should everywhere be as great as the general degree of improvement of the community will allow; and that nothing less can be ultimately desirable than the admission of all to a share in the sovereign power of the state. But since all cannot, in a community exceeding a single small town, participate personally in any but some very minor portions of the public business, it follows that the ideal type of a perfect government must be representative.

CHAPTER IV

UNDER WHAT SOCIAL CONDITIONS REPRESENTATIVE GOVERNMENT IS INAPPLICABLE

WE HAVE recognized in representative government the ideal type of the most perfect polity, for which, in consequence, any portion of mankind are better adapted in proportion to their degree of general improvement. As they range lower and lower in development, that form of government will be, generally speaking, less suitable to them, though this is not true universally; for the adaptation of a people to representative government does not depend so much upon the place they occupy in the general scale of humanity as upon the degree in which they possess certain special requisites; requisites, however, so closely connected with their degree of general advancement that any variation between the two is rather the exception than the rule. Let us examine at what point in the descending series representative government ceases altogether to be admissible, either through its own unfitness or the superior fitness of some other regimen.

First, then, representative, like any other government, must be unsuitable in any case in which it cannot permanently subsist—i.e., in which it does not fulfill the three fundamental conditions enumerated in the first chapter. These were: (1) that the people should be willing to receive it; (2) that they should be willing and able to do what is necessary for its preservation; (3) that they should be willing and able to fulfill the duties and discharge the functions which it imposes on them.

The willingness of the people to accept representative government only becomes a practical question when an enlightened ruler, or a foreign nation or nations who have gained power over the country, are disposed to offer it the boon. To individual reformers the question is almost irrelevant since, if no other objection can be made to their enterprise than that the opinion of the nation is not yet on their side, they have the ready and proper answer, that to bring it over to their side is the very end they aim at. When opinion is really adverse, its hostility is usually to the fact of change rather than to representative government in itself. The contrary case is not indeed unexampled; there has sometimes been a religious repugnance to any limitation of the power of a particular line of rulers; but, in general, the doctrine of passive obedience meant only submission to the will of the powers that be, whether monarchical or popular. In any case in which the attempt to introduce representative government is at all likely to be made, indifference to it, and inability to understand its processes and requirements rather than positive opposition are the obstacles to be expected. These, however, are as fatal, and may be as hard to be got rid of, as actual aversion, it being easier, in most cases, to change the direction of an active feeling than to create one in a state previously passive. When a people have no sufficient value for, and attachment to, a representative constitution, they have next to no chance of retaining it. In every country the executive is the branch of the government which wields the immediate power, and is in direct contact with the public; to it, principally, the hopes and fears of individuals are directed, and by it both the benefits and the terrors and *prestige* of government are mainly represented to the public eye. Unless, therefore, the authorities whose office it is to check the executive are backed by an effective opinion and feeling in the country, the executive has always the means of setting them aside or compelling them to subservience, and is sure to be well supported in doing so. Representative institutions necessarily depend for permanence upon the readiness of the people to fight for them in case of their being endangered. If too little valued for this, they

seldom obtain a footing at all, and if they do, are almost sure
to be overthrown as soon as the head of the government, or
any party leader who can muster force for a *coup de main*, is
willing to run some small risk for absolute power.

These considerations relate to the first two causes of failure
in a representative government. The third is, when the people
want either the will or the capacity to fulfill the part which
belongs to them in a representative constitution. When nobody, or only some small fraction, feels the degree of interest
in the general affairs of the State necessary to the formation
of a public opinion, the electors will seldom make any use of
the right of suffrage but to serve their private interest, or the
interest of their locality, or of someone with whom they are
connected as adherents or dependents. The small class who, in
this state of public feeling, gain the command of the representative body for the most part use it solely as a means of
seeking their fortune. If the executive is weak, the country is
distracted by mere struggles for place; if strong, it makes
itself despotic at the cheap price of appeasing the representatives, or such of them as are capable of giving trouble, by a
share of the spoil; and the only fruit produced by national
representation is that in addition to those who really govern
there is an assembly quartered on the public, and no abuse in
which a portion of the assembly are interested is at all likely
to be removed. When, however, the evil stops here, the price
may be worth paying, for the publicity and discussion which,
though not an invariable, are a natural accompaniment of
any, even nominal, representation. In the modern kingdom of
Greece, for example,[1] it can hardly be doubted that the place-
hunters who chiefly compose the representative assembly,
though they contribute little or nothing directly to good government, nor even much temper the arbitrary power of the
executive, yet keep up the idea of popular rights and conduce

[1] Written before the salutary revolution of 1862, which, provoked by
popular disgust at the system of governing by corruption, and the general
demoralization of political men, has opened to that rapidly improving
people a new and hopeful chance of real constitutional government.

greatly to the real liberty of the press which exists in that country. This benefit, however, is entirely dependent on the coexistence with the popular body of a hereditary king. If, instead of struggling for the favors of the chief ruler, these selfish and sordid factions struggled for the chief place itself, they would certainly, as in Spanish America, keep the country in a state of chronic revolution and civil war. A despotism, not even legal, but of illegal violence, would be alternately exercised by a succession of political adventurers, and the name and forms of representation would have no effect but to prevent despotism from attaining the stability and security by which alone its evils can be mitigated or its few advantages realized.

The preceding are the cases in which representative government cannot permanently exist. There are others in which it possibly might exist, but in which some other form of government would be preferable. These are principally when the people, in order to advance in civilization, have some lesson to learn, some habit not yet acquired, to the acquisition of which representative government is likely to be an impediment.

The most obvious of these cases is the one already considered, in which the people have still to learn the first lesson of civilization, that of obedience. A race who have been trained in energy and courage by struggles with nature and their neighbors, but who have not yet settled down into permanent obedience to any common superior, would be little likely to acquire this habit under the collective government of their own body. A representative assembly drawn from among themselves would simply reflect their own turbulent insubordination. It would refuse its authority to all proceedings which would impose, on their savage independence, any improving restraint. The mode in which such tribes are usually brought to submit to the primary conditions of civilized society is through the necessities of warfare and the despotic authority indispensable to military command. A military leader is the only superior to whom they will submit, except occasionally some prophet supposed to be inspired from above or conjurer regarded as possessing miraculous power. These may exercise a temporary ascendancy, but as it is merely personal it rarely effects any change in the general habits of the people unless the prophet, like Mohammed, is also a military chief and goes forth the armed apostle of a new religion; or unless the military chiefs ally themselves with his influence and turn it into a prop for their own government.

A people are no less unfitted for representative government by the contrary fault to that last specified—by extreme passiveness and ready submission to tyranny. If a people thus prostrated by character and circumstances could obtain representative institutions, they would inevitably choose their tyrants as their representatives, and the yoke would be made heavier on them by the contrivance which *prima facie* might be expected to lighten it. On the contrary, many a people has gradually emerged from this condition by the aid of a central authority whose position has made it the rival, and has ended by making it the master, of the local despots, and which, above all, has been single. French history from Hugh Capet to Richelieu and Louis XIV [2] is a continued example of this course of things. Even when the king was scarcely so powerful as many of his chief feudatories, the great advantage which he derived from being but one has been recognized by French historians. To him the eyes of *all* the locally oppressed were turned; he was the object of hope and reliance throughout the kingdom, while each local potentate was only powerful within a more or less confined space. At his hands refuge and protection were sought from every part of the country, against first one, then another, of the immediate oppressors. His progress to ascendancy was slow; but it resulted from successively taking advantage of opportunities which offered themselves only to him. It was, therefore, sure, and, in proportion as it was accomplished, it abated in the oppressed portion of the community the habit of submitting to oppression. The king's interest lay in encouraging all partial attempts on the part of the serfs to emancipate them-

2 [These names span France's development from a national beginning to the most centralized power of the monarchy. See also biographical index.]

selves from their masters and place themselves in immediate
subordination to himself. Under his protection numerous communities were formed which knew no one above them but the
king. Obedience to a distant monarch is liberty itself compared
with the dominion of the lord of the neighboring castle: and the
monarch was long compelled by necessities of position to exert
his authority as the ally, rather than the master, of the classes
whom he had aided in effecting their liberation. In this manner
a central power, despotic in principle though generally much
restricted in practice, was mainly instrumental in carrying the
people through a necessary stage of improvement, which representative government, if real, would most likely have prevented them from entering upon. Nothing short of despotic
rule, or a general massacre, could have effected the emancipation of the serfs in the Russian empire.

The same passages of history forcibly illustrate another
mode in which unlimited monarchy overcomes obstacles to
the progress of civilization which representative government
would have had a decided tendency to aggravate. One of the
strongest hindrances to improvement, up to a rather advanced
stage, is an inveterate spirit of locality. Portions of mankind,
in many other respects capable of, and prepared for, freedom,
may be unqualified for amalgamating into even the smallest
nation. Not only may jealousies and antipathies repel them
from one another and bar all possibility of voluntary union,
but they may not yet have acquired any of the feelings or
habits which would make the union real, supposing it to be
nominally accomplished. They may, like the citizens of an
ancient community or those of an Asiatic village, have had
considerable practice in exercising their faculties on village
or town interests, and have even realized a tolerably effective
popular government on that restricted scale, and may yet have
but slender sympathies with anything beyond, and no habit
or capacity of dealing with, interests common to many such
communities. I am not aware that history furnishes any example in which a number of these political atoms or corpuscles

have coalesced into a body and learned to feel themselves one people, except through previous subjection to a central authority common to all.[3] It is through the habit of deferring to that authority, entering into its plans and subserving its purposes, that a people such as we have supposed receive into their minds the conception of large interests common to a considerable geographical extent. Such interests, on the contrary, are necessarily the predominant consideration in the mind of the central ruler; and through the relations, more or less intimate, which he progressively establishes with the localities they become familiar to the general mind. The most favorable concurrence of circumstances under which this step in improvement could be made would be one which should raise up representative institutions without representative government—a representative body, or bodies, drawn from the localities, making itself the auxiliary and instrument of the central power, but seldom attempting to thwart or control it. The people being thus taken, as it were, into council, though not sharing the supreme power, the political education given by the central authority is carried home much more effectually than it could otherwise be, to the local chiefs and to the population generally, while at same time a tradition is kept up of government by general consent, or at least, the sanction of tradition is not given to government without it, which, when consecrated by custom, has so often put a bad end to a good beginning, and is one of the most frequent causes of the sad fatality which in most countries has stopped improvement in so early a stage, because the work of some one period has been so done as to bar the needful work of the ages following. Meanwhile it may be laid down as a political truth that by irresponsible monarchy rather than by representative government can a multitude of insignificant political units be welded into a people, with common feelings of cohesion, power

[3] Italy, which alone can be quoted as an exception, is only so in regard to the final stage of its transformation. The more difficult previous advance from the city isolation of Florence, Pisa, or Milan to the provincial unity of Tuscany or Lombardy took place in the usual manner.

enough to protect itself against conquest or foreign aggression, and affairs sufficiently various and considerable of its own to occupy worthily and expand to fit proportions the social and political intelligence of the population.

For these several reasons kingly government, free from the control (though perhaps strengthened by the support) of representative institutions, is the most suitable form of polity for the earliest stages of any community, not excepting a city-community like those of ancient Greece, where, accordingly, the government of kings, under some real but no ostensible or constitutional control by public opinion, did historically precede by an unknown and probably great duration all free institutions, and gave place at last, during a considerable lapse of time, to oligarchies of a few families.

A hundred other infirmities or shortcomings in a people might be pointed out, which *pro tanto* disqualify them from making the best use of representative government; but in regard to these it is not equally obvious that the government of *one* or a *few* would have any tendency to cure or alleviate the evil. Strong prejudices of any kind, obstinate adherence to old habits, positive defects of national character, or mere ignorance, and deficiency of mental cultivation, if prevalent in a people, will be in general faithfully reflected in their representative assemblies, and should it happen that the executive administration, the direct management of public affairs, is in the hands of persons comparatively free from these defects, more good would frequently be done by them when not hampered by the necessity of carrying with them the voluntary assent of such bodies. But the mere position of the rulers does not in these, as it does in the other cases which we have examined, of itself invest them with interests and tendencies operating in the beneficial direction. From the general weaknesses of the people or of the state of civilization, the One and his counselors, or the Few, are not likely to be habitually exempt, except in the case of their being foreigners, belonging to a superior people or a more advanced state of society. Then, indeed, the rulers may be, to almost any extent, superior in civilization to those over whom they rule; and subjection to a foreign government of this description, notwithstanding its inevitable evils, is often of the greatest advantage to a people, carrying them rapidly through several stages of progress and clearing away obstacles to improvement which might have lasted indefinitely if the subject population had been left unassisted to its native tendencies and chances. In a country not under the dominion of foreigners, the only cause adequate to producing similar benefits is the rare accident of a monarch of extraordinary genius. There have been in history a few of these who, happily for humanity, have reigned long enough to render some of their improvements permanent by leaving them under the guardianship of a generation which had grown up under their influence. Charlemagne may be cited as one instance; Peter the Great is another. Such examples however are so unfrequent that they can only be classed with the happy accidents which have so often decided at a critical moment whether some leading portion of humanity should make a sudden start or sink back toward barbarism—chances like the existence of Themistocles at the time of the Persian invasion, or of the first or third William of Orange. It would be absurd to construct institutions for the mere purpose of taking advantage of such possibilities, especially as men of this caliber, in any distinguished position, do not require despotic power to enable them to exert great influence, as is evidenced by the three last mentioned. The case most requiring consideration in reference to institutions is the not very uncommon one in which a small but leading portion of the population, from difference of race, more civilized origin, or other peculiarities of circumstance, are markedly superior in civilization and general character to the remainder. Under those conditions government by the representatives of the mass would stand a chance of depriving them of much of the benefit they might derive from the greater civilization of the superior ranks, while government by the representatives of those ranks would probably rivet the degradation of the multitude and leave them no hope of decent treatment except by ridding themselves of one of the most valuable elements of future advance-ment. The best prospect of improvement for a people thus composed lies in the existence of a constitutionally unlimited, or at least a practically preponderant, authority in the chief ruler of the dominant class. He alone has by his position an interest in raising and improving the mass of whom he is not jealous, as a counterpoise to his associates of whom he is. And if fortunate circumstances place beside him, not as controllers but as subordinates, a body representative of the superior caste, which by its objections and questionings, and by its occasional outbreaks of spirit, keeps alive habits of collective resistance, and may admit of being, in time and by degrees, expanded into a really national representation (which is in substance the history of the English Parliament), the nation has then the most favorable prospects of improvement which can well occur to a community thus circumstanced and con-stituted.

Among the tendencies which, without absolutely rendering a people unfit for representative government, seriously inca-pacitate them from reaping the full benefit of it, one deserves particular notice. There are two states of the inclinations, intrinsically very different, but which have something in com-mon, by virtue of which they often coincide in the direction they give to the efforts of individuals and of nations: one is the desire to exercise power over others; the other is disincli-nation to have power exercised over themselves. The difference between different portions of mankind in the relative strength of these two dispositions is one of the most important elements in their history. There are nations in whom the passion for governing others is so much stronger than the desire of per-sonal independence that for the mere shadow of the one they are found ready to sacrifice the whole of the other. Each one of their number is willing, like the private soldier in an army, to abdicate his personal freedom of action into the hands of his general, provided the army is triumphant and victorious and he is able to flatter himself that he is one of a conquering host, though the notion that he has himself any share in the domination exercised over the conquered is an illusion. A government strictly limited in its powers and attributions, required to hold its hands from overmeddling, and to let most things go on without its assuming the part of guardian or director, is not to the taste of such a people. In their eyes the possessors of authority can hardly take too much upon themselves, provided the authority itself is open to general competition. An average individual among them prefers the chance, however distant or improbable, of wielding some share of power over his fellow citizens, above the certainty, to himself and others, of having no unnecessary power exercised over them. These are the elements of a people of place hunters, in whom the course of politics is mainly determined by place hunting; where equality alone is cared for, but not liberty; where the contests of political parties are but struggles to decide whether the power of meddling in everything shall belong to one class or another, perhaps merely to one knot of public men or another; where the idea entertained of democracy is merely that of opening offices to the competition of all instead of a few; where the more popular the institutions, the more innumerable are the places created, and the more monstrous the overgovernment exercised by all over each, and by the executive over all. It would be as unjust as it would be ungenerous to offer this, or anything approaching to it, as an unexaggerated picture of the French people, yet the degree in which they do participate in this type of character has caused representative government by a limited class to break down by excess of corruption, and the attempt at representative government by the whole male population to end in giving one man the power of consigning any number of the rest, without trial, to Lambessa or Cayenne,[4] provided he allows all of them to think themselves not excluded from the possibility of sharing his favors. The point of character which, beyond any other, fits the people of this country for representative government

4 [Lambessa, Algerian village, site of a prison colony; Cayenne, capital of French Guiana, location of another notorious penal colony; today both places have become synonyms for inhuman imprisonment.]

is that they have almost universally the contrary characteristic. They are very jealous of any attempt to exercise power over them not sanctioned by long usage and by their own opinion of right; but they in general care very little for the exercise of power over others. Not having the smallest sympathy with the passion for governing, while they are but too well acquainted with the motives of private interest from which that office is sought, they prefer that it should be performed by those to whom it comes without seeking, as a consequence of social position. If foreigners understood this, it would account to them for some of the apparent contradictions in the political feelings of Englishmen; their unhesitating readiness to let themselves be governed by the higher classes, coupled with so little personal subservience to them that no people are so fond of resisting authority when it oversteps certain prescribed limits, or so determined to make their rulers always remember that they will only be governed in the way they themselves like best. Place hunting, accordingly, is a form of ambition to which the English, considered nationally, are almost strangers. If we except the few families or connections of whom official employment lies directly in the way, Englishmen's views of advancement in life take an altogether different direction—that of success in business or in a profession. They have the strongest distaste for any mere struggle for office by political parties or individuals: and there are few things to which they have a greater aversion than to the multiplication of public employments—a thing, on the contrary, always popular with the bureaucracy-ridden nations of the Continent, who would rather pay higher taxes than diminish by the smallest fraction their individual chances of a place for themselves or their relatives, and among whom a cry for retrenchment never means abolition of offices, but the reduction of the salaries of those which are too considerable for the ordinary citizen to have any chance of being appointed to them.

CHAPTER V

OF THE PROPER FUNCTIONS OF
REPRESENTATIVE BODIES

IN TREATING of representative government it is above all
necessary to keep in view the distinction between its idea
or essence and the particular forms in which the idea has
been clothed by accidental historical developments or by the
notions current at some particular period.

The meaning of representative government is that the
whole people, or some numerous portion of them, exercise
through deputies periodically elected by themselves the ultimate controlling power, which in every constitution must reside somewhere. This ultimate power they must possess in all
its completeness. They must be masters, whenever they please,
of all the operations of government. There is no need that
the constitutional law should itself give them this mastery. It
does not in the British Constitution. But what it does give
practically amounts to this. The power of final control is as
essentially single, in a mixed and balanced government, as in
a pure monarchy or democracy. This is the portion of truth in
the opinion of the ancients, revived by great authorities in
our own time, that a balanced constitution is impossible.
There is almost always a balance, but the scales never hang
exactly even. Which of them preponderates is not always apparent on the face of the political institution. In the British
Constitution each of the three co-ordinate members of the
sovereignty is invested with powers which, if fully exercised,
would enable it to stop all the machinery of government.
Nominally, therefore, each is invested with equal power of
thwarting and obstructing the others; and if, by exerting that
power, any of the three could hope to better its position, the
ordinary course of human affairs forbids us to doubt that the

power would be exercised. There can be no question that the full powers of each would be employed defensively if it found itself assailed by one or both of the others. What then prevents the same powers from being exerted aggressively? The unwritten maxims of the constitution—in other words, the positive political morality of the country; and this positive political morality is what we must look to if we would know in whom the really supreme power in the Constitution resides.

By constitutional law the Crown can refuse its assent to any Act of Parliament and can appoint to office and maintain in it any Minister, in opposition to the remonstrances of Parliament. But the constitutional morality of the country nullifies these powers, preventing them from being ever used; and, by requiring that the head of the Administration should always be virtually appointed by the House of Commons, makes that body the real sovereign of the State. These unwritten rules, which limit the use of lawful powers, are, however, only effectual and maintain themselves in existence on condition of harmonizing with the actual distribution of real political strength. There is in every constitution a strongest power—one which would gain the victory if the compromises by which the Constitution habitually works were suspended and there came a trial of strength. Constitutional maxims are adhered to, and are practically operative, so long as they give the predominance in the Constitution to that one of the powers which has the preponderance of active power out of doors. This, in England, is the popular power. If, therefore, the legal provisions of the British Constitution, together with the unwritten maxims by which the conduct of the different political authorities is in fact regulated, did not give to the popular element in the Constitution that substantial supremacy over every department of the government which corresponds to its real power in the country, the Constitution would not possess the stability which characterizes it; either the laws or the unwritten maxims would soon have to be changed. The British government is thus a representative government in the correct sense of the term; and the powers which it leaves in hands not directly accountable to the people can only be considered as precautions which the ruling power is willing should be taken against its own errors. Such precautions have existed in all well-constructed democracies. The Athenian constitution had many such provisions; and so has that of the United States.

But while it is essential to representative government that the practical supremacy in the state should reside in the representatives of the people, it is an open question what actual functions, what precise part in the machinery of government, shall be directly and personally discharged by the representative body. Great varieties in this respect are compatible with the essence of representative government, provided the functions are such as secure to the representative body the control of everything in the last resort.

There is a radical distinction between controlling the business of government and actually doing it. The same person or body may be able to control everything, but cannot possibly do everything; and in many cases its control over everything will be more perfect the less it personally attempts to do. The commander of an army could not direct its movements effectually if he himself fought in the ranks or led an assault. It is the same with bodies of men. Some things cannot be done except by bodies; other things cannot be well done by them. It is one question, therefore, what a popular assembly should control, another what it should itself do. It should, as we have already seen, control all the operations of government. But in order to determine through what channel this general control may most expediently be exercised, and what portion of the business of government the representative assembly should hold in its own hands, it is necessary to consider what kinds of business a numerous body is competent to perform properly. That alone which it can do well it ought to take personally upon itself. With regard to the rest, its proper province is not to do it, but to take means for having it well done by others.

For example, the duty which is considered as belonging more peculiarly than any other to an assembly representative of the people is that of voting the taxes. Nevertheless, in no country does the representative body undertake, by itself or its delegated officers, to prepare the estimates. Though the supplies can only be voted by the House of Commons, and though the sanction of the House is also required for the appropriation of the revenues to the different items of the public expenditure, it is the maxim and the uniform practice of the Constitution that money can be granted only on the proposition of the Crown. It has, no doubt, been felt that moderation as to the amount, and care and judgment in the detail of its application, can only be expected when the executive government through whose hands it is to pass is made responsible for the plans and calculations on which the disbursements are grounded. Parliament, accordingly, is not expected, nor even permitted, to originate directly either taxation or expenditure. All it is asked for is its consent, and the sole power it possesses is that of refusal.

The principles which are involved and recognized in this constitutional doctrine, if followed as far as they will go, are a guide to the limitation and definition of the general functions of representative assemblies. In the first place, it is admitted in all countries in which the representative system is practically understood that numerous representative bodies ought not to administer. The maxim is grounded not only on the most essential principles of good government, but on those of the successful conduct of business of any description. No body of men, unless organized and under command, is fit for action, in the proper sense. Even a select board composed of few members, and these specially conversant with the business to be done, is always an inferior instrument to some one individual who could be found among them, and would be improved in character if that one person were made the chief, and all the others reduced to subordinates. What can be done better by a body than by any individual is deliberation. When it is necessary or important to secure hearing and consideration to many conflicting opinions, a deliberative body is indispensable. Those bodies, therefore, are frequently useful, even for administrative business, but in general only as advisers; such business being, as a rule, better conducted under the responsibility of one. Even a joint-stock company has always in practice, if not in theory, a managing director; its good or bad management depends essentially on some one person's qualifications, and the remaining directors, when of any use, are so by their suggestions to him or by the power they possess of watching him, and restraining or removing him in case of misconduct. That they are ostensibly equal sharers with him in the management is no advantage, but a considerable setoff against any good which they are capable of doing: it weakens greatly the sense in his own mind, and in those of other people, of that individual responsibility in which he should stand forth personally and undividedly.

But a popular assembly is still less fitted to administer or to dictate in detail to those who have the charge of administration. Even when honestly meant, the interference is almost always injurious. Every branch of public administration is a skilled business, which has its own peculiar principles and traditional rules, many of them not even known, in any effectual way, except to those who have at some time had a hand in carrying on the business, and none of them likely to be duly appreciated by persons not practically acquainted with the department. I do not mean that the transaction of public business has esoteric mysteries, only to be understood by the initiated. Its principles are all intelligible to any person of good sense, who has in his mind a true picture of the circumstances and conditions to be dealt with; but to have this he must know those circumstances and conditions; and the knowledge does not come by intuition. There are many rules of the greatest importance in every branch of public business (as there are in every private occupation) of which a person fresh to the subject neither knows the reason nor even suspects the existence, because they are intended to meet dangers or provide against inconveniences which never entered into his thoughts. I have known public men, ministers, of more than ordinary natural capacity who on their first introduction to a department of business new to them have excited the mirth of their inferiors by the air with which they announced as a truth hitherto set at nought, and brought to light by themselves, something which was probably the first thought of everybody who ever looked at the subject, given up as soon as he had got on to a second. It is true that a great statesman is he who knows when to depart from traditions as well as when to adhere to them. But it is a great mistake to suppose that he will do this better for being ignorant of the traditions. No one who does not thoroughly know the modes of action which common experience has sanctioned is capable of judging of the circumstances which require a departure from those ordinary modes of action. The interests dependent on the acts done by a public department, the consequences liable to follow from any particular mode of conducting it, require for weighing and estimating them a kind of knowledge, and of specially exercised judgment, almost as rarely found in those not bred to it as the capacity to reform the law in those who have not professionally studied it. All these difficulties are sure to be ignored by a representative assembly which attempts to decide on special acts of administration. At its best, it is inexperience sitting in judgment on experience, ignorance on knowledge—ignorance which, never suspecting the existence of what it does not know, is equally careless and supercilious, making light of, if not resenting, all pretensions to have a judgment better worth attending to than its own. Thus it is when no interested motives intervene; but when they do, the result is jobbery more unblushing and audacious than the worst corruption which can well take place in a public office under a government of publicity. It is not necessary that the interested bias should extend to the majority of the assembly. In any particular case it is often enough that it affects two or three of their number. Those two or three will have a greater interest in misleading the body than any other of its members are likely to have in putting it right. The bulk of the assembly may keep their hands clean, but they cannot keep their minds vigilant or their judgments discerning in matters they know nothing about; and an indolent majority, like an indolent individual, belongs to the person who takes most pains with it. The bad measures or bad appointments of a minister may be checked by Parliament; and the interest of ministers in defending, and of rival partisans in attacking, secures a tolerably equal discussion; but *quis custodiet custodes?* who shall check the Parliament? A minister, a head of an office, feels himself under some responsibility. An assembly in such cases feels under no responsibility at all; for when did any member of Parliament lose his seat for the vote he gave on any detail of administration? To a minister, or the head of an office, it is of more importance what will be thought of his proceedings some time hence than what is thought of them at the instant; but an assembly, if the cry of the moment goes with it, however hastily raised or artificially stirred up, thinks itself and is thought by everybody to be completely exculpated however disastrous may be the consequences. Besides, an assembly never personally experiences the inconveniences of its bad measures until they have reached the dimensions of national evils. Ministers and administrators see them approaching, and have to bear all the annoyance and trouble of attempting to ward them off.

The proper duty of a representative assembly in regard to matters of administration is not to decide them by its own vote, but to take care that the persons who have to decide them shall be the proper persons. Even this they cannot advantageously do by nominating the individuals. There is no act which more imperatively requires to be performed under a strong sense of individual responsibility than the nomination to employments. The experience of every person conversant with public affairs bears out the assertion that there is scarcely any act respecting which the conscience of an average man is less sensitive; scarcely any case in which less consideration is paid to qualifications, partly because men do not know, and partly because they do not care for, the difference in qualifications between one person and another. When a minister makes what is meant to be an honest appointment, that is, when he does not actually job it for his personal connections or his party, an ignorant person might suppose that he would try to give it to the person best qualified. No such thing. An ordinary minister thinks himself a miracle of virtue if he gives it to a person of merit or who has a claim on the public on any account, though the claim or the merit may be of the most opposite description to that required. *Il fallait un calculateur, ce fut un danseur qui l'obtint,*[1] is hardly more of a caricature than in the days of Figaro; and the minister doubtless thinks himself not only blameless but meritorious if the man dances well. Besides, the qualifications which fit special individuals for special duties can only be recognized by those who know the individuals, or who make it their business to examine and judge of persons from what they have done, or from the evidence of those who are in a position to judge. When these conscientious obligations are so little regarded by great public officers who can be made responsible for their appointments, how must it be with assemblies who cannot? Even now, the worst appointments are those which are made for the sake of gaining support or disarming opposition in the representative body; what might we expect if they were made by the body itself? Numerous bodies never regard special qualifications at all. Unless a man is fit for the gallows, he is thought to be about as fit as other people for almost anything for which he can offer himself as a candidate. When appointments made by a public body are not decided, as they almost always are, by party connection or private jobbing, a man is appointed either because he has a reputation, often quite undeserved, for *general* ability, or frequently for no better reason than that he is personally popular.

It has never been thought desirable that Parliament should itself nominate even the members of a Cabinet. It is enough that it virtually decides who shall be prime minister, or who shall be the two or three individuals from whom the prime minister shall be chosen. In doing this it merely recognizes the fact that a certain person is the candidate of the party whose

[1] ["An accountant was needed, but a dancer obtained it (the appointment)."]

general policy commands its support. In reality, the only thing which Parliament decides is, which of two, or at most three, parties or bodies of men shall furnish the executive government; the opinion of the party itself decides which of its members is fittest to be placed at the head. According to the existing practice of the British Constitution, these things seem to be on as good a footing as they can be. Parliament does not nominate any minister, but the Crown appoints the head of the administration in conformity to the general wishes and inclinations manifested by Parliament, and the other ministers on the recommendation of the chief; while every minister has the undivided moral responsibility of appointing fit persons to the other offices of administration which are not permanent. In a republic, some other arrangement would be necessary; but the nearer it approached in practice to that which has long existed in England, the more likely it would be to work well. Either, as in the American republic, the head of the Executive must be elected by some agency entirely independent of the representative body or the body must content itself with naming the prime minister and making him responsible for the choice of his associates and subordinates. To all these considerations, at least theoretically, I fully anticipate a general assent, though, practically, the tendency is strong in representative bodies to interfere more and more in the details of administration, by virtue of the general law, that whoever has the strongest power is more and more tempted to make an excessive use of it; and this is one of the practical dangers to which the futurity of representative governments will be exposed.

But it is equally true, though only of late and slowly beginning to be acknowledged, that a numerous assembly is as little fitted for the direct business of legislation as for that of administration. There is hardly any kind of intellectual work which so much needs to be done, not only by experienced and exercised minds, but by minds trained to the task through long and laborious study, as the business of making laws. This is a sufficient reason, were there no other, why they can never

be well made but by a committee of very few persons. A reason
no less conclusive is that every provision of a law requires to be
framed with the most accurate and long-sighted perception of
its effect on all the other provisions; and the law when made
should be capable of fitting into a consistent whole with the
previously existing laws. It is impossible that these conditions
should be in any degree fulfilled when laws are voted clause
by clause in a miscellaneous assembly. The incongruity of
such a mode of legislating would strike all minds were it not
that our laws are already, as to form and construction, such a
chaos that the confusion and contradiction seem incapable of
being made greater by any addition to the mass. Yet even now,
the utter unfitness of our legislative machinery for its purpose
is making itself practically felt every year more and more. The
mere time necessarily occupied in getting through Bills renders Parliament more and more incapable of passing any, except on detached and narrow points. If a Bill is prepared
which even attempts to deal with the whole of any subject
(and it is impossible to legislate properly on any part without
having the whole present to the mind), it hangs over from
session to session through sheer impossibility of finding time to
dispose of it. It matters not though the Bill may have been deliberately drawn up by the authority deemed the best qualified,
with all appliances and means to boot; or by a select commission, chosen for their conversancy with the subject, and having employed years in considering and digesting the particular measure; it cannot be passed because the House of Commons will not forego the precious privilege of tinkering it
with their clumsy hands. The custom has of late been to some
extent introduced, when the principle of a Bill has been affirmed on the second reading, of referring it for consideration
in detail to a Select Committee; but it has not been found
that this practice causes much less time to be lost afterwards
in carrying it through the Committee of the whole House; the
opinions or private crotchets which have been overruled by
knowledge always insist on giving themselves a second chance
before the tribunal of ignorance. Indeed, the practice itself has

been adopted principally by the House of Lords, the members of which are less busy and fond of meddling, and less jealous of the importance of their individual voices, than those of the elective House. And when a Bill of many clauses does succeed in getting itself discussed in detail, what can depict the state in which it comes out of Committee! Clauses omitted which are essential to the working of the rest; incongruous ones inserted to conciliate some private interest or some crotchety member who threatens to delay the Bill; articles foisted in on the motion of some sciolist with a mere smattering of the subject, leading to consequences which the member who introduced or those who supported the Bill did not at the moment foresee, and which need an amending Act in the next session to correct their mischiefs. It is one of the evils of the present mode of managing these things that the explaining and defending of a Bill, and of its various provisions, is scarcely ever performed by the person from whose mind they emanated, who probably has not a seat in the House. Their defense rests upon some minister or member of Parliament who did not frame them, who is dependent on cramming for all his arguments but those which are perfectly obvious, who does not know the full strength of his case, nor the best reasons by which to support it, and is wholly incapable of meeting unforeseen objections. This evil, as far as Government bills are concerned, admits of remedy, and has been remedied in some representative constitutions, by allowing the Government to be represented in either House by persons in its confidence, having a right to speak, though not to vote.

If that, as yet considerable, majority of the House of Commons who never desire to move an amendment or make a speech would no longer leave the whole regulation of business to those who do; if they would bethink themselves that better qualifications for legislation exist, and may be found if sought for, than a fluent tongue and the faculty of getting elected by a constituency; it would soon be recognized that, in legislation as well as administration, the only task to which a representative assembly can possibly be competent is not that of doing work, but of causing it to be done; of determining to whom or to what sort of people it shall be confided, and giving or withholding the national sanction to it when performed. Any government fit for a high state of civilization would have as one of its fundamental elements a small body, not exceeding in number the members of a Cabinet, who should act as a Commission of legislation, having for its appointed office to make the laws. If the laws of this country were, as surely they will soon be, revised and put into a connected form, the Commission of Codification by which this is effected should remain as a permanent institution, to watch over the work, protect it from deterioration, and make further improvements as often as required. No one would wish that this body should of itself have any power of *enacting* laws; the Commission would only embody the element of intelligence in their construction; Parliament would represent that of will. No measure would become a law until expressly sanctioned by Parliament; and Parliament, or either House, would have the power not only of rejecting but of sending back a Bill to the Commission for reconsideration or improvement. Either House might also exercise its initiative, by referring any subject to the Commission, with directions to prepare a law. The Commission, of course, would have no power of refusing its instrumentality to any legislation which the country desired. Instructions, concurred in by both Houses, to draw up a Bill which should effect a particular purpose would be imperative on the Commissioners, unless they preferred to resign their office. Once framed, however, Parliament should have no power to alter the measure, but solely to pass or reject it; or, if partially disapproved of, remit it to the Commission for reconsideration. The Commissioners should be appointed by the Crown, but should hold their offices for a time certain, say, five years, unless removed on an address from the two Houses of Parliament, grounded either on personal misconduct (as in the case of judges), or on refusal to draw up a Bill in obedience to the demands of Parliament. At the expiration of the five years a member should cease to hold office unless reap-

pointed, in order to provide a convenient mode of getting rid
of those who had not been found equal to their duties, and of
infusing new and younger blood into the body.

The necessity of some provision corresponding to this was
felt even in the Athenian democracy where, in the time of its
most complete ascendancy, the popular *ecclesia* could pass
psephisms (mostly decrees on single matters of policy), but
laws, so called, could only be made or altered by a different
and less numerous body, renewed annually, called the *no-
mothetae,* whose duty it also was to revise the whole of the
laws and keep them consistent with one another. In the English Constitution there is great difficulty in introducing any
arrangement which is new both in form and in substance, but
comparatively little repugnance is felt to the attainment of
new purposes by an adaptation of existing forms and traditions. It appears to me that the means might be devised of enriching the Constitution with this great improvement through
the machinery of the House of Lords. A Commission for preparing Bills would in itself be no more an innovation on the
Constitution than the Board for the administration of the
Poor Laws or the Inclosure Commission. If, in consideration
of the great importance and dignity of the trust, it were made
a rule that every person appointed a member of the Legislative Commission, unless removed from office on an address
from Parliament, should be a Peer for life, it is probable that
the same good sense and taste which leave the judicial functions of the Peerage practically to the exclusive care of the
law lords would leave the business of legislation, except on
questions involving political principles and interests, to the
professional legislators; that Bills originating in the Upper
House would always be drawn up by them; that the Government would devolve on them the framing of all its Bills; and
that private members of the House of Commons would gradually find it convenient, and likely to facilitate the passing of
their measures through the two Houses if, instead of bringing
in a Bill and submitting it directly to the House, they obtained leave to introduce it and have it referred to the Legis-

lative Commission. For it would, of course, be open to the House to refer for the consideration of that body not a subject merely, but any specific proposal, or a Draft of a Bill *in extenso,* when any member thought himself capable of preparing one such as ought to pass; and the House would doubtless refer every such draft to the Commission, if only as materials and for the benefit of the suggestions it might contain, as they would, in like manner, refer every amendment or objection which might be proposed in writing by any member of the House after a measure had left the Commissioners' hands. The alteration of Bills by a Committee of the whole House would cease, not by formal abolition, but by desuetude; the right not being abandoned, but laid up in the same armory with the royal veto, the right of withholding the supplies and other ancient instruments of political warfare, which no one desires to see used, but no one likes to part with, lest they should at any time be found to be still needed in an extraordinary emergency. By such arrangements as these, legislation would assume its proper place as a work of skilled labor and special study and experience; while the most important liberty of the nation, that of being governed only by laws assented to by its elected representatives, would be fully preserved and made more valuable by being detached from the serious, but by no means unavoidable, drawbacks which now accompany it in the form of ignorant and ill-considered legislation.

Instead of the function of governing, for which it is radically unfit, the proper office of a representative assembly is to watch and control the government: to throw the light of publicity on its acts; to compel a full exposition and justification of all of them which anyone considers questionable; to censure them if found condemnable and, if the men who compose the government abuse their trust or fulfill it in a manner which conflicts with the deliberate sense of the nation, to expel them from office, and either expressly or virtually appoint their successors. This is surely ample power and security enough for the liberty of the nation. In addition to this, the

Parliament has an office, not inferior even to this in importance: to be at once the nation's Committee of Grievances and
its Congress of Opinions—an arena in which not only the general opinion of the nation, but that of every section of it, and
as far as possible of every eminent individual whom it contains, can produce itself in full light and challenge discussion;
where every person in the country may count upon finding
somebody who speaks his mind, as well or better than he
could speak it himself, not to friends and partisans exclusively,
but in the face of opponents, to be tested by adverse controversy; where those whose opinion is overruled feel satisfied
that it is heard and set aside not by a mere act of will, but for
what are thought superior reasons, and commend themselves
as such to the representatives of the majority of the nation;
where every party or opinion in the country can muster its
strength, and be cured of any illusion concerning the number
or power of its adherents; where the opinion which prevails
in the nation makes itself manifest as prevailing, and marshals
its hosts in the presence of the government, which is thus enabled and compelled to give way to it on the mere manifestation, without the actual employment, of its strength; where
statesmen can assure themselves, far more certainly than by
any other signs, what elements of opinion and power are growing, and what declining, and are enabled to shape their measures with some regard not solely to present exigencies, but to
tendencies in progress. Representative assemblies are often
taunted by their enemies with being places of mere talk and
bavardage. There has seldom been more misplaced derision.
I know not how a representative assembly can more usefully
employ itself than in talk, when the subject of talk is the great
public interests of the country, and every sentence of it represents the opinion either of some important body of persons in
the nation or of an individual in whom some such body have
reposed their confidence. A place where every interest and
shade of opinion in the country can have its cause even pas-
sionately pleaded, in the face of the government and of all
other interests and opinions can compel them to listen and

either comply or state clearly why they do not, is in itself, if it answered no other purpose, one of the most important political institutions that can exist anywhere, and one of the foremost benefits of free government. Such "talking" would never be looked upon with disparagement if it were not allowed to stop "doing," which it never would, if assemblies knew and acknowledged that talking and discussion are their proper business, while *doing,* as the result of discussion, is the task not of a miscellaneous body but of individuals specially trained to it; that the fit office of an assembly is to see that those individuals are honestly and intelligently chosen, and to interfere no further with them except by unlimited latitude of suggestion and criticism, and by applying or withholding the final seal of national assent. It is for want of this judicious reserve that popular assemblies attempt to do what they cannot do well—to govern and legislate—and provide no machinery but their own for much of it, when, of course, every hour spent in talk is an hour withdrawn from actual business. But the very fact which most unfits such bodies for a Council of Legislation qualifies them the more for their other office—namely, that they are not a selection of the greatest political minds in the country, from whose opinions little could with certainty be inferred concerning those of the nation, but are, when properly constituted, a fair sample of every grade of intellect among the people which is at all entitled to a voice in public affairs. Their part is to indicate wants, to be an organ for popular demands, and a place of adverse discussion for all opinions relating to public matters, both great and small; and, along with this, to check by criticism, and eventually by withdrawing their support, those high public officers who really conduct the public business or who appoint those by whom it is conducted. Nothing but the restriction of the function of representative bodies within these rational limits will enable the benefits of popular control to be enjoyed in conjunction with the no less important requisites (growing ever more important as human affairs increase in scale and in complexity) of skilled legislation and administration. There are no means of combining these benefits except by separating the functions which guarantee the one from those which essentially require the other; by disjoining the office of control and criticism from the actual conduct of affairs, and devolving the former on the representatives of the Many, while securing for the latter, under strict responsibility to the nation, the acquired knowledge and practiced intelligence of a specially trained and experienced Few.

The preceding discussion of the functions which ought to devolve on the sovereign representative assembly of the nation would require to be followed by an inquiry into those properly vested in the minor representative bodies, which ought to exist for purposes that regard only localities. And such an inquiry forms an essential part of the present treatise; but many reasons require its postponement until we have considered the most proper composition of the great representative body destined to control as sovereign the enactment of laws and the administration of the general affairs of the nation.

CHAPTER VI

OF THE INFIRMITIES AND DANGERS TO WHICH REPRESENTATIVE GOVERNMENT IS LIABLE

THE defects of any form of government may be either negative or positive. It is negatively defective if it does not concentrate in the hands of the authorities power sufficient to fulfill the necessary offices of a government; or if it does not sufficiently develop by exercise the active capacities and social feelings of the individual citizens. On neither of these points is it necessary that much should be said at this stage of our inquiry.

The want of an amount of power in the government, adequate to preserve order and allow of progress in the people, is incident rather to a wild and rude state of society generally than to any particular form of political union. When the people are too much attached to savage independence to be tolerant of the amount of power to which it is for their good that they should be subject, the state of society (as already observed) is not yet ripe for representative government. When the time for that government has arrived, sufficient power for all needful purposes is sure to reside in the sovereign assembly; and if enough of it is not entrusted to the executive, this can only arise from a jealous feeling on the part of the assembly toward the administration, never likely to exist but where the constitutional power of the assembly to turn them out of office has not yet sufficiently established itself. Wherever that constitutional right is admitted in principle, and fully operative in practice, there is no fear that the assembly will not be willing to trust its own ministers with any amount of power really desirable; the danger is, on the contrary, lest they should grant it too ungrudgingly, and too indefinite in extent, since the power of the minister is the power of the body who make and who keep him so. It is, however, very likely, and is one of the dangers of a controlling assembly, that it may be lavish of powers, but afterwards interfere with their exercise; may give power by wholesale, and take it back in detail, by multiplied single acts of interference in the business of administration. The evils arising from this assumption of the actual function of governing, in lieu of that of criticizing and checking those who govern, have been sufficiently dwelt upon in the preceding chapter. No safeguard can in the nature of things be provided against this improper meddling except a strong and general conviction of its injurious character.

The other negative defect which may reside in a government, that of not bringing into sufficient exercise the individual faculties, moral, intellectual, and active, of the people, has been exhibited generally in setting forth the distinctive mischiefs of despotism. As between one form of popular government and another, the advantage in this respect lies with that which most widely diffuses the exercise of public functions; on the one hand, by excluding fewest from the suffrage; on the other, by opening to all classes of private citizens, so far as is consistent with other equally important objects, the widest participation in the details of judicial and administrative business; as by jury trial, admission to municipal offices, and above all by the utmost possible publicity and liberty of discussion, whereby not merely a few individuals in succession, but the whole public, are made, to a certain extent, participants in the government and sharers in the instruction and mental exercise derivable from it. The further illustration of these benefits, as well as of the limitations under which they must be aimed at, will be better deferred until we come to speak of the details of administration.

The *positive* evils and dangers of the representative, as of every other form of government, may be reduced to two heads: first, general ignorance and incapacity, or, to speak more moderately, insufficient mental qualifications, in the controlling body; secondly, the danger of its being under the influence of interests not identical with the general welfare of the community.

The former of these evils, deficiency in high mental qualifications, is one to which it is generally supposed that popular government is liable in a greater degree than any other. The energy of a monarch, the steadiness and prudence of an aristocracy, are thought to contrast most favorably with the vacillation and shortsightedness of even a qualified democracy. These propositions, however, are not by any means so well founded as they at first sight appear.

Compared with simple monarchy, representative government is in these respects at no disadvantage. Except in a rude age, hereditary monarchy, when it is really such, and not aristocracy in disguise, far surpasses democracy in all the forms of incapacity supposed to be characteristic of the last. I say, except in a rude age, because in a really rude state of society there is a considerable guarantee for the intellectual and active capacities of the sovereign. His personal will is constantly encountering obstacles from the willfulness of his subjects, and of powerful individuals among their number. The circumstances of society do not afford him much temptation to mere luxurious self-indulgence; mental and bodily activity, especially political and military, are his principal excitements; and among turbulent chiefs and lawless followers he has little authority and is seldom long secure even of his throne, unless he possesses a considerable amount of personal daring, dexterity, and energy. The reason why the average of talent is so high among the Henries and Edwards of our history may be read in the tragical fate of the second Edward and the second Richard, and the civil wars and disturbances of the reigns of John and his incapable successor.[1] The troubled period of the Reformation also produced several eminent hereditary monarchs, Elizabeth, Henri Quatre, Gustavus Adolphus; but they were mostly bred up in adversity, succeeded to the throne by the unexpected failure of nearer heirs, or had to contend with great difficulties in the commencement of their reign. Since European life assumed a settled aspect, anything above mediocrity in a hereditary king has become extremely rare, while the general average has been even below mediocrity, both in talent and in vigor of character. A monarchy constitutionally absolute now only maintains itself in existence (except temporarily in the hands of some active-minded usurper) through the mental qualifications of a permanent bureaucracy. The Russian and Austrian Governments, and even the French Government in its normal condition, are oligarchies of officials, of whom the head of the State does little more than select the chiefs. I am speaking of the regular course of their administration, for the will of the master, of course, determines many of their particular acts.

The governments which have been remarkable in history for sustained mental ability and vigor in the conduct of affairs have generally been aristocracies. But they have been,

---

[1] [These four kings had to contend with internal strife and political opposition by their barons throughout their reigns; Edward II was deposed and Richard II died in prison, probably murdered.]

without any exception, aristocracies of public functionaries. The ruling bodies have been so narrow that each member, or at least each influential member, of the body was able to make, and did make, public business an active profession and the principal occupation of his life. The only aristocracies which have manifested high governing capacities and acted on steady maxims of policy, through many generations, are those of Rome and Venice. But at Venice, though the privileged order was numerous, the actual management of affairs was rigidly concentrated in a small oligarchy within the oligarchy, whose whole lives were devoted to the study and conduct of the affairs of the state. The Roman government partook more of the character of an open aristocracy like our own. But the really governing body, the Senate, was in general exclusively composed of persons who had exercised public functions and had either already filled or were looking forward to fill the higher offices of the state, at the peril of a severe responsibility in case of incapacity and failure. When once members of the Senate, their lives were pledged to the conduct of public affairs; they were not permitted even to leave Italy except in the discharge of some public trust; and unless turned out of the Senate by the censors for character or conduct deemed disgraceful, they retained their powers and responsibilities to the end of life. In an aristocracy thus constituted, every member felt his personal importance entirely bound up with the dignity and estimation of the commonwealth which he administered, and with the part he was able to play in its councils. This dignity and estimation were quite different things from the prosperity or happiness of the general body of the citizens, and were often wholly incompatible with it. But they were closely linked with the external success and aggrandizement of the State: and it was, consequently, in the pursuit of that object almost exclusively that either the Roman or the Venetian aristocracies manifested the systematically wise collective policy and the great individual capacities for government for which history has deservedly given them credit.

It thus appears that the only governments, not representative, in which high political skill and ability have been other than exceptional, whether under monarchical or aristocratic forms, have been essentially bureaucracies. The work of government has been in the hands of governors by profession, which is the essence and meaning of bureaucracy. Whether the work is done by them because they have been trained to it or they are trained to it because it is to be done by them makes a great difference in many respects, but none at all as to the essential character of the rule. Aristocracies, on the other hand, like that of England, in which the class who possessed the power derived it merely from their social position, without being specially trained or devoting themselves exclusively to it (and in which, therefore, the power was not exercised directly, but through representative institutions oligarchically constituted) have been, in respect to intellectual endowments, much on a par with democracies; that is, they have manifested such qualities in any considerable degree only during the temporary ascendancy which great and popular talents, united with a distinguished position, have given to some one man. Themistocles and Pericles, Washington and Jefferson, were not more completely exceptions in their several democracies, and were assuredly much more splendid exceptions than the Chathams and Peels of the representative aristocracy of Great Britain, or even the Sullys and Colberts of the aristocratic monarchy of France. A great minister, in the aristocratic governments of modern Europe, is almost as rare a phenomenon as a great king.

The comparison, therefore, as to the intellectual attributes of a government has to be made between a representative democracy and a bureaucracy; all other governments may be left out of the account. And here it must be acknowledged that a bureaucratic government has, in some important respects, greatly the advantage. It accumulates experience, acquires well-tried and well-considered traditional maxims, and makes provision for appropriate practical knowledge in those who have the actual conduct of affairs. But it is not equally favorable to individual energy of mind. The disease which afflicts bureaucratic governments, and which they usually die of, is routine. They perish by the immutability of their maxims; and, still more, by the universal law that whatever becomes a routine loses its vital principle and, having no longer a mind acting within it, goes on revolving mechanically though the work it is intended to do remains undone. A bureaucracy always tends to become a pedantocracy. When the bureaucracy is the real government, the spirit of the corps (as with the Jesuits) bears down the individuality of its more distinguished members. In the profession of government, as in other professions, the sole idea of the majority is to do what they have been taught; and it requires a popular government to enable the conceptions of the man of original genius among them to prevail over the obstructive spirit of trained mediocrity. Only in a popular government (setting apart the accident of a highly intelligent despot) could Sir Rowland Hill have been victorious over the Post Office. A popular government installed him *in* the Post Office and made the body, in spite of itself, obey the impulse given by the man who united special knowledge with individual vigor and originality. That the Roman aristocracy escaped this characteristic disease of a bureaucracy was evidently owing to its popular element. All special offices, both those which gave a seat in the Senate and those which were sought by senators, were conferred by popular election. The Russian government is a characteristic exemplification of both the good and bad side of bureaucracy; its fixed maxims, directed with Roman perseverance to the same unflinchingly-pursued ends from age to age; the remarkable skill with which those ends are generally pursued; the frightful internal corruption and the permanent organized hostility to improvements from without, which even the autocratic power of a vigorous-minded emperor is seldom or never sufficient to overcome, the patient obstructiveness of the body being in the long run more than a match for the fitful energy of one man. The Chinese government, a bureaucracy of Mandarins, is, as far as known to us, another apparent example of the same qualities and defects.

In all human affairs conflicting influences are required to
keep one another alive and efficient even for their own proper
uses; and the exclusive pursuit of one good object, apart from
some other which should accompany it, ends not in excess
of one and defect of the other, but in the decay and loss even
of that which has been exclusively cared for. Government by
trained officials cannot do, for a country, the things which
can be done by a free government, but it might be supposed
capable of doing some things which free government, of itself,
cannot do. We find, however, that an outside element of freedom is necessary to enable it to do effectually or permanently
even its own business. And so, also, freedom cannot produce
its best effects, and often breaks down altogether, unless means
can be found of combining it with trained and skilled administration. There could not be a moment's hesitation between
representative government, among a people in any degree
ripe for it, and the most perfect imaginable bureaucracy.
But it is, at the same time, one of the most important ends
of political institutions to attain as many of the qualities of
the one as are consistent with the other; to secure, as far as
they can be made compatible, the great advantage of the conduct of affairs by skilled persons, bred to it as an intellectual
profession, along with that of a general control vested in, and
seriously exercised by, bodies representative of the entire
people. Much would be done toward this end by recognizing
the line of separation, discussed in the preceding chapter,
between the work of government properly so called, which can
only be well performed after special cultivation, and that
of selecting, watching, and, when needful, controlling the
governors, which in this case, as in others, properly devolves,
not on those who do the work, but on those for whose benefit
it ought to be done. No progress at all can be made toward
obtaining a skilled democracy unless the democracy are willing
that the work which requires skill should be done by those
who possess it. A democracy has enough to do in providing
itself with an amount of mental competency sufficient for its
own proper work, that of superintendence and check.

How to obtain and secure this amount is one of the questions to be taken into consideration in judging of the proper constitution of a representative body. In proportion as its composition fails to secure this amount, the assembly will encroach, by special acts, on the province of the executive; it will expel a good, or elevate and uphold a bad, ministry; it will connive at, or overlook in them, abuses of trust, will be deluded by their false pretenses, or will withhold support from those who endeavor to fulfill their trust conscientiously; it will countenance, or impose, a selfish, a capricious and impulsive, a shortsighted, ignorant, and prejudiced general policy, foreign and domestic; it will abrogate good laws, or enact bad ones, let in new evils, or cling with perverse obstinacy to old; it will even, perhaps, under misleading impulses, momentary or permanent, emanating from itself or from its constituents, tolerate or connive at proceedings which set law aside altogether, in cases where equal justice would not be agreeable to popular feeling. Such are among the dangers of representative government arising from a constitution of the representation which does not secure an adequate amount of intelligence and knowledge in the representative assembly.

We next proceed to the evils arising from the prevalence of modes of action in the representative body dictated by sinister interests (to employ the useful phrase introduced by Bentham), that is, interests conflicting more or less with the general good of the community.

It is universally admitted that, of the evils incident to monarchical and aristocratic governments, a large proportion arise from this cause. The interest of the monarch or the interest of the aristocracy, either collective or that of its individual members, is promoted, or they themselves think that it will be promoted, by conduct opposed to that which the general interest of the community requires. The interest, for example, of the government is to tax heavily; that of the community is to be as little taxed as the necessary expenses of good government permit. The interest of the king, and of the governing aristocracy, is to possess, and exercise, unlimited power over the people, to enforce, on their part, complete conformity to the will and preferences of the rulers. The interest of the people is to have as little control exercised over them in any respect as is consistent with attaining the legitimate ends of government. The interest, or apparent and supposed interest, of the king or aristocracy is to permit no censure of themselves, at least in any form which they may consider either to threaten their power or seriously to interfere with their free agency. The interest of the people is that there should be full liberty of censure on every public officer and on every public act or measure. The interest of a ruling class, whether in an aristocracy or an aristocratic monarchy, is to assume to themselves an endless variety of unjust privileges, sometimes benefiting their pockets at the expense of the people, sometimes merely tending to exalt them above others or, what is the same thing in different words, to degrade others below themselves. If the people are disaffected, which under such a government they are very likely to be, it is the interest of the king or aristocracy to keep them at a low level of intelligence and education, foment dissensions among them, and even prevent them from being too well off, lest they should "wax fat, and kick," agreeably to the maxim of Cardinal Richelieu in his celebrated *Testament Politique*.[2] All these things are for the interest of a king or aristocracy, in a purely selfish point of view, unless a sufficiently strong counterinterest is created by the fear of provoking resistance. All these evils have been, and many of them still are, produced by the sinister interests of kings and aristocracies, where their power is sufficient to raise them above the opinion of the rest of the community; nor is it rational to expect, as the consequence of such a position, any other conduct.

These things are superabundantly evident in the case of a monarchy or an aristocracy; but it is sometimes rather gratuitously assumed that the same kind of injurious influences

2 [*Testament politique d'Armand du Plessis* (Amsterdam, 1687).]

do not operate in a democracy. Looking at democracy in the way in which it is commonly conceived, as the rule of the numerical majority, it is surely possible that the ruling power may be under the dominion of sectional or class interests, pointing to conduct different from that which would be dictated by impartial regard for the interest of all. Suppose the majority to be whites, the minority Negroes, or *vice versa:* is it likely that the majority would allow equal justice to the minority? Suppose the majority Catholics, the minority Protestants, or the reverse: will there not be the same danger? Or let the majority be English, the minority Irish, or the contrary: is there not a great probability of similar evil? In all countries there is a majority of poor, a minority who, in contradistinction, may be called rich. Between these two classes, on many questions, there is complete opposition of apparent interest. We will suppose the majority sufficiently intelligent to be aware that it is not for their advantage to weaken the security of property, and that it would be weakened by any act of arbitrary spoliation. But is there not a considerable danger lest they should throw upon the possessors of what is called realized property, and upon the larger incomes, an unfair share, or even the whole, of the burden of taxation; and having done so, add to the amount without scruple, expending the proceeds in modes supposed to conduce to the profit and advantage of the laboring class? Suppose again a minority of skilled laborers, a majority of unskilled: the experience of many trade unions, unless they are greatly calumniated, justifies the apprehension that equality of earnings might be imposed as an obligation, and that piecework, payment by the hour, and all practices which enable superior industry or abilities to gain a superior reward might be put down. Legislative attempts to raise wages, limitation of competition in the labor market, taxes or restrictions on machinery, and on improvements of all kinds tending to dispense with any of the existing labor—even, perhaps, protection of the home producer against foreign industry—are very natural (I do not venture to say whether probable) results of a feeling of class interest in a governing majority of manual laborers.

It will be said that none of these things are for the *real* interest of the most numerous class; to which I answer that if the conduct of human beings was determined by no other interested considerations than those which constitute their "real" interest, neither monarchy nor oligarchy would be such bad governments as they are; for assuredly very strong arguments may be, and often have been, adduced to show that either a king or a governing senate are in much the most enviable position when ruling justly and vigilantly over an active, wealthy, enlightened, and high-minded people. But a king only now and then, and an oligarchy in no known instance, have taken this exalted view of their self-interest; and why should we expect a loftier mode of thinking from the laboring classes? It is not what their interest is, but what they suppose it to be, that is the important consideration with respect to their conduct; and it is quite conclusive against any theory of government that it assumes the numerical majority to do habitually what is never done, nor expected to be done, save in very exceptional cases, by any other depositaries of power—namely, to direct their conduct by their real ultimate interest, in opposition to their immediate and apparent interest. No one, surely, can doubt that many of the pernicious measures above enumerated, and many others as bad, would be for the immediate interest of the general body of unskilled laborers. It is quite possible that they would be for the selfish interest of the whole existing generation of the class. The relaxation of industry and activity, and diminished encouragement to saving which would be their ultimate consequence, might perhaps be little felt by the class of unskilled laborers in the space of a single lifetime. Some of the most fatal changes in human affairs have been, as to their more manifest immediate effects, beneficial. The establishment of the despotism of the Caesars was a great benefit to the entire generation in which it took place. It put a stop to civil war, abated a vast amount of malversation and tyranny by praetors and proconsuls; it fostered many of the graces of life and intellectual cultivation in all departments not political; it produced monuments of literary genius dazzling to the imaginations of shallow readers of history, who do not reflect that the men to whom the despotism of Augustus (as well as of Lorenzo de' Medici and of Louis XIV) owes its brilliancy were all formed in the generation preceding. The accumulated riches and the mental energy and activity, produced by centuries of freedom, remained for the benefit of the first generation of slaves. Yet this was the commencement of a *régime* by whose gradual operation all the civilization which had been gained insensibly faded away, until the Empire, which had conquered and embraced the world in its grasp, so completely lost even its military efficiency that invaders whom three or four legions had always sufficed to coerce were able to overrun and occupy nearly the whole of its vast territory. The fresh impulse given by Christianity came but just in time to save arts and letters from perishing, and the human race from sinking back into perhaps endless night.

When we talk of the interest of a body of men, or even of an individual man, as a principle determining their actions, the question what would be considered their interest by an unprejudiced observer is one of the least important parts of the whole matter. As Coleridge observes, the man makes the motive, not the motive the man. What it is the man's interest to do or refrain from depends less on any outward circumstances than upon what sort of man he is. If you wish to know what is practically a man's interest, you must know the cast of his habitual feelings and thoughts. Everybody has two kinds of interests—interests which he cares for, and interests which he does not care for. Everybody has selfish and unselfish interests, and a selfish man has cultivated the habit of caring for the former, and not caring for the latter. Everyone has present and distant interests, and the improvident man is he who cares for the present interests and does not care for the distant. It matters little that on any correct calculation the latter may be the more considerable if the habits of his mind lead him to fix his thoughts and wishes solely on the former. It would be vain to attempt to persuade a man who beats his wife and ill-treats his children that he would be happier if he lived in love and kindness with them. He would be happier if he were the kind of person who *could* so live, but he is not, and it is probably too late for him to become, that kind of person. Being what he is, the gratification of his love of domineering and the indulgence of his ferocious temper are to his perceptions a greater good to himself than he would be capable of deriving from the pleasure and affection of those dependent on him. He has no pleasure in their pleasure, and does not care for their affection. His neighbor, who does, is probably a happier man than he, but could he be persuaded of this, the persuasion would, most likely, only still further exasperate his malignity or his irritability. On the average, a person who cares for other people, for his country, or for mankind, is a happier man than one who does not; but of what use is it to preach this doctrine to a man who cares for nothing but his own ease or his own pocket? He cannot care for other people if he would. It is like preaching to the worm who crawls on the ground how much better it would be for him if he were an eagle.

Now it is a universally observed fact that the two evil dispositions in question, the disposition to prefer a man's selfish interests to those which he shares with other people, and his immediate and direct interests to those which are indirect and remote, are characteristics most especially called forth and fostered by the possession of power. The moment a man, or a class of men, find themselves with power in their hands, the man's individual interest, or the class's separate interest, acquires an entirely new degree of importance in their eyes. Finding themselves worshiped by others, they become worshipers of themselves and think themselves entitled to be counted at a hundred times the value of other people, while the facility they acquire of doing as they like without regard to consequences insensibly weakens the habits which make

men look forward even to such consequences as affect themselves. This is the meaning of the universal tradition, grounded
on universal experience, of men's being corrupted by power.
Everyone knows how absurd it would be to infer from what
a man is or does when in a private station, that he will be
and do exactly the like when a despot on a throne, where the
bad parts of his human nature, instead of being restrained
and kept in subordination by every circumstance of his life
and by every person surrounding him, are courted by all persons and ministered to by all circumstances. It would be quite
as absurd to entertain a similar expectation in regard to a
class of men, the demos, or any other. Let them be ever so
modest and amenable to reason while there is a power over
them stronger than they, we ought to expect a total change in
this respect when they themselves become the strongest power.

Governments must be made for human beings as they are
or as they are capable of speedily becoming; and in any state
of cultivation which mankind, or any class among them, have
yet attained, or are likely soon to attain, the interests by which
they will be led, when they are thinking only of self-interest,
will be almost exclusively those which are obvious at first sight,
and which operate on their present condition. It is only a
disinterested regard for others, and especially for what comes
after them, for the idea of posterity, of their country, or of
mankind, whether grounded on sympathy or on a conscientious feeling, which ever directs the minds and purposes of
classes or bodies of men toward distant or unobvious interests.
And it cannot be maintained that any form of government
would be rational which required as a condition that these
exalted principles of action should be the guiding and master
motives in the conduct of average human beings. A certain
amount of conscience, and of disinterested public spirit, may
fairly be calculated on in the citizens of any community ripe
for representative government. But it would be ridiculous to
expect such a degree of it, combined with such intellectual discernment, as would be proof against any plausible fallacy
tending to make that which was for their class interest appear

the dictate of justice and of the general good. We all know what specious fallacies may be urged in defense of every act of injustice yet proposed for the imaginary benefit of the mass. We know how many, not otherwise fools or bad men, have thought it justifiable to repudiate the national debt. We know how many, not destitute of ability, and of considerable popular influence, think it fair to throw the whole burden of taxation upon savings, under the name of realized property, allowing those whose progenitors and themselves have always spent all they received to remain, as a reward for such exemplary conduct, wholly untaxed. We know what powerful arguments, the more dangerous because there is a portion of truth in them, may be brought against all inheritance, against the power of bequest, against every advantage which one person seems to have over another. We know how easily the uselessness of almost every branch of knowledge may be proved to the complete satisfaction of those who do not possess it. How many, not altogether stupid men, think the scientific study of languages useless, think ancient literature useless, all erudition useless, logic and metaphysics useless, poetry and the fine arts idle and frivolous, political economy purely mischievous? Even history has been pronounced useless and mischievous by able men. Nothing but that acquaintance with external nature, empirically acquired, which serves directly for the production of objects necessary to existence or agreeable to the senses, would get its utility recognized if people had the least encouragement to disbelieve it. Is it reasonable to think that even much more cultivated minds than those of the numerical majority can be expected to be will have so delicate a conscience, and so just an appreciation of what is against their own apparent interest, that they will reject these and the innumerable other fallacies which will press in upon them from all quarters as soon as they come into power to induce them to follow their own selfish inclinations and shortsighted notions of their own good, in opposition to justice, at the expense of all other classes and of posterity?

One of the greatest dangers, therefore, of democracy, as of

all other forms of government, lies in the sinister interest of the holders of power: it is the danger of class legislation, of government intended for (whether really effecting it or not) the immediate benefit of the dominant class to the lasting detriment of the whole. And one of the most important questions demanding consideration in determining the best constitution of a representative government is how to provide efficacious securities against this evil.

If we consider as a class, politically speaking, any number of persons who have the same sinister interest—that is, whose direct and apparent interest points toward the same description of bad measures—the desirable object would be that no class, and no combination of classes likely to combine, should be able to exercise a preponderant influence in the government. A modern community, not divided within itself by strong antipathies of race, language, or nationality, may be considered as in the main divisible into two sections, which, in spite of partial variations, correspond on the whole with two divergent directions of apparent interest. Let us call them (in brief general terms) laborers, on the one hand, employers of labor, on the other, including, however, along with employers of labor not only retired capitalists and the possessors of inherited wealth, but all that highly paid description of laborers (such as the professions) whose education and way of life assimilate them with the rich, and whose prospect and ambition it is to raise themselves into that class. With the laborers, on the other hand, may be ranked those smaller employers of labor who by interests, habits, and educational impressions are assimilated in wishes, tastes, and objects to the laboring classes, comprehending a large proportion of petty tradesmen. In a state of society thus composed, if the representative system could be made ideally perfect, and if it were possible to maintain it in that state, its organization must be such that these two classes, manual laborers and their affinities on one side, employers of labor and their affinities on the other, should be in the arrangement of the representative system equally balanced, each influencing about an equal number of votes in Parliament; since, assuming that the majority of each class, in any difference between them, would be mainly governed by their class interests, there would be a minority of each in whom that consideration would be subordinate to reason, justice, and the good of the whole; and this minority of either, joining with the whole of the other, would turn the scale against any demands of their own majority which were not such as ought to prevail. The reason why, in any tolerably constituted society, justice and the general interest mostly in the end carry their point is that the separate and selfish interests of mankind are almost always divided, some are interested in what is wrong, but some, also, have their private interest on the side of what is right; and those who are governed by higher considerations, though too few and weak to prevail against the whole of the others, usually after sufficient discussion and agitation become strong enough to turn the balance in favor of the body of private interests which is on the same side with them. The representative system ought to be so constituted as to maintain this state of things: it ought not to allow any of the various sectional interests to be so powerful as to be capable of prevailing against truth and justice and the other sectional interests combined. There ought always to be such a balance preserved among personal interests as may render any one of them dependent for its successes on carrying with it at least a large proportion of those who act on higher motives and more comprehensive and distant views.

CHAPTER VII

OF TRUE AND FALSE DEMOCRACY;
REPRESENTATION OF ALL, AND
REPRESENTATION OF THE
MAJORITY ONLY

I T HAS been seen that the dangers incident to a representative democracy are of two kinds: danger of a low grade of intelligence in the representative body and in the popular opinion which controls it, and danger of class legislation on the part of the numerical majority, these being all composed of the same class. We have next to consider how far it is possible so to organize the democracy as, without interfering materially with the characteristic benefits of democratic government, to do away with these two great evils, or at least to abate them in the utmost degree attainable by human contrivance.

The common mode of attempting this is by limiting the democratic character of the representation through a more or less restricted suffrage. But there is a previous consideration which, duly kept in view, considerably modifies the circumstances which are supposed to render such a restriction necessary. A completely equal democracy, in a nation in which a single class composes the numerical majority, cannot be divested of certain evils, but those evils are greatly aggravated by the fact that the democracies which at present exist are not equal but systematically unequal in favor of the predominant class. Two very different ideas are usually confounded under the name democracy. The pure idea of democracy, according to its definition, is the government of the whole people by the whole people, equally represented. Democracy as commonly conceived and hitherto practiced is the government of the whole people by a mere majority of the people, exclusively represented. The former is synonymous with the equality of all citizens; the latter, strangely confounded with it, is a government of privilege, in favor of the numerical majority, who alone possess practically any voice in the State. This is the inevitable consequence of the manner in which the votes are now taken, to the complete disfranchisement of minorities.

The confusion of ideas here is great, but it is so easily cleared up that one would suppose the slightest indication would be sufficient to place the matter in its true light before any mind of average intelligence. It would be so but for the power of habit, owing to which the simplest idea, if unfamiliar, has as great difficulty in making its way to the mind as a far more complicated one. That the minority must yield to the majority, the smaller number to the greater, is a familiar idea; and accordingly men think there is no necessity for using their minds any further, and it does not occur to them that there is any medium between allowing the smaller number to be equally powerful with the greater and blotting out the smaller number altogether. In a representative body actually deliberating, the minority must of course be overruled; and in any equal democracy (since the opinions of the constituents, when they insist on them, determine those of the representative body) the majority of the people, through their representatives, will outvote and prevail over the minority and their representatives. But does it follow that the minority should have no representatives at all? Because the majority ought to prevail over the minority, must the majority have all the votes, the minority none? Is it necessary that the minority should not even be heard? Nothing but habit and old association can reconcile any reasonable being to the needless injustice. In a really equal democracy every or any section would be represented, not disproportionately, but proportionately. A majority of the electors would always have a majority of the representatives, but a minority of the electors would always have a minority of the representatives. Man for man they would be as fully represented as the majority. Unless they are, there is not equal government, but a government of inequality and privilege: one part of the people rule over the rest; there is a part whose fair and equal share of influence in the representation is withheld from them, contrary to all just government, but, above all, contrary to the principle of democracy, which professes equality as its very root and foundation.

The injustice and violation of principle are not less flagrant because those who suffer by them are a minority; for there is not equal suffrage where every single individual does not count for as much as any other single individual in the community. But it is not only a minority who suffer. Democracy, thus constituted, does not even attain its ostensible object, that of giving the powers of government in all cases to the numerical majority. It does something very different: it gives them to a majority of the majority, who may be, and often are, but a minority of the whole. All principles are most effectually tested by extreme cases. Suppose then that, in a country governed by equal and universal suffrage, there is a contested election in every constituency, and every election is carried by a small majority. The Parliament thus brought together represents little more than a bare majority of the people. This Parliament proceeds to legislate and adopts important measures by a bare majority of itself. What guarantee is there that these measures accord with the wishes of a majority of the people? Nearly half the electors, having been outvoted at the hustings, have had no influence at all in the decision; and the whole of these may be, a majority of them probably are, hostile to the measures, having voted against those by whom they have been carried. Of the remaining electors, nearly half have chosen representatives who, by supposition, have voted against the measures. It is possible, therefore, and not at all improbable, that the opinion which has prevailed was agreeable only to a minority of the nation, though a majority of that portion of it whom the institutions of the country have erected into a ruling class. If democracy means the certain ascendancy of the majority, there are no means of insuring that but by allowing every individual figure to tell equally in the summing up. Any minority left out, either purposely or by the play of the machinery, gives the power not to the majority but to a minority in some other part of the scale.

The only answer which can possibly be made to this reasoning is that, as different opinions predominate in different localities, the opinion which is in a minority in some places has a majority in others, and on the whole every opinion which exists in the constituencies obtains its fair share of voices in the representation. And this is roughly true in the present state of the constituency; if it were not, the discordance of the House with the general sentiment of the country would soon become evident. But it would be no longer true if the present constituency were much enlarged; still less, if made coextensive with the whole population, for in that case the majority in every locality would consist of manual laborers; and when there was any question pending on which these classes were at issue with the rest of the community, no other class could succeed in getting represented anywhere. Even now, is it not a great grievance that in every Parliament a very numerous portion of the electors, willing and anxious to be represented, have no member in the House for whom they have voted? Is it just that every elector of Marylebone is obliged to be represented by two nominees of the vestries, every elector of Finsbury or Lambeth by those (as is generally believed) of the publicans? 1 The constituencies to which most of the highly educated and public spirited persons in the country belong, those of the large towns, are now, in great part, either unrepresented or misrepresented. The electors who are on a different side in party politics from the local majority are unrepresented. Of those who are on the same side, a large proportion are misrepresented, having been obliged to accept the man who had the greatest number of supporters in their political party, though his opinions may differ from theirs on

1 [In ancient Rome, the publicans were tax collectors of ill repute (Matt. 9:10).]

every other point. The state of things is, in some respects, even worse than if the minority were not allowed to vote at all, for then at least the majority might have a member who would represent their own best mind, while now the necessity of not dividing the party, for fear of letting in its opponents, induces all to vote either for the first person who presents himself wearing their colors or for the one brought forward by their local leaders; and these, if we pay them the compliment, which they very seldom deserve, of supposing their choice to be unbiased by their personal interests, are compelled, that they may be sure of mustering their whole strength, to bring forward a candidate whom none of the party will strongly object to—that is, a man without any distinctive peculiarity, any known opinions except the shibboleth of the party. This is strikingly exemplified in the United States, where at the election of President the strongest party never dares put forward any of its strongest men, because every one of these, from the mere fact that he has been long in the public eye, has made himself objectionable to some portion or other of the party, and is therefore not so sure a card for rallying all their votes as a person who has never been heard of by the public at all until he is produced as the candidate. Thus the man who is chosen, even by the strongest party, represents perhaps the real wishes only of the narrow margin by which that party outnumbers the other. Any section whose support is necessary to success possesses a veto on the candidate. Any section which holds out more obstinately than the rest can compel all the others to adopt its nominee; and this superior pertinacity is unhappily more likely to be found among those who are holding out for their own interest than for that of the public. The choice of the majority is therefore very likely to be determined by that portion of the body who are the most timid, the most narrow-minded and prejudiced, or who cling most tenaciously to the exclusive class interest; in which case the electoral rights of the minority, while useless for the purposes for which votes are given, serve only for compelling the majority to accept the candidate of the weakest or worst portion of themselves.

That, while recognizing these evils, many should consider them as the necessary price paid for a free government is in no way surprising: it was the opinion of all the friends of freedom up to a recent period. But the habit of passing them over as irremediable has become so inveterate that many persons seem to have lost the capacity of looking at them as things which they would be glad to remedy if they could. From despairing of a cure, there is too often but one step to denying the disease; and from this follows dislike to having a remedy proposed, as if the proposer were creating a mischief instead of offering relief from one. People are so inured to the evils that they feel as if it were unreasonable, if not wrong, to complain of them. Yet, avoidable or not, he must be a purblind lover of liberty on whose mind they do not weigh, who would not rejoice at the discovery that they could be dispensed with. Now nothing is more certain than that the virtual blotting-out of the minority is no necessary or natural consequence of freedom; that, far from having any connection with democracy, it is diametrically opposed to the first principle of democracy—representation in proportion to numbers. It is an essential part of democracy that minorities should be adequately represented. No real democracy, nothing but a false show of democracy, is possible without it.

Those who have seen and felt, in some degree, the force of these considerations have proposed various expedients by which the evil may be, in a greater or less degree, mitigated. Lord John Russell, in one of his Reform Bills, introduced a provision that certain constituencies should return three members, and that in these each elector should be allowed to vote only for two; and Mr. Disraeli, in the recent debates, revived the memory of the fact by reproaching him for it, being of opinion, apparently, that it befits a Conservative statesman to regard only means, and to disown scornfully all fellow-feeling with anyone who is betrayed, even once, into thinking of ends.[2] Others have proposed that each elector should be allowed to vote only for one. By either of these plans, a minority equaling or exceeding a third of the local constituency would be able, if it attempted no more, to return one out of three members. The same result might be attained in a still better way if, as proposed in an able pamphlet by Mr. James Garth Marshall, the elector retained his three votes, but was at liberty to bestow them all upon the same candidate. These schemes, though infinitely better than none at all, are yet but makeshifts and attain the end in a very imperfect manner, since all local minorities of less than a third, and all minorities, however numerous, which are made up from several constituencies, would remain unrepresented. It is much to be lamented, however, that none of these plans have been carried into effect, as any of them would have recognized the right principle and prepared the way for its more complete application. But real equality of representation is not obtained unless any set of electors amounting to the average number of a constituency, wherever in the country they happen to reside, have the power of combining with one another to return a representative. This degree of perfection in representation appeared impracticable until a man of great capacity, fitted alike for

2 This blunder of Mr. Disraeli (from which, greatly to his credit, Sir John Pakington took an opportunity, soon after, of separating himself) is a speaking instance among many, how little the Conservative leaders understand Conservative principles. Without presuming to require from political parties such an amount of virtue and discernment as that they should comprehend, and know when to apply, the principles of their opponents, we may yet say that it would be a great improvement if each party understood and acted upon its own. Well would it be for England if Conservatives voted consistently for everything conservative, and Liberals for everything liberal. We should not then have to wait long for things which, like the present and many other great measures, are eminently both the one and the other. The Conservatives, as being by the law of their existence the stupidest party, have much the greatest sins of this description to answer for; and it is a melancholy truth that, if any measure were proposed, on any subject, truly, largely, and far-sightedly conservative, even if Liberals were willing to vote for it, the great bulk of the Conservative party would rush blindly in and prevent it from being carried.

large general views and for the contrivance of practical details—Mr. Thomas Hare—had proved its possibility by drawing up a scheme for its accomplishment, embodied in a draft of an act of Parliament—a scheme which has the almost unparalleled merit of carrying out a great principle of government in a manner approaching to ideal perfection as regards the special object in view, while it attains incidentally several other ends of scarcely inferior importance.

According to this plan, the unit of representation—the quota of electors who would be entitled to have a member to themselves—would be ascertained by the ordinary process of taking averages, the number of voters being divided by the number of seats in the House; and every candidate who obtained that quota would be returned, from however great a number of local constituencies it might be gathered. The votes would, as at present, be given locally; but any elector would be at liberty to vote for any candidate in whatever part of the country he might offer himself. Those electors, therefore, who did not wish to be represented by any of the local candidates might aid by their vote in the return of the person they liked best among all those throughout the country who had expressed a willingness to be chosen. This would, so far, give reality to the electoral rights of the otherwise virtually disfranchised minority. But it is important that not those alone who refuse to vote for any of the local candidates, but those also who vote for one of them and are defeated, should be enabled to find elsewhere the representation which they have not succeeded in obtaining in their own district. It is therefore provided that an elector may deliver a voting paper, containing other names in addition to the one which stands foremost in his preference. His vote would only be counted for one candidate; but if the object of his first choice failed to be returned, from not having obtained the quota, his second perhaps might be more fortunate. He may extend his list to a greater number, in the order of his preference, so that if the names which stand near the top of the list either cannot make up the quota, or are able to make it up without his vote, the

110 REPRESENTATIVE GOVERNMENT

vote may still be used for someone whom it may assist in re-
turning. To obtain the full number of members required to
complete the House, as well as to prevent very popular candidates from engrossing nearly all the suffrages, it is necessary,
however many votes a candidate may obtain, that no more of
them than the quota should be counted for his return, the remainder of those who voted for him would have their votes
counted for the next person on their respective lists who
needed them and could by their aid complete the quota. To
determine which of a candidate's votes should be used for his
return, and which set free for others, several methods are proposed, into which we shall not here enter. He would, of course,
retain the votes of all those who would not otherwise be represented; and for the remainder, drawing lots, in default of better, would be an unobjectionable expedient. The voting papers would be conveyed to a central office, where the votes
would be counted, the number of first, second, third, and
other votes given for each candidate ascertained, and the
quota would be allotted to everyone who could make it up,
until the number of the House was complete: first votes being
preferred to second, second to third, and so forth. The voting
papers and all the elements of the calculation would be placed
in public repositories, accessible to all whom they concerned;
and if anyone who had obtained the quota was not duly returned it would be in his power easily to prove it.

These are the main provisions of the scheme. For a more
minute knowledge of its very simple machinery, I must refer
to Mr. Hare's *Treatise on the Election of Representatives* (a
small volume published in 1859),[3] and to a pamphlet by Mr.
Henry Fawcett (now Professor of Political Economy in the
University of Cambridge), published in 1860, and entitled *Mr.
Hare's Reform Bill simplified and explained.* This last is a
very clear and concise exposition of the plan, reduced to its
simplest elements, by the omission of some of Mr. Hare's

[3] In a second edition, published recently, Mr. Hare has made important
improvements in some of the detailed provisions.

original provisions which, though in themselves beneficial, were thought to take more from the simplicity of the scheme than they added to its practical usefulness. The more these works are studied, the stronger, I venture to predict, will be the impression of the perfect feasibility of the scheme and its transcendent advantages. Such and so numerous are these that, in my conviction, they place Mr. Hare's plan among the very greatest improvements yet made in the theory and practice of government.

In the first place, it secures a representation, in proportion to numbers, of every division of the electoral body—not two great parties alone, with perhaps a few large sectional minorities in particular places, but every minority in the whole nation, consisting of a sufficiently large number to be, on principles of equal justice, entitled to a representative. Secondly, no elector would, as at present, be nominally represented by someone whom he had not chosen. Every member of the House would be the representative of a unanimous constitu‧ ency. He would represent a thousand electors, or two thou‧ sand, or five thousand, or ten thousand, as the quota might be, every one of whom would have not only voted for him, but selected him from the whole country, not merely from the assortment of two or three perhaps rotten oranges which may be the only choice offered to him in his local market. Under this relation the tie between the elector and the representative would be of a strength, and a value, of which at present we have no experience. Every one of the electors would be personally identified with his representative, and the representative with his constituents. Every elector who voted for him would have done so either because, among all the candidates for Parliament who are favorably known to a certain number of electors, he is the one who best expresses the voter's own opinions, or because he is one of those whose abilities and character the voter most respects and whom he most willingly trusts to think for him. The member would represent persons, not the mere bricks and mortar of the town—the voters them‧

selves, not a few vestrymen or parish notabilities merely. All, however, that is worth preserving in the representation of places would be preserved. Though the Parliament of the nation ought to have as little as possible to do with purely local affairs, yet, while it has to do with them, there ought to be members specially commissioned to look after the interests of every important locality; and these there would still be. In every locality which could make up the quota within itself, the majority would generally prefer to be represented by one of themselves, by a person of local knowledge and residing in the locality, if there is any such person to be found among the candidates who is otherwise well qualified to be their representative. It would be the minorities chiefly who, being unable to return the local member, would look out elsewhere for a candidate likely to obtain other votes in addition to their own.

Of all modes in which a national representation can possibly be constituted, this one affords the best security for the intellectual qualifications desirable in the representatives. At present, by universal admission, it is becoming more and more difficult for anyone who has only talents and character to gain admission into the House of Commons. The only persons who can get elected are those who possess local influence or make their way by lavish expenditure, or who, on the invitation of three or four tradesmen or attorneys, are sent down by one of the two great parties from their London clubs as men whose votes the party can depend on under all circumstances. On Mr. Hare's system, those who did not like the local candidates, or who could not succeed in carrying the local candidate they preferred, would have the power to fill up their voting papers by a selection from all the persons of national reputation, on the list of candidates, with whose general political principles they were in sympathy. Almost every person, therefore, who had made himself in any way honorably distinguished, though devoid of local influence, and having sworn allegiance to no political party, would have a fair chance of making up the quota; and with this encouragement such persons might be expected to offer themselves, in numbers hitherto undreamed of. Hundreds of able men of independent thought, who would have no chance whatever of being chosen by the majority of any existing constituency, have by their writings or their exertions in some field of public usefulness made themselves known and approved by a few persons in almost every district of the kingdom; and if every vote that would be given for them in every place could be counted for their election, they might be able to complete the number of the quota. In no other way which it seems possible to suggest would Parliament be so certain of containing the very *élite* of the country.

And it is not solely through the votes of minorities that this system of election would raise the intellectual standard of the House of Commons. Majorities would be compelled to look out for members of a much higher caliber. When the individuals composing the majority would no longer be reduced to Hobson's choice,[4] of either voting for the person brought forward by their local leaders or not voting at all; when the nominee of the leaders would have to encounter the competition not solely of the candidate of the minority, but of all the men of established reputation in the country who were willing to serve, it would be impossible any longer to foist upon the electors the first person who presents himself with the catchwords of the party in his mouth and three or four thousand pounds in his pocket. The majority would insist on having a candidate worthy of their choice or they would carry their votes somewhere else, and the minority would prevail. The slavery of the majority to the least estimable portion of their number would be at an end; the very best and most capable of the local notabilities would be put forward by preference; if possible, such as were known in some advantageous

4 [An involuntary choice that leaves no alternative, derived from Thomas Hobson (d. 1631), a stable owner of Cambridge, England, who forced his patrons to take whichever horse was nearest the door.]

way beyond the locality, that their local strength might have a chance of being fortified by stray votes from elsewhere. Constituencies would become competitors for the best candidates and would vie with one another in selecting from among the men of local knowledge and connections those who were most distinguished in every other respect.

The natural tendency of representative government, as of modern civilization, is toward collective mediocrity; and this tendency is increased by all reductions and extensions of the franchise, their effect being to place the principal power in the hands of classes more and more below the highest level of instruction in the community. But though the superior intellects and characters will necessarily be outnumbered, it makes a great difference whether or not they are heard. In the false democracy which, instead of giving representation to all, gives it only to the local majorities, the voice of the instructed minority may have no organs at all in the representative body. It is an admitted fact that in the American democracy, which is constructed on this faulty model, the highly-cultivated members of the community, except such of them as are willing to sacrifice their own opinions and modes of judgment, and become the servile mouthpieces of their inferiors in knowledge, seldom even offer themselves for Congress or the State Legislatures, so little likelihood have they of being returned. Had a plan like Mr. Hare's by good fortune suggested itself to the enlightened and patriotic founders of the American Republic, the Federal and State Assemblies would have contained many of these distinguished men, and democracy would have been spared its greatest reproach and one of its most formidable evils. Against this evil the system of personal representation, proposed by Mr. Hare, is almost a specific. The minority of instructed minds scattered through the local constituencies would unite to return a number, proportioned to their own numbers, of the very ablest men the country contains. They would be under the strongest inducement to choose such men, since in no other mode could they make their small numerical strength tell for anything considerable. The representatives of the majority, besides that they would themselves be improved in quality by the operation of the system, would no longer have the whole field to themselves. They would indeed outnumber the others, as much as the one class of electors outnumbers the other in the country; they could always outvote them, but they would speak and vote in their presence, and subject to their criticism. When any difference arose, they would have to meet the arguments of the instructed few by reasons, at least apparently, as cogent; and since they could not, as those do who are speaking to persons already unanimous, simply assume that they are in the right, it would occasionally happen to them to become convinced that they were in the wrong. As they would in general be well-meaning (for thus much may reasonably be expected from a fairly-chosen national representation), their own minds would be insensibly raised by the influence of the minds with which they were in contact, or even in conflict. The champions of unpopular doctrines would not put forth their arguments merely in books and periodicals, read only by their own side; the opposing ranks would meet face to face and hand to hand, and there would be a fair comparison of their intellectual strength in the presence of the country. It would then be found out whether the opinion which prevailed by counting votes would also prevail if the votes were weighed as well as counted. The multitude have often a true instinct for distinguishing an able man when he has the means of displaying his ability in a fair field before them. If such a man fails to obtain at least some portion of his just weight, it is through institutions or usages which keep him out of sight. In the old democracies there were no means of keeping out of sight any able man: the bema [5] was open to him; he needed nobody's consent to become a public adviser. It is not so in a representative government; and the best friends of represent-

[5] [A platform for public speaking, derived from the name of the platform of the Pnyx at Athens. (See note 1, p. 9.)]

ative democracy can hardly be without misgivings that the Themistocles or Demosthenes,[6] whose counsels would have saved the nation, might be unable during his whole life ever to obtain a seat. But if the presence in the representative assembly can be insured of even a few of the first minds in the country, though the remainder consist only of average minds, the influence of these leading spirits is sure to make itself sensibly felt in the general deliberations, even though they be known to be, in many respects, opposed to the tone of popular opinion and feeling. I am unable to conceive any mode by which the presence of such minds can be so positively insured as by that proposed by Mr. Hare.

This portion of the Assembly would also be the appropriate organ of a great social function, for which there is no provision in any existing democracy, but which in no government can remain permanently unfulfilled without condemning that government to infallible degeneracy and decay. This may be called the function of antagonism. In every government there is some power stronger than all the rest, and the power which is strongest tends perpetually to become the sole power. Partly by intention, and partly unconsciously, it is ever striving to make all other things bend to itself, and is not content while there is anything which makes permanent head against it, any influence not in agreement with its spirit. Yet if it succeeds in suppressing all rival influences, and molding everything after its own model, improvement, in that country, is at an end and decline commences. Human improvement is a product of many factors, and no power ever yet constituted among mankind includes them all; even the most beneficent power only contains in itself some of the requisites of good, and the remainder, if progress is to continue, must be derived from some other source. No community has ever long con-

6 [Themistocles (c. 528-c. 462 B.C.), Athenian statesman, and Demosthenes (384-322 B.C.), the famous orator. Their (unfortunately for Athens) rejected counsels mentioned by Mill were (a) Themistocles' advice to increase their fleet and land defenses in their struggle against the Persians; (b) Demosthenes' warnings against the danger of Philip of Macedon.]

tinued progressive but while a conflict was going on between
the strongest power in the community and some rival power:
between the spiritual and temporal authorities; the military
or territorial and the industrious classes; the king and the
people; the orthodox and religious reformers. When the victory on either side was so complete as to put an end to the
strife, and no other conflict took its place, first stagnation
followed, and then decay. The ascendancy of the numerical
majority is less unjust, and on the whole less mischievous,
than many others, but it is attended with the very same kind
of dangers, and even more certainly; for when the government is in the hands of One or a Few, the Many are always
existent as a rival power, which may not be strong enough ever
to control the other, but whose opinion and sentiment are a
moral, and even a social, support to all who, either from conviction or contrariety of interest, are opposed to any of the
tendencies of the ruling authority. But when the Democracy
is supreme, there is no One or Few strong enough for dis-
sentient opinions and injured or menaced interests to lean
upon. The great difficulty of democratic government has
hitherto seemed to be, how to provide, in a democratic society,
what circumstances have provided hitherto in all the societies
which have maintained themselves ahead of others—a social
support, *a point d'appui,* for individual resistance to the tendencies of the ruling power: a protection, a rallying point,
for opinions and interests which the ascendant public opinion
views with disfavor. For want of such a *point d'appui,* the older
societies, and all but a few modern ones, either fell into dissolution or became stationary (which means slow deterioration) through the exclusive predominance of a part only of
the conditions of social and mental well-being.

Now this great want the system of personal representation
is fitted to supply in the most perfect manner which the circumstances of modern society admit of. The only quarter in
which to look for a supplement, or completing corrective, to
the instincts of a democratic majority is the instructed minority; but in the ordinary mode of constituting democracy this

minority has no organ; Mr. Hare's system provides one. The representatives who would be returned to Parliament by the aggregate of minorities would afford that organ in its greatest perfection. A separate organization of the instructed classes, even if practicable, would be invidious and could only escape from being offensive by being totally without influence. But if the *élite* of these classes formed part of the Parliament, by the same title as any other of its members—by representing the same number of citizens, the same numerical fraction of the national will—their presence could give umbrage to nobody, while they would be in the position of highest vantage, both for making their opinions and counsels heard on all important subjects and for taking an active part in public business. Their abilities would probably draw to them more than their numerical share of the actual administration of government; as the Athenians did not confide responsible public functions to Cleon or Hyperbolus (the employment of Cleon at Pylos and Amphipolis was purely exceptional), but Nicias, and Theramenes, and Alcibiades, were in constant employment both at home and abroad, though known to sympathize more with oligarchy than with democracy.[7] The instructed minority would, in the actual voting, count only for their numbers, but as a moral power they would count for much more, in virtue of their knowledge, and of the influence it would give them over the rest. An arrangement better adapted to keep popular opinion within reason and justice, and to guard it from the various deteriorating influences which assail the weak side of democracy, could scarely by human ingenuity be devised. A democratic people would in this way be provided with what in any other way it would almost certainly

[7] [All prominent in political and military events of the war with Sparta after the death of Pericles. Cleon (d. 422 B.C.) opposed and succeeded Pericles and led successful expeditions against Sparta. Hyperbolus (d. 411 B.C.) became leader of the war party after the death of Cleon. Nicias (*c.* 470-413 B.C.) was appointed a joint commander of the Sicilian expedition. Theramenes (b. *c.* 455 B.C.) became one of the Thirty Tyrants. Alcibiades (*c.* 450-404 B.C.), who was brought up by his guardian Pericles and was an intimate friend of Socrates, was also a leader of the Sicilian expedition.]

miss—leaders of a higher grade of intellect and character than itself. Modern democracy would have its occasional Pericles, and its habitual group of superior and guiding minds.

With all this array of reasons, of the most fundamental character, on the affirmative side of the question, what is there on the negative? Nothing that will sustain examination when people can once be induced to bestow any real examination upon a new thing. Those indeed, if any such there be, who under pretense of equal justice aim only at substituting the class ascendancy of the poor for that of the rich will, of course, be unfavorable to a scheme which places both on a level. But I do not believe that any such wish exists at present among the working classes of this country, though I would not answer for the effect which opportunity and demagogic artifices may hereafter have in exciting it. In the United States, where the numerical majority have long been in full possession of collective despotism, they would probably be as unwilling to part with it as a single despot or an aristocracy. But I believe that the English democracy would as yet be content with protection against the class legislation of others, without claiming the power to exercise it in their turn.

Among the ostensible objectors to Mr. Hare's scheme, some profess to think the plan unworkable; but these, it will be found, are generally people who have barely heard of it or have given it a very slight and cursory examination. Others are unable to reconcile themselves to the loss of what they term the local character of the representation. A nation does not seem to them to consist of persons, but of artificial units, the creation of geography and statistics. Parliament must represent towns and counties, not human beings. But no one seeks to annihilate towns and counties. Towns and counties, it may be presumed, are represented when the human beings who inhabit them are represented. Local feelings cannot exist without somebody who feels them; nor local interests without somebody interested in them. If the human beings whose feelings and interests these are have their proper share of representation, these feelings and interests are represented in common with all other feelings and interests of those persons. But I cannot see why the feelings and interests which arrange mankind according to localities should be the only ones thought worthy of being represented, or why people who have other feelings and interests, which they value more than they do their geographical ones, should be restricted to these as the sole principle of their political classification. The notion that Yorkshire and Middlesex have rights apart from those of their inhabitants, or that Liverpool and Exeter are the proper objects of the legislator's care, in contradistinction to the population of those places, is a curious specimen of delusion produced by words.

In general, however, objectors cut the matter short by affirming that the people of England will never consent to such a system. What the people of England are likely to think of those who pass such a summary sentence on their capacity of understanding and judgment, deeming it superfluous to consider whether a thing is right or wrong before affirming that they are certain to reject it, I will not undertake to say. For my own part, I do not think that the people of England have deserved to be, without trial, stigmatized as insurmountably prejudiced against anything which can be proved to be good either for themselves or for others. It also appears to me that, when prejudices persist obstinately, it is the fault of nobody so much as of those who make a point of proclaiming them insuperable, as an excuse to themselves for never joining in an attempt to remove them. Any prejudice whatever will be insurmountable if those who do not share it themselves truckle to it, and flatter it, and accept it as a law of nature. I believe, however, that in this case there is in general, among those who have yet heard of the proposition, no other hostility to it than the natural and healthy distrust attaching to all novelties which have not been sufficiently canvassed to make generally manifest all the pros and cons of the question. The only serious obstacle is the unfamiliarity; this, indeed, is a formidable one, for the imagination much more easily reconciles itself to a great alteration in substance than to a very small one in names and forms. But unfamiliarity is a disadvantage which, when there is any real value in an idea, it only requires time to remove. And in these days of discussion, and generally awakened interest in improvement, what formerly was the work of centuries often requires only years.

Since the first publication of this Treatise several adverse criticisms have been made on Mr. Hare's plan which indicate at least a careful examination of it and a more intelligent consideration than had previously been given to its pretensions. This is the natural progress of the discussion of great improvements. They are at first met by a blind prejudice, and by arguments to which only blind prejudice could attach any value. As the prejudice weakens, the arguments it employs for some time increase in strength since, the plan being better understood, its inevitable inconveniences, and the circumstances which militate against its at once producing all the benefits it is intrinsically capable of, come to light along with its merits. But of all the objections, having any semblance of reason, which have come under my notice, there is not one which had not been foreseen, considered, and canvassed by the supporters of the plan and found either unreal or easily surmountable.

The most serious, in appearance, of the objections may be the most briefly answered; the assumed impossibility of guarding against fraud, or suspicion of fraud, in the operations of the Central Office. Publicity and complete liberty of inspecting the voting papers after the election were the securities provided, but these, it is maintained, would be unavailing because, to check the returns, a voter would have to go over all the work that had been done by the staff of clerks. This would be a very weighty objection if there were any necessity that the returns should be verified individually by every voter. All that a simple voter could be expected to do in the way of verification would be to check the use made of his own voting paper; for which purpose every paper would be returned, after a proper interval, to the place from whence it came. But what he could not do would be done for him by the unsuccessful candidates and their agents. Those among the defeated who thought that they ought to have been returned would, singly or a number together, employ an agency for verifying the entire process of the election; and if they detected material error, the documents would be referred to a Committee of the House of Commons, by whom the entire electoral operations of the nation would be examined and verified, at a tenth part the expense of time and money necessary for the scrutiny of a single return before an Election Committee under the system now in force.

Assuming the plan to be workable, two modes have been alleged in which its benefits might be frustrated and injurious consequences produced in lieu of them. First, it said that undue power would be given to knots or cliques; sectarian combinations, associations for special objects, such as the Maine Law League, the Ballot or Liberation Society; or bodies united by class interests or community of religious persuasion. It is in the second place objected that the system would admit of being worked for party purposes. A central organ of each political party would send its list of 658 candidates all through the country, to be voted for by the whole of its supporters in every constituency. Their votes would far outnumber those which could ever be obtained by any independent candidate. The "ticket" system, it is contended, would, as it does in America, operate solely in favor of the great organized parties, whose tickets would be accepted blindly and voted for in their integrity; and would hardly ever be outvoted, except occasionally, by the sectarian groups, or knots of men bound together by a common crotchet, who have been already spoken of.

The answer to this appears to be conclusive. No one pretends that under Mr. Hare's or any other plan organization would cease to be an advantage. Scattered elements are always at a disadvantage compared with organized bodies. As Mr. Hare's plan cannot alter the nature of things, we must expect

that all parties or sections, great or small, which possess organization, would avail themselves of it to the utmost to
strengthen their influence. But under the existing system those
influences are everything. The scattered elements are absolutely nothing. The voters who are neither bound to the great
political nor to any of the little sectarian divisions have no
means of making their votes available. Mr. Hare's plan gives
them the means. They might be more, or less, dexterous in
using it. They might obtain their share of influence, or much
less than their share. But whatever they did acquire would
be clear gain. And when it is assumed that every petty interest,
or combination for a petty object, would give itself an organization, why should we suppose that the great interest of
national intellect and character would alone remain unorganized? If there would be Temperance tickets, and Ragged
School tickets,[8] and the like, would not one public-spirited
person in a constituency be sufficient to put forth a "personal
merit" ticket and circulate it through a whole neighborhood?
And might not a few such persons, meeting in London, select
from the list of candidates the most distinguished names,
without regard to technical divisions of opinion, and publish
them at a trifling expense through all the constituencies? It
must be remembered that the influence of the two great
parties, under the present mode of election, is unlimited; in
Mr. Hare's scheme it would be great, but confined within
bounds. Neither they nor any of the smaller knots would be
able to elect more members than in proportion to the relative
number of their adherents. The ticket system in America
operates under conditions the reverse of this. In America electors vote for the party ticket because the election goes by a
mere majority, and a vote for anyone who is certain not to
obtain the majority is thrown away. But on Mr. Hare's system
a vote given to a person of known worth has almost as much
chance of obtaining its object as one given to a party candi-

---

8 [Various temperance societies flourished in England during the nineteenth century. The Ragged Schools Union was one of several organiza-
tions providing education for the London poor before 1870.]

date. It might be hoped, therefore, that every Liberal or Conservative who was anything besides a Liberal or a Conservative—who had any preferences of his own in addition to those
of his party—would scratch through the names of the more
obscure and insignificant party candidates and inscribe in their
stead some of the men who are an honor to the nation. And
the probability of this fact would operate as a strong inducement with those who drew up the party lists not to confine
themselves to pledged party men, but to include along with
these, in their respective tickets, such of the national notabilities as were more in sympathy with their side than with the
opposite.

The real difficulty, for it is not to be dissembled that there
is a difficulty, is that the independent voters, those who are
desirous of voting for unpatronized persons of merit, would
be apt to put down the names of a few such persons and to
fill up the remainder of their list with mere party candidates,
thus helping to swell the numbers against those by whom they
would prefer to be represented. There would be an easy
remedy for this, should it be necessary to resort to it, namely,
to impose a limit to the number of secondary or contingent
votes. No voter is likely to have an independent preference,
grounded on knowledge, for 658, or even for 100 candidates.
There would be little objection to his being limited to twenty,
fifty, or whatever might be the number in the selection of
whom there was some probability that his own choice would
be exercised—that he would vote as an individual, and not as
one of the mere rank and file of a party. But even without
this restriction, the evil would be likely to cure itself as soon
as the system came to be well understood. To counteract it
would become a paramount object with all the knots and
cliques whose influence is so much deprecated. From these,
each in itself a small minority, the word would go forth,
"Vote for your *special* candidates only; or at least put their
names foremost, so as to give them the full chance which
your numerical strength warrants, of obtaining the quota by
means of first votes, or without descending low in the scale."

And those voters who did not belong to any clique would profit by the lesson.

The minor groups would have precisely the amount of power which they ought to have. The influence they could exercise would be exactly that which their number of voters entitled them to; not a particle more; while, to ensure even that, they would have a motive to put up, as representatives of their special objects, candidates whose other recommendations would enable them to obtain the suffrages of voters not of the sect or clique. It is curious to observe how the popular line of argument in defense of existing systems veers round, according to the nature of the attack made upon them. Not many years ago it was the favorite argument in support of the then existing system of representation that under it all "interests" or "classes" were represented. And certainly all interests or classes of any importance ought to be represented, that is, ought to have spokesmen, or advocates, in Parliament. But from thence it was argued that a system ought to be supported which gave to the partial interests not advocates merely, but the tribunal itself. Now behold the change. Mr. Hare's system makes it impossible for partial interests to have the command of the tribunal, but it ensures them advocates, and for doing even this it is reproached. Because it unites the good points of class representation and the good points of numerical representation, it is attacked from both sides at once.

But it is not such objections as these that are the real difficulty in getting the system accepted; it is the exaggerated notion entertained of its complexity, and the consequent doubt whether it is capable of being carried into effect. The only complete answer to this objection would be actual trial. When the merits of the plan shall have become more generally known, and shall have gained for it a wider support among impartial thinkers, an effort should be made to obtain its introduction experimentally in some limited field, such as the municipal election of some great town. An opportunity was lost when the decision was taken to divide the West Riding of Yorkshire for the purpose of giving it four members, instead of trying the new principle, by leaving the constituency undivided, and allowing a candidate to be returned on obtaining either in first or secondary votes a fourth part of the whole number of votes given. Such experiments would be a very imperfect test of the worth of the plan, but they would be an exemplification of its mode of working; they would enable people to convince themselves that it is not impracticable, would familiarize them with its machinery, and afford some materials for judging whether the difficulties which are thought to be so formidable are real or only imaginary. The day when such a partial trial shall be sanctioned by Parliament will, I believe, inaugurate a new era of Parliamentary Reform, destined to give to Representative Government a shape fitted to its mature and triumphant period, when it shall have passed through the militant stage in which alone the world has yet seen it.[9]

[9] In the interval between the last and present editions of this treatise, it has become known that the experiment here suggested has actually been made on a larger than any municipal or provincial scale, and has been in course of trial for several years. In the Danish Constitution (not that of Denmark proper, but the Constitution framed for the entire Danish kingdom) the equal representation of minorities was provided for on a plan so nearly identical with Mr. Hare's as to add another to the many examples how the ideas which resolve difficulties arising out of a general situation of the human mind or of society present themselves, without communication, to several superior minds at once. This feature of the Danish electoral law has been brought fully and clearly before the British public in an able paper by Mr. Robert Lytton, forming one of the valuable reports by Secretaries of Legation, printed by order of the House of Commons in 1864. Mr. Hare's plan, which may now be also called M. Andrae's, has thus advanced from the position of a simple project to that of a realized political fact.

Though Denmark is as yet the only country in which *personal* representation has become an institution, the progress of the idea among thinking minds has been very rapid. In almost all the countries in which universal suffrage is now regarded as a necessity the scheme is rapidly making its way with the friends of democracy, as a logical consequence of their principle; with those who rather accept than prefer democratic government, as an indispensable corrective of its inconveniences. The po-

CHAPTER VIII

OF THE EXTENSION OF THE SUFFRAGE

S UCH a representative democracy as has now been sketched, representative of all, and not solely of the majority—in which the interests, the opinions, the grades of intellect which are outnumbered would nevertheless be heard, and would have a chance of obtaining by weight of character and strength of argument an influence which would not belong to their numerical force—this democracy, which is alone equal, alone impartial, alone the government of all by all, the only true type of democracy, would be free from the greatest evils of the falsely-called democracies which now prevail, and from which the current idea of democracy is exclusively derived. But even in this democracy, absolute power, if they chose to

---

litical thinkers of Switzerland led the way. Those of France followed. To mention no others, within a very recent period two of the most influential and authoritative political writers in France, one belonging to the moderate liberal and the other to the extreme democratic school, have given in a public adhesion to the plan. Among its German supporters is numbered one of the most eminent political thinkers in Germany, who is also a distinguished member of the liberal Cabinet of the Grand Duke of Baden. This subject, among others, has its share in the important awakening of thought in the American republic, which is already one of the fruits of the great pending contest for human freedom. In the two principal of our Australian colonies Mr. Hare's plan has been brought under the consideration of their respective legislatures and, though not yet adopted, has already a strong party in its favor; while the clear and complete understanding of its principles, shown by the majority of the speakers both on the Conservative and on the Radical side of general politics, shows how unfounded is the notion of its being too complicated to be capable of being generally comprehended and acted on. Nothing is required to make both the plan and its advantages perfectly intelligible to all, except that the time should have come when they will think it worth their while to take the trouble of really attending to it.

exercise it, would rest with the numerical majority; and these would be composed exclusively of a single class, alike in biases, prepossessions, and general modes of thinking, and a class, to say no more, not the most highly cultivated. The constitution would, therefore, still be liable to the characteristic evils of class government: in a far less degree, assuredly, than that exclusive government by a class which now usurps the name of democracy, but still under no effective restraint except what might be found in the good sense, moderation, and forbearance of the class itself. If checks of this description are sufficient, the philosophy of constitutional government is but solemn trifling. All trust in constitutions is grounded on the assurance they may afford, not that the depositaries of power will not, but that they cannot, misemploy it. Democracy is not the ideally best form of government unless this weak side of it can be strengthened, unless it can be so organized that no class, not even the most numerous, shall be able to reduce all but itself to political insignificance and direct the course of legislation and administration by its exclusive class interest. The problem is to find the means of preventing this abuse, without sacrificing the characteristic advantages of popular government.

These twofold requisites are not fulfilled by the expedient of a limitation of the suffrage involving the compulsory exclusion of any portion of the citizens from a voice in the representation. Among the foremost benefits of free government is that education of the intelligence and of the sentiments which is carried down to the very lowest ranks of the people when they are called to take a part in acts which directly affect the great interests of their country. On this topic I have already dwelt so emphatically that I only return to it because there are few who seem to attach to this effect of popular institutions all the importance to which it is entitled. People think it fanciful to expect so much from what seems so slight a cause—to recognize a potent instrument of mental improvement in the exercise of political franchises by manual laborers. Yet, unless substantial mental cultivation in the mass of mankind is to be a mere vision, this is the road by which it must come. If anyone supposes that this road will not bring it, I call to witness the entire contents of M. de Tocqueville's great work, and especially his estimate of the Americans.[1] Almost all travellers are struck by the fact that every American is in some sense both a patriot and a person of cultivated intelligence; and M. de Tocqueville has shown how close the connection is between these qualities and their democratic institutions. No such wide diffusion of the ideas, tastes, and sentiments of educated minds has ever been seen elsewhere, or even conceived as attainable.[2] Yet this is nothing to what we might look for in a government equally democratic in its unexclusiveness, but better organized in other important points. For political life is indeed in America a most valuable school, but it is a school from which the ablest teachers are excluded; the first minds in the country being as effectually shut out from the national representation, and from public functions generally, as if they were under a formal disqualification. The demos, too, being in America the one source of power, all the selfish ambition of the country gravitates toward it, as

[1] [La Démocratie en Amérique (2 vols., 1835, 1840).]

[2] The following "extract from the Report of the English Commissioner to the New York Exhibition," which I quote from Mr. Carey's Principles of Social Science, bears striking testimony to one part, at least, of the assertion in the text:

"We have a few great engineers and mechanics, and a large body of clever workmen; but the Americans seem likely to become a whole nation of such people. Already, their rivers swarm with steamboats; their valleys are becoming crowded with factories; their towns, surpassing those of every state of Europe, except Belgium, Holland, and England, are the abodes of all the skill which now distinguishes a town population; and there is scarcely an art in Europe not carried on in America with equal or greater skill than in Europe, though it has been here cultivated and improved through ages. A whole nation of Franklins, Stephensons, and Watts in prospect, is something wonderful for other nations to contemplate. In contrast with the comparative inertness and ignorance of the bulk of the people of Europe, whatever may be the superiority of a few well-instructed and gifted persons, the great intelligence of the whole people of America is the circumstance most worthy of public attention."

it does in despotic countries toward the monarch: the people,
like the despot, is pursued with adulation and sycophancy,
and the corrupting effects of power fully keep pace with its improving and ennobling influences. If, even with this alloy,
democratic institutions produce so marked a superiority of
mental development in the lowest class of Americans, compared with the corresponding classes in England and elsewhere, what would it be if the good portion of the influence
could be retained without the bad? And this, to a certain extent, may be done; but not by excluding that portion of the
people who have fewest intellectual stimuli of other kinds
from so inestimable an introduction to large, distant, and complicated interests as is afforded by the attention they may be
induced to bestow on political affairs. It is by political discussion that the manual laborer, whose employment is a routine,
and whose way of life brings him in contact with no variety
of impressions, circumstances, or ideas, is taught that remote
causes and events which take place far off have a most sensible effect even on his personal interests; and it is from political discussion and collective political action that one whose
daily occupations concentrate his interests in a small circle
round himself learns to feel for and with his fellow citizens
and becomes consciously a member of a great community. But
political discussions fly over the heads of those who have no
votes and are not endeavoring to acquire them. Their position, in comparison with the electors, is that of the audience
in a court of justice compared with the twelve men in the
jury box. It is not *their* suffrages that are asked, it is not their
opinion that is sought to be influenced; the appeals are made,
the arguments addressed, to others than them; nothing depends on the decision they may arrive at, and there is no
necessity and very little inducement to them to come to any.
Whoever, in an otherwise popular government, has no vote
and no prospect of obtaining it will either be a permanent
malcontent or will feel as one whom the general affairs of
society do not concern; for whom they are to be managed by
others; who "has no business with the laws except to obey

them," nor with public interests and concerns except as a looker-on. What he will know or care about them from this position may partly be measured by what an average woman of the middle class knows and cares about politics, compared with her husband or brothers.

Independently of all these considerations it is a personal injustice to withhold from anyone, unless for the prevention of greater evils, the ordinary privilege of having his voice reckoned in the disposal of affairs in which he has the same interest as other people. If he is compelled to pay, if he may be compelled to fight, if he is required implicitly to obey, he should be legally entitled to be told what for, to have his consent asked and his opinion counted at its worth, though not at more than its worth. There ought to be no pariahs in a full-grown and civilized nation, no persons disqualified, except through their own default. Everyone is degraded, whether aware of it or not, when other people, without consulting him, take upon themselves unlimited power to regulate his destiny. And even in a much more improved state than the human mind has ever yet reached it is not in nature that they who are thus disposed of should meet with as fair play as those who have a voice. Rulers and ruling classes are under a necessity of considering the interests and wishes of those who have the suffrage; but of those who are excluded, it is in their option whether they will do so or not, and, however honestly disposed, they are in general too fully occupied with things which they *must* attend to, to have much room in their thoughts for anything which they can with impunity disregard. No arrangement of the suffrage, therefore, can be permanently satisfactory in which any person or class is peremptorily excluded, in which the electoral privilege is not open to all persons of full age who desire to obtain it.

There are, however, certain exclusions, required by positive reasons, which do not conflict with this principle, and which, though an evil in themselves, are only to be got rid of by the cessation of the state of things which requires them. I regard it as wholly inadmissible that any person should partici-

pate in the suffrage without being able to read, write, and, I
will add, perform the common operations of arithmetic. Justice demands, even when the suffrage does not depend on it,
that the means of attaining these elementary acquirements
should be within the reach of every person, either gratuitously
or at an expense not exceeding what the poorest who earn
their own living can afford. If this were really the case, people
would no more think of giving the suffrage to a man who
could not read than of giving it to a child who could not
speak; and it would not be society that would exclude him,
but his own laziness. When society has not performed its duty
by rendering this amount of instruction accessible to all, there
is some hardship in the case, but it is a hardship that ought
to be borne. If society has neglected to discharge two solemn
obligations, the more important and more fundamental of the
two must be fulfilled first: universal teaching must precede
universal enfranchisement. No one but those in whom an *a
priori* theory has silenced common sense will maintain that
power over others, over the whole community, should be im-
parted to people who have not acquired the commonest and
most essential requisites for taking care of themselves, for
pursuing intelligently their own interests and those of the
persons most nearly allied to them. This argument, doubtless,
might be pressed further and made to prove much more. It
would be eminently desirable that other things besides reading,
writing, and arithmetic could be made necessary to the suffrage; that some knowledge of the conformation of the earth,
its natural and political divisions, the elements of general
history, and of the history and institutions of their own country could be required from all electors. But these kinds of
knowledge, however indispensable to an intelligent use of
the suffrage, are not, in this country, nor probably anywhere
save in the northern United States, accessible to the whole
people; nor does there exist any trustworthy machinery for ascertaining whether they have been acquired or not. The attempt, at present, would lead to partiality, chicanery, and
every kind of fraud. It is better that the suffrage should be

conferred indiscriminately, or even withheld indiscriminately, than that it should be given to one and withheld from another at the discretion of a public officer. In regard, however, to reading, writing, and calculating there need be no difficulty. It would be easy to require from everyone who presented himself for registry that he should, in the presence of the registrar, copy a sentence from an English book and perform a sum in the rule of three, and to secure, by fixed rules and complete publicity, the honest application of so very simple a test. This condition, therefore, should in all cases accompany universal suffrage; and it would after a few years exclude none but those who cared so little for the privilege that their vote, if given, would not in general be an indication of any real political opinion.

It is also important that the assembly which votes the taxes, either general or local, should be elected exclusively by those who pay something toward the taxes imposed. Those who pay no taxes, disposing by their votes of other people's money, have every motive to be lavish and none to economize. As far as money matters are concerned, any power of voting possessed by them is a violation of the fundamental principle of free government—a severance of the power of control from the interest in its beneficial exercise. It amounts to allowing them to put their hands into other people's pockets for any purpose which they think fit to call a public one; which in some of the great towns of the United States is known to have produced a scale of local taxation onerous beyond example and wholly borne by the wealthier classes. That representation should be coextensive with taxation, not stopping short of it, but also not going beyond it, is in accordance with the theory of British institutions. But to reconcile this, as a condition annexed to the representation, with universality, it is essential, as it is on many other accounts desirable, that taxation, in a visible shape, should descend to the poorest class. In this country, and in most others, there is probably no laboring family which does not contribute to the indirect taxes by the purchase of tea, coffee, sugar, not to mention narcotics or stimulants. But this mode of defraying a share of the public expenses is hardly felt; the payer, unless a person of education and reflection, does not identify his interest with a low scale of public expenditure as closely as when money for its support is demanded directly from himself; and even supposing him to do so, he would doubtless take care that, however lavish an expenditure he might, by his vote, assist in imposing upon the government, it should not be defrayed by any additional taxes on the articles which he himself consumes. It would be better that a direct tax, in the simple form of a capitation, should be levied on every grown person in the community; or that every such person should be admitted an elector on allowing himself to be rated *extra ordinem* to the assessed taxes; or that a small annual payment, rising and falling with the gross expenditure of the country, should be required from every registered elector; that so everyone might feel that the money which he assisted in voting was partly his own, and that he was interested in keeping down its amount.

However this may be, I regard it as required by first principles that the receipt of parish relief should be a peremptory disqualification for the franchise. He who cannot by his labor suffice for his own support has no claim to the privilege of helping himself to the money of others. By becoming dependent on the remaining members of the community for actual subsistence, he abdicates his claim to equal rights with them in other respects. Those to whom he is indebted for the continuance of his very existence may justly claim the exclusive management of those common concerns to which he now brings nothing, or less than he takes away. As a condition of the franchise a term should be fixed, say five years previous to the registry, during which the applicant's name has not been on the parish books as a recipient of relief. To be an uncertified bankrupt, or to have taken the benefit of the Insolvent Act, should disqualify for the franchise until the person has paid his debts, or at least proved that he is not now, and has not for some long period been, dependent on eleemosynary support. Nonpayment of taxes, when so long persisted in that it cannot have arisen from inadvertence, should disqualify while it lasts. These exclusions are not in their nature permanent. They exact such conditions only as all are able, or ought to be able, to fulfill if they choose. They leave the suffrage accessible to all who are in the normal condition of a human being; and if anyone has to forego it, he either does not care sufficiently for it to do for its sake what he is already bound to do or he is in a general condition of depression and degradation in which this slight addition, necessary for the security of others, would be unfelt, and on emerging from which, this mark of inferiority would disappear with the rest.

In the long run, therefore (supposing no restrictions to exist but those of which we have now treated), we might expect that all, except that (it is to be hoped) progressively diminishing class, the recipients of parish relief, would be in possession of votes, so that the suffrage would be, with that slight abatement, universal. That it should be thus widely expanded is, as we have seen, absolutely necessary to an enlarged and elevated conception of good government. Yet in this state of things the great majority of voters, in most countries, and emphatically in this, would be manual laborers; and the twofold danger—that of too low a standard of political intelligence, and that of class legislation—would still exist in a very perilous degree. It remains to be seen whether any means exist by which these evils can be obviated.

They are capable of being obviated if men sincerely wish it, not by any artificial contrivance, but by carrying out the natural order of human life, which recommends itself to everyone in things in which he has no interest or traditional opinion running counter to it. In all human affairs, every person directly interested, and not under positive tutelage, has an admitted claim to a voice and, when his exercise of it is not inconsistent with the safety of the whole, cannot justly be excluded from it. But though everyone ought to have a voice —that everyone should have an equal voice is a totally different proposition. When two persons who have a joint interest in any business differ in opinion, does justice require that both opinions should be held of exactly equal value? If, with equal virtue, one is superior to the other in knowledge and intelligence, or if, with equal intelligence, one excels the other in virtue, the opinion, the judgment of the higher moral or intellectual being is worth more than that of the inferior: and if the institutions of the country virtually assert that they are of the same value, they assert a thing which is not. One of the two, as the wiser or better man, has a claim to superior weight; the difficulty is in ascertaining which of the two it is— a thing impossible as between individuals, but, taking men in bodies and in numbers, it can be done with a certain approach to accuracy. There would be no pretense for applying this doctrine to any case which could with reason be considered as one of individual and private right. In an affair which concerns only one of two persons, that one is entitled to follow his own opinion, however much wiser the other may be than himself. But we are speaking of things which equally concern them both; where, if the more ignorant does not yield his share of the matter to the guidance of the wiser man, the wiser man must resign his to that of the more ignorant. Which of these modes of getting over the difficulty is most for the interest of both and most conformable to the general fitness of things? If it be deemed unjust that either should have to give way, which injustice is greatest: that the better judgment should give way to the worse, or the worse to the better?

Now national affairs are exactly such a joint concern, with the difference that no one needs ever be called upon for a complete sacrifice of his own opinion. It can always be taken into the calculation and counted at a certain figure, a higher figure being assigned to the suffrages of those whose opinion is entitled to greater weight. There is not, in this arrangement, anything necessarily invidious to those to whom it assigns the lower degrees of influence. Entire exclusion from a voice in the common concerns is one thing, the concession to others of a more potential voice, on the ground of greater capacity for the management of the joint interests, is another. The two things are not merely different, they are incommensurable. Everyone has a right to feel insulted by being made a nobody and stamped as of no account at all. No one but a fool, and only a fool of a peculiar description, feels offended by the acknowledgment that there are others whose opinion, and even whose wish, is entitled to a greater amount of consideration than his. To have no voice in what are partly his own concerns is a thing which nobody willingly submits to; but when what is partly his concern is also partly another's, and he feels the other to understand the subject better than himself, that the other's opinion should be counted for more than his own accords with his expectations, and with the course of things which in all other affairs of life he is accustomed to acquiesce in. It is only necessary that this superior influence should be assigned on grounds which he can comprehend, and of which he is able to perceive the justice.

I hasten to say that I consider it entirely inadmissible, unless as a temporary makeshift, that the superiority of influence should be conferred in consideration of property. I do not deny that property is a kind of test; education in most countries, though anything but proportional to riches, is on the average better in the richer half of society than in the poorer. But the criterion is so imperfect; accident has so much more to do than merit with enabling men to rise in the world; and it is so impossible for anyone, by acquiring any amount of instruction, to make sure of the corresponding rise in station, that this foundation of electoral privilege is always, and will continue to be, supremely odious. To connect plurality of votes with any pecuniary qualification would be not only objectionable in itself, but a sure mode of discrediting the principle and making its permanent maintenance impracticable. The democracy, at least of this country, are not at present jealous of personal superiority, but they are naturally and most justly so of that which is grounded on mere pecuniary circumstances. The only thing which can justify reckoning one person's opinion as equivalent to more than one is individual mental superiority; and what is wanted is some approximate means of ascertaining

that. If there existed such a thing as a really national education or a trustworthy system of general examination, education
might be tested directly. In the absence of these, the nature of
a person's occupation is some test. An employer of labor is on
the average more intelligent than a laborer; for he must labor
with his head, and not solely with his hands. A foreman is
generally more intelligent than an ordinary laborer, and a
laborer in the skilled trades than in the unskilled. A banker,
merchant, or manufacturer is likely to be more intelligent than
a tradesman, because he has larger and more complicated interests to manage. In all these cases it is not the having merely
undertaken the superior function, but the successful performance of it, that tests the qualifications; for which reason, as
well as to prevent persons from engaging nominally in an occupation for the sake of the vote, it would be proper to require that the occupation should have been persevered in for
some length of time (say three years). Subject to some such condition, two or more votes might be allowed to every person
who exercises any of these superior functions. The liberal professions, when really and not nominally practiced, imply, of
course, a still higher degree of instruction; and wherever a sufficient examination, or any serious conditions of education, are
required before entering on a profession, its members could
be admitted at once to a plurality of votes. The same rule
might be applied to graduates of universities; and even to
those who bring satisfactory certificates of having passed
through the course of study required by any school at which
the higher branches of knowledge are taught, under proper
securities that the teaching is real, and not a mere pretense.
The "local" or "middle class" examination for the degree of
Associate, so laudably and public-spiritedly established by the
Universities of Oxford and Cambridge, and any similar ones
which may be instituted by other competent bodies (provided
they are fairly open to all comers), afford a ground on which
plurality of votes might with great advantage be accorded to
those who have passed the test. All these suggestions are open
to much discussion in the detail, and to objections which it is

of no use to anticipate. The time is not come for giving to such plans a practical shape, nor should I wish to be bound by the particular proposals which I have made. But it is to me evident that in this direction lies the true ideal of representative government; and that to work toward it, by the best practical contrivances which can be found, is the path of real political improvement.

If it be asked to what length the principle admits of being carried, or how many votes might be accorded to an individual on the ground of superior qualifications, I answer that this is not in itself very material provided the distinctions and gradations are not made arbitrarily, but are such as can be understood and accepted by the general conscience and understanding. But it is an absolute condition not to overpass the limit prescribed by the fundamental principle laid down in a former chapter as the condition of excellence in the constitution of a representative system. The plurality of votes must on no account be carried so far that those who are privileged by it, or the class (if any) to which they mainly belong, shall outweigh by means of it all the rest of the community. The distinction in favor of education, right in itself, is further and strongly recommended by its preserving the educated from the class legislation of the uneducated, but it must stop short of enabling them to practice class legislation on their own account. Let me add that I consider it an absolutely necessary part of the plurality scheme that it be open to the poorest individual in the community to claim its privileges if he can prove that, in spite of all difficulties and obstacles, he is, in point of intelligence, entitled to them. There ought to be voluntary examinations at which any person whatever might present himself, might prove that he came up to the standard of knowledge and ability laid down as sufficient, and be admitted, in consequence, to the plurality of votes. A privilege which is not refused to anyone who can show that he has realized the conditions on which in theory and principle it is dependent would not necessarily be repugnant to anyone's sentiment of justice; but it would certainly be so if, while conferred on general presumptions not always infallible, it were denied to direct proof.

Plural voting, though practiced in vestry elections and those of poor-law guardians, is so unfamiliar in elections to Parliament that it is not likely to be soon or willingly adopted; but as the time will certainly arrive when the only choice will be between this and equal universal suffrage, whoever does not desire the last cannot too soon begin to reconcile himself to the former. In the meantime, though the suggestion, for the present, may not be a practical one, it will serve to mark what is best in principle, and enable us to judge of the eligibility of any indirect means, either existing or capable of being adopted, which may promote in a less perfect manner the same end. A person may have a double vote by other means than that of tendering two votes at the same hustings: he may have a vote in each of two different constituencies; and though this exceptional privilege at present belongs rather to superiority of means than of intelligence, I would not abolish it where it exists, since until a truer test of education is adopted it would be unwise to dispense with even so imperfect a one as is afforded by pecuniary circumstances. Means might be found of giving a further extension to the privilege, which would connect it in a more direct manner with superior education. In any future Reform Bill which lowers greatly the pecuniary conditions of the suffrage, it might be a wise provision to allow all graduates of universities, all persons who have passed creditably through the higher schools, all members of the liberal professions, and perhaps some others, to be registered specifically in those characters and to give their votes as such in any constituency in which they choose to register, retaining, in addition, their votes as simple citizens in the localities in which they reside.

Until there shall have been devised, and until opinion is willing to accept, some mode of plural voting which may assign to education, as such, the degree of superior influence due to it, and sufficient as a counterpoise to the numerical weight of the least educated class; for so long the benefits of completely universal suffrage cannot be obtained without bringing with them, as it appears to me, a chance of more than equivalent evils. It is possible, indeed (and this is perhaps one of the transitions through which we may have to pass in our progress to a really good representative system), that the barriers which restrict the suffrage might be entirely levelled in some particular constituencies, whose members, consequently, would be returned principally by manual laborers; the existing electoral qualification being maintained elsewhere, or any alteration in it being accompanied by such a grouping of the constituencies as to prevent the laboring class from becoming preponderant in Parliament. By such a compromise, the anomalies in the representation would not only be retained, but augmented; this, however, is not a conclusive objection, for if the country does not choose to pursue the right ends by a regular system directly leading to them, it must be content with an irregular makeshift, as being greatly preferable to a system free from irregularities, but regularly adapted to wrong ends, or in which some ends equally necessary with the others have been left out. It is a far graver objection that this adjustment is incompatible with the intercommunity of local constituencies which Mr. Hare's plan requires; that under it every voter would remain imprisoned within the one or more constituencies in which his name is registered and, unless willing to be represented by one of the candidates for those localities, would not be represented at all.

So much importance do I attach to the emancipation of those who already have votes, but whose votes are useless because always outnumbered; so much should I hope from the natural influence of truth and reason, if only secured a hearing and a competent advocacy—that I should not despair of the operation even of equal and universal suffrage if made real by the proportional representation of all minorities, on Mr. Hare's principle. But if the best hopes which can be formed on this subject were certainties, I should still contend for the principle of plural voting. I do not propose the plurality as a thing in itself undesirable, which, like the exclusion of part of the community from the suffrage, may be temporarily tolerated while necessary to prevent greater evils. I do not look upon equal voting as among the things which are good in themselves, provided they can be guarded against inconveniences. I look upon it as only relatively good—less objectionable than inequality of privilege grounded on irrelevant or adventitious circumstances, but in principle wrong, because recognizing a wrong standard and exercising a bad influence on the voter's mind. It is not useful, but hurtful, that the constitution of the country should declare ignorance to be entitled to as much political power as knowledge. The national institutions should place all things that they are concerned with before the mind of the citizen in the light in which it is for his good that he should regard them; and as it is for his good that he should think that everyone is entitled to some influence, but the better and wiser to more than others, it is important that this conviction should be professed by the State and embodied in the national institutions. Such things constitute the *spirit* of the institutions of a country: that portion of their influence which is least regarded by common, and especially by English, thinkers, though the institutions of every country not under great positive oppression produce more effect by their spirit than by any of their direct provisions, since by it they shape the national character. The American institutions have imprinted strongly on the American mind that any one man (with a white skin) is as good as any other; and it is felt that this false creed is nearly connected with some of the more unfavorable points in American character. It is not a small mischief that the constitution of any country should sanction this creed, for the belief in it, whether express or tacit, is almost as detrimental to moral and intellectual excellence as any effect which most forms of government can produce.

It may, perhaps, be said that a constitution which gives equal influence, man for man, to the most and to the least instructed is nevertheless conducive to progress, because the appeals constantly made to the less instructed classes, the exercise given to their mental powers, and the exertions which the more instructed are obliged to make for enlightening their judgment and ridding them of errors and prejudices are powerful stimulants to their advance in intelligence. That this most desirable effect really attends the admission of the less educated classes to some, and even to a large, share of power, I admit and have already strenuously maintained. But theory and experience alike prove that a countercurrent sets in when they are made the possessors of all power. Those who are supreme over everything, whether they be One, or Few, or Many, have no longer need of the arms of reason; they can make their mere will prevail, and those who cannot be resisted are usually far too well satisfied with their own opinions to be willing to change them or listen without impatience to anyone who tells them that they are in the wrong. The position which gives the strongest stimulus to the growth of intelligence is that of rising into power, not that of having achieved it; and of all resting points, temporary or permanent, in the way to ascendancy, the one which develops the best and highest qualities is the position of those who are strong enough to make reason prevail, but not strong enough to prevail against reason. This is the position in which, according to the principles we have laid down, the rich and the poor, the much and the little educated, and all the other classes and denominations which divide society between them ought as far as practicable to be placed. And by combining this principle with the otherwise just one of allowing superiority of weight to superiority of mental qualities, a political constitution would realize that kind of relative perfection which is alone compatible with the complicated nature of human affairs.

In the preceding argument for universal but graduated suffrage I have taken no account of difference of sex. I consider it to be as entirely irrelevant to political rights as difference in height or in the color of the hair. All human beings have the same interest in good government; the welfare of all is alike affected by it, and they have equal need of a voice in it to secure their share of its benefits. If there be any difference,

women require it more than men, since, being physically
weaker, they are more dependent on law and society for protection. Mankind have long since abandoned the only premises
which will support the conclusion that women ought not to
have votes. No one now holds that women should be in personal servitude, that they should have no thought, wish, or
occupation, but to be the domestic drudges of husbands, fa-
thers, or brothers. It is allowed to unmarried, and wants but little of being conceded to married, women to hold property and
have pecuniary and business interests in the same manner as
men. It is considered suitable and proper that women should
think, and write, and be teachers. As soon as these things are
admitted, the political disqualification has no principle to rest
on. The whole mode of thought of the modern world is with
increasing emphasis pronouncing against the claim of society
to decide for individuals what they are and are not fit for, and
what they shall and shall not be allowed to attempt. If the
principles of modern politics and political economy are good
for anything, it is for proving that these points can only be
rightly judged of by the individuals themselves; and that, under complete freedom of choice, wherever there are real diversities of aptitude, the great number will apply themselves
to the things for which they are on the average fittest, and the
exceptional course will only be taken by the exceptions. Either
the whole tendency of modern social improvements has been
wrong or it ought to be carried out to the total abolition of all
exclusions and disabilities which close any honest employment
to a human being.

But it is not even necessary to maintain so much in order to
prove that women should have the suffrage. Were it as right,
as it is wrong, that they should be a subordinate class, confined to domestic occupations and subject to domestic authority, they would not the less require the protection of the suffrage to secure them from the abuse of that authority. Men, as
well as women, do not need political rights in order that they
may govern, but in order that they may not be misgoverned.
The majority of the male sex are, and will be all their lives,

nothing else than laborers in cornfields and manufactories, but this does not render the suffrage less desirable for them, nor their claim to it less irresistible, when not likely to make a bad use of it. Nobody pretends to think that women would make a bad use of the suffrage. The worst that is said is that they would vote as mere dependents, at the bidding of their male relations. If it be so, so let it be. If they think for themselves, great good will be done, and if they do not, no harm. It is a benefit to human beings to take off their fetters, even if they do not desire to walk. It would already be a great improvement in the moral position of women to be no longer declared by law incapable of an opinion, and not entitled to a preference, respecting the most important concerns of humanity. There would be some benefit to them individually in having something to bestow which their male relatives cannot exact, and are yet desirous to have. It would also be no small benefit that the husband would necessarily discuss the matter with his wife, and that the vote would not be his exclusive affair, but a joint concern. People do not sufficiently consider how markedly the fact that she is able to have some action on the outward world independently of him raises her dignity and value in a vulgar man's eyes, and makes her the object of a respect which no personal qualities would ever obtain for one whose social existence he can entirely appropriate. The vote itself, too, would be improved in quality. The man would often be obliged to find honest reasons for his vote, such as might induce a more upright and impartial character to serve with him under the same banner. The wife's influence would often keep him true to his own sincere opinion. Often, indeed, it would be used, not on the side of public principle, but of the personal interest or worldly vanity of the family. But wherever this would be the tendency of the wife's influence, it is exerted to the full already in that bad direction; and with the more certainty, since under the present law and custom she is generally too utter a stranger to politics in any sense in which they involve principle to be able to realize to herself that there is a point of honor in them, and most people have as little sympathy in the point of honor of others when their own is not placed in the same thing, as they have in the religious feelings of those whose religion differs from theirs. Give the woman a vote, and she comes under the operation of the political point of honor. She learns to look on politics as a thing on which she is allowed to have an opinion, and in which if one has an opinion it ought to be acted upon; she acquires a sense of personal accountability in the matter, and will no longer feel, as she does at present, that whatever amount of bad influence she may exercise, if the man can but be persuaded, all is right, and his responsibility covers all. It is only by being herself encouraged to form an opinion and obtain an intelligent comprehension of the reasons which ought to prevail with the conscience against the temptations of personal or family interest that she can ever cease to act as a disturbing force on the political conscience of the man. Her indirect agency can only be prevented from being politically mischievous by being exchanged for direct.

I have supposed the right of suffrage to depend, as in a good state of things it would, on personal conditions. Where it depends, as in this and most other countries, on conditions of property, the contradiction is even more flagrant. There is something more than ordinarily irrational in the fact that when a woman can give all the guarantees required from a male elector, independent circumstances, the position of a householder and head of a family, payment of taxes or whatever may be the conditions imposed, the very principle and system of a representation based on property is set aside, and an exceptionally personal disqualification is created for the mere purpose of excluding her. When it is added that in the country where this is done a woman now reigns, and that the most glorious ruler whom that country ever had was a woman, the picture of unreason, and scarcely disguised injustice, is complete.[3] Let us hope that as the work proceeds of pulling down, one after another, the remains of the moldering fabric

[3] [Reference is, of course, to Great Britain and Queen Victoria (1819-1901). The "most glorious ruler" is Queen Elizabeth I (1533-1603).]

of monopoly and tyranny, this one will not be the last to disappear; that the opinion of Bentham, of Mr. Samuel Bailey,
of Mr. Hare, and many other of the most powerful political
thinkers of this age and country (not to speak of others), will
make its way to all minds not rendered obdurate by selfishness
or inveterate prejudice; and that, before the lapse of another
generation, the accident of sex, no more than the accident of
skin, will be deemed a sufficient justification for depriving its
possessor of the equal protection and just privileges of a citizen.[4]

CHAPTER IX

SHOULD THERE BE TWO STAGES OF ELECTION?

IN SOME representative constitutions the plan has been adopted of choosing the members of the representative body
by a double process, the primary electors only choosing
other electors, and these electing the member of parliament.
This contrivance was probably intended as a slight impediment to the full sweep of popular feeling, giving the suffrage,
and with it the complete ultimate power, to the many, but
compelling them to exercise it through the agency of a comparatively few who, it was supposed, would be less moved than
the demos by the gusts of popular passion; and as the electors,
being already a select body, might be expected to exceed in intellect and character the common level of their constituents,
the choice made by them was thought likely to be more careful and enlightened, and would in any case be made under a
greater feeling of responsibility, than election by the masses

4 [Jeremy Bentham (1748-1832), English political philosopher, was a
close friend of James Mill and very influential in John Stuart Mill's intellectual training. Samuel Bailey (1791-1870) was an English philosopher
and economist. Mill treats of the inequality of women in a number of his
writings, most particularly in *The Subjection of Women* (1869).]

themselves. This plan of filtering, as it were, the popular suffrage through an intermediate body admits of a very plausible
defense: since it may be said, with great appearance of reason,
that less intellect and instruction are required for judging who
among our neighbors can be most safely trusted to choose a
member of parliament than who is himself fittest to be one.

In the first place, however, if the dangers incident to popular power may be thought to be in some degree lessened by this
indirect arrangement, so also are its benefits; and the latter effect is much more certain than the former. To enable the system to work as desired it must be carried into effect in the
spirit in which it is planned: the electors must use the suffrage
in the manner supposed by the theory, that is, each of them
must not ask himself who the member of parliament should be,
but only whom he would best like to choose one for him. It is
evident that the advantages which indirect is supposed to have
over direct election require this disposition of mind in the
voter, and will only be realized by his taking the doctrine *au
sérieux,* that his sole business is to choose the choosers, not the
member himself. The supposition must be that he will not occupy his thoughts with political opinions and measures, or political men, but will be guided by his personal respect for some
private individual to whom he will give a general power of attorney to act for him. Now if the primary electors adopt this
view of their position, one of the principal uses of giving them
a vote at all is defeated—the political function to which they
are called fails of developing public spirit and political intelligence; of making public affairs an object of interest to their
feelings and of exercise to their faculties. The supposition,
moreover, involves inconsistent conditions; for if the voter feels
no interest in the final result, how or why can he be expected
to feel any in the process which leads to it? To wish to have a
particular individual for his representative in parliament is
possible to a person of a very moderate degree of virtue and
intelligence; and to wish to choose an elector who will elect
that individual is a natural consequence; but for a person who
does not care who is elected, or feels bound to put that consid-

eration in abeyance, to take any interest whatever in merely
naming the worthiest person to elect another according to his
own judgment, implies a zeal for what is right in the abstract,
a habitual principle of duty for the sake of duty, which is
possible only to persons of a rather high grade of cultivation,
who, by the very possession of it, show that they may be, and
deserve to be, trusted with political power in a more direct
shape. Of all public functions which it is possible to confer on
the poorer members of the community this surely is the least
calculated to kindle their feelings, and holds out least natural
inducement to care for it, other than a virtuous determination
to discharge conscientiously whatever duty one has to perform;
and if the mass of electors cared enough about political affairs
to set any value on so limited a participation in them, they
would not be likely to be satisfied without one much more extensive.

In the next place, admitting that a person who, from his narrow range of cultivation, cannot judge well of the qualifications of a candidate for parliament may be a sufficient judge
of the honesty and general capacity of somebody whom he may
depute to choose a member of Parliament for him, I may remark that if the voter acquiesces in this estimate of his capabilities and really wishes to have the choice made for him by
a person in whom he places reliance, there is no need of any
constitutional provision for the purpose; he has only to ask
this confidential person privately what candidate he had better vote for. In that case the two modes of election coincide in
their result, and every advantage of indirect election is obtained under direct. The systems only diverge in their operation if we suppose that the voter would prefer to use his own
judgment in the choice of a representative, and only lets another choose for him because the law does not allow him a
more direct mode of action. But if this be his state of mind; if
his will does not go along with the limitation which the law
imposes, and he desires to make a direct choice, he can do so
notwithstanding the law. He has only to choose as elector a
known partisan of the candidate he prefers, or someone who

will pledge himself to vote for that candidate. And this is so much the natural working of election by two stages that, except in a condition of complete political indifference, it can scarcely be expected to act otherwise. It is in this way that the election of the President of the United States practically takes place. Nominally, the election is indirect: the population at large does not vote for the President; it votes for electors who choose the President. But the electors are always chosen under an express engagement to vote for a particular candidate, nor does a citizen ever vote for an elector because of any preference for the man; he votes for the Lincoln ticket, or the Breckenridge ticket. It must be remembered that the electors are not chosen in order that they may search the country and find the fittest person in it to be President or to be a member of Parliament. There would be something to be said for the practice if this were so; but it is not so, nor ever will be until mankind in general are of opinion, with Plato, that the proper person to be entrusted with power is the person most unwilling to accept it. The electors are to make choice of one of those who have offered themselves as candidates; and those who choose the electors already know who these are. If there is any political activity in the country, all electors who care to vote at all have made up their minds which of these candidates they would like to have, and will make that the sole consideration in giving their vote. The partisans of each candidate will have their list of electors ready, all pledged to vote for that individual; and the only question practically asked of the primary elector will be which of these lists he will support.

The case in which election by two stages answers well in practice is when the electors are not chosen solely as electors, but have other important functions to discharge, which precludes their being selected solely as delegates to give a particular vote. This combination of circumstances exemplifies itself in another American institution, the Senate of the United States. That assembly, the Upper House, as it were, of Congress, is considered to represent not the people directly, but the States as such, and to be the guardian of that portion of their

sovereign rights which they have not alienated. As the internal
sovereignty of each State is, by the nature of an equal federation, equally sacred whatever be the size or importance of the
State, each returns to the Senate the same number of members (two), whether it be little Delaware or the "Empire State"
of New York. These members are not chosen by the population, but by the State Legislatures, themselves elected by the
people of each State; but as the whole ordinary business of a
legislative assembly, internal legislation and the control of the
executive, devolves upon these bodies, they are elected with a
view to those objects more than to the other; and in naming
two persons to represent the State in the Federal Senate they
for the most part exercise their own judgment, with only that
general reference to public opinion necessary in all acts of the
government of a democracy. The elections, thus made, have
proved eminently successful and are conspicuously the best of
all the elections in the United States, the Senate invariably
consisting of the most distinguished men among those who
have made themselves sufficiently known in public life.[1] After
such an example it cannot be said that indirect popular election is never advantageous. Under certain conditions it is the
very best system that can be adopted. But those conditions are
hardly to be obtained in practice, except in a federal government like that of the United States, where the election can be
entrusted to local bodies whose other functions extend to the
most important concerns of the nation. The only bodies in any
analogous position which exist, or are likely to exist, in this
country are the municipalities, or any other boards which have
been or may be created for similar local purposes. Few persons, however, would think it any improvement in our parliamentary constitution if the members for the City of London
were chosen by the Aldermen and Common Council, and those
for the borough of Marylebone avowedly, as they already are
virtually, by the vestries of the component parishes. Even if

[1] [Experience and popular sentiment do not bear out Mill's contention.
Today all senators are elected by popular vote, with the proviso that
temporary vacancies are filled by gubernatorial appointment.]

those bodies, considered merely as local boards, were far less objectionable than they are, the qualities that would fit them for the limited and peculiar duties of municipal or parochial aedileship are no guarantee of any special fitness to judge of the comparative qualifications of candidates for a seat in Parliament. They probably would not fulfill this duty any better than it is fulfilled by the inhabitants voting directly, while, on the other hand, if fitness for electing members of Parliament had to be taken into consideration in selecting persons for the office of vestrymen or town councilors, many of those who are fittest for that more limited duty would inevitably be excluded from it, if only by the necessity there would be of choosing persons whose sentiments in general politics agreed with those of the voters who elected them. The mere indirect political influence of town councils has already led to a considerable perversion of municipal elections from their intended purpose, by making them a matter of party politics. If it were part of the duty of a man's bookkeeper or steward to choose his physician, he would not be likely to have a better medical attendant than if he chose one for himself, while he would be restricted in his choice of a steward or bookkeeper to such as might without too great danger to his health be entrusted with the other office.

It appears, therefore, that every benefit of indirect election which is attainable at all is attainable under direct; that such of the benefits expected from it as would not be obtained under direct election will just as much fail to be obtained under indirect, while the latter has considerable disadvantages peculiar to itself. The mere fact that it is an additional and superfluous wheel in the machinery is no trifling objection. Its decided inferiority as a means of cultivating public spirit and political intelligence has already been dwelt upon; and if it had any effective operation at all—that is, if the primary electors did to any extent leave to their nominees the selection of their parliamentary representative—the voter would be prevented from identifying himself with his member of Parliament, and the member would feel a much less active sense of responsibility to his constituents. In addition to all this, the comparatively small number of persons in whose hands, at last, the election of a member of Parliament would reside could not but afford great additional facilities to intrigue and to every form of corruption compatible with the station in life of the electors. The constituencies would universally be reduced, in point of conveniences for bribery, to the condition of the small boroughs at present. It would be sufficient to gain over a small number of persons to be certain of being returned. If it be said that the electors would be responsible to those who elected them, the answer is obvious that, holding no permanent office or position in the public eye, they would risk nothing by a corrupt vote except what they would care little for, not to be appointed electors again; and the main reliance must still be on the penalties for bribery, the insufficiency of which reliance, in small constituencies, experience has made notorious to all the world. The evil would be exactly proportional to the amount of discretion left to the chosen electors. The only case in which they would probably be afraid to employ their vote for the promotion of their personal interest would be when they were elected under an express pledge, as mere delegates, to carry, as it were, the votes of their constituents to the hustings. The moment the double stage of election began to have any effect, it would begin to have a bad effect. And this we shall find true of the principle of indirect election however applied, except in circumstances similar to those of the election of senators in the United States.

The best which could be said for this political contrivance is that in some states of opinion it might be a more practicable expedient than that of plural voting for giving to every member of the community a vote of some sort, without rendering the mere numerical majority predominant in Parliament: as, for instance, if the present constituency of this country were increased by the addition of a numerous and select portion of the laboring classes, elected by the remainder. Circumstances might render such a scheme a convenient mode of temporary compromise, but it does not carry out any principle sufficiently thoroughly to be likely to recommend itself to any class of thinkers as a permanent arrangement.

CHAPTER X

OF THE MODE OF VOTING

THE question of greatest moment in regard to modes of voting is that of secrecy or publicity; and to this we will at once address ourselves.

It would be a great mistake to make the discussion turn on sentimentalities about skulking or cowardice. Secrecy is justifiable in many cases, imperative in some, and it is not cowardice to seek protection against evils which are honestly avoidable. Nor can it be reasonably maintained that no cases are conceivable in which secret voting is preferable to public. But I must contend that these cases, in affairs of a political character, are the exception, not the rule.

The present is one of the many instances in which, as I have already had occasion to remark, the *spirit* of an institution, the impression it makes on the mind of the citizen, is one of the most important parts of its operation. The spirit of vote by ballot—the interpretation likely to be put on it in the mind of an elector—is that the suffrage is given to him for himself, for his particular use and benefit, and not as a trust for the public. For if it is indeed a trust; if the public are entitled to his vote, are not they entitled to know his vote? This false and pernicious impression may well be made on the generality, since it has been made on most of those who of late years have been conspicuous advocates of the ballot. The doctrine was not so understood by its earlier promoters, but the effect of a doctrine on the mind is best shown, not in those who form it, but in those who are formed by it. Mr. Bright and his school of democrats think themselves greatly concerned in maintaining that the franchise is what they term a right, not a trust.

Now this one idea, taking root in the general mind, does a moral mischief outweighing all the good that the ballot could do at the highest possible estimate of it. In whatever way we define or understand the idea of a right, no person can have a right (except in the purely legal sense) to power over others; every such power which he is allowed to possess is morally, in the fullest force of the term, a trust. But the exercise of any political function, either as an elector or as a representative, is power over others. Those who say that the suffrage is not a trust but a right will scarcely accept the conclusions to which their doctrine leads. If it is a right, if it belongs to the voter for his own sake, on what ground can we blame him for selling it or using it to recommend himself to anyone whom it is his interest to please? A person is not expected to consult exclusively the public benefit in the use he makes of his house, or his three-per-cent stock, or anything else to which he really has a right. The suffrage is indeed due to him, among other reasons, as a means to his own protection, but only against treatment from which he is equally bound, so far as depends on his vote, to protect every one of his fellow citizens. His vote is not a thing in which he has an option; it has no more to do with his personal wishes than the verdict of a juryman. It is strictly a matter of duty; he is bound to give it according to his best and most conscientious opinion of the public good. Whoever has any other idea of it is unfit to have the suffrage; its effect on him is to pervert, not to elevate, his mind. Instead of opening his heart to an exalted patriotism and the obligation of public duty, it awakens and nourishes in him the disposition to use a public function for his own interest, pleasure, or caprice—the same feelings and purposes, on a humbler scale, which actuate a despot and oppressor. Now an ordinary citizen in any public position, or on whom there devolves any social function, is certain to think and feel, respecting the obligations it imposes on him, exactly what society appears to think and feel in conferring it. What seems to be expected from him by society forms a standard which he may fall below, but which he will seldom rise above. And the interpretation which he is almost sure to put upon secret voting is that he is not bound to give his vote with any reference to those who are not allowed to know how he gives it; but may bestow it simply as he feels inclined.

This is the decisive reason why the argument does not hold, from the use of the ballot in clubs and private societies, to its adoption in parliamentary elections. A member of a club is really, what the elector falsely believes himself to be, under no obligation to consider the wishes or interests of anyone else. He declares nothing by his vote but that he is or is not willing to associate, in a manner more or less close, with a particular person. This is a matter on which, by universal admission, his own pleasure or inclination is entitled to decide; and that he should be able so to decide it without risking a quarrel is best for everybody, the rejected person included. An additional reason rendering the ballot unobjectionable in these cases is that it does not necessarily or naturally lead to lying. The persons concerned are of the same class or rank, and it would be considered improper in one of them to press another with questions as to how he had voted. It is far otherwise in parliamentary elections, and is likely to remain so, as long as the social relations exist which produce the demand for the ballot; as long as one person is sufficiently the superior of another to think himself entitled to dictate his vote. And while this is the case, silence or an evasive answer is certain to be construed as proof that the vote given has not been that which was desired.

In any political election, even by universal suffrage (and still more obviously in the case of a restricted suffrage), the voter is under an absolute moral obligation to consider the interest of the public, not his private advantage, and give his vote, to the best of his judgment, exactly as he would be bound to do if he were the sole voter and the election depended upon him alone. This being admitted, it is at least a *prima facie* consequence that the duty of voting, like any other public duty, should be performed under the eye and criticism of the public; every one of whom has not only an interest in its performance, but a good title to consider himself wronged if it is performed otherwise than honestly and carefully. Undoubtedly neither this nor any other maxim of political morality is absolutely inviolable; it may be overruled by still more cogent considerations. But its weight is such that the cases which admit of a departure from it must be of a strikingly exceptional character.

It may, unquestionably, be the fact that if we attempt, by publicity, to make the voter responsible to the public for his vote, he will practically be made responsible for it to some powerful individual, whose interest is more opposed to the general interest of the community than that of the voter himself would be if, by the shield of secrecy, he were released from responsibility altogether. When this is the condition, in a high degree, of a large proportion of the voters, the ballot may be the smaller evil. When the voters are slaves, anything may be tolerated which enables them to throw off the yoke. The strongest case for the ballot is when the mischievous power of the Few over the Many is increasing. In the decline of the Roman republic the reasons for the ballot were irresistible. The oligarchy was yearly becoming richer and more tyrannical, the people poorer and more dependent, and it was necessary to erect stronger and stronger barriers against such abuse of the franchise as rendered it but an instrument the more in the hands of unprincipled persons of consequence. As little can it be doubted that the ballot, so far as it existed, had a beneficial operation in the Athenian constitution. Even in the least unstable of the Grecian commonwealths freedom might be for the time destroyed by a single unfairly obtained popular vote; and though the Athenian voter was not sufficiently dependent to be habitually coerced, he might have been bribed or intimidated by the lawless outrages of some knot of individuals, such as were not uncommon even at Athens among the youth of rank and fortune. The ballot was in these cases a valuable instrument of order, and conduced to the Eunomia [1] by which Athens was distinguished among the ancient commonwealths.

But in the more advanced states of modern Europe, and especially in this country, the power of coercing voters has de-

1 [A well-ordered community.]

clined and is declining; and bad voting is now less to be apprehended from the influences to which the voter is subject at the
hands of others than from the sinister interests and discreditable feelings which belong to himself, either individually or as
a member of a class. To secure him against the first, at the
cost of removing all restraint from the last, would be to exchange a smaller and a diminishing evil for a greater and increasing one. On this topic, and on the question generally, as
applicable to England at the present date, I have, in a pamphlet on Parliamentary Reform, expressed myself in terms
which, as I do not feel that I can improve upon, I will venture
here to transcribe:

"Thirty years ago it was still true that in the election of
members of Parliament the main evil to be guarded against
was that which the ballot would exclude—coercion by landlords, employers, and customers. At present, I conceive a much
greater source of evil is the selfishness or the selfish partialities
of the voter himself. A base and mischievous vote is now, I am
convinced, much oftener given from the voter's personal interest, or class interest, or some mean feeling in his own mind,
than from any fear of consequences at the hands of others: and
to these influences the ballot would enable him to yield himself up, free from all sense of shame or responsibility.

"In times not long gone by, the higher and richer classes
were in complete possession of the government. Their power
was the master grievance of the country. The habit of voting
at the bidding of an employer, or of a landlord, was so firmly
established that hardly anything was capable of shaking it but
a strong popular enthusiasm, seldom known to exist but in a
good cause. A vote given in opposition to those influences was
therefore, in general, an honest, a public-spirited vote; but in
any case, and by whatever motive dictated, it was almost sure
to be a good vote, for it was a vote against the monster evil,
the overruling influence of oligarchy. Could the voter at that
time have been enabled, with safety to himself, to exercise his
privilege freely, even though neither honestly nor intelligently,
it would have been a great gain to reform for it would have

broken the yoke of the then ruling power in the country—the power which had created and which maintained all that was bad in the institutions and the administration of the State— the power of landlords and boroughmongers.

"The ballot was not adopted, but the progress of circumstances has done and is doing more and more, in this respect, the work of the ballot. Both the political and the social state of the country, as they affect this question, have greatly changed, and are changing every day. The higher classes are not now masters of the country. A person must be blind to all the signs of the times who could think that the middle classes are as subservient to the higher, or the working classes as dependent on the higher and middle as they were a quarter of a century ago. The events of that quarter of a century have not only taught each class to know its own collective strength, but have put the individuals of a lower class in a condition to show a much bolder front to those of a higher. In a majority of cases, the vote of the electors, whether in opposition to or in accordance with the wishes of their superiors, is not now the effect of coercion, which there are no longer the same means of applying, but the expression of their own personal or political partialities. The very vices of the present electoral system are a proof of this. The growth of bribery, so loudly complained of, and the spread of the contagion to places formerly free from it are evidence that the local influences are no longer paramount; that the electors now vote to please themselves, and not other people. There is, no doubt, in counties, and in the smaller boroughs, a large amount of servile dependence still remaining, but the temper of the times is adverse to it, and the force of events is constantly tending to diminish it. A good tenant can now feel that he is as valuable to his landlord as his landlord is to him; a prosperous tradesman can afford to feel independent of any particular customer. At every election the votes are more and more the voter's own. It is their minds, far more than their personal circumstances, that now require to be emancipated. They are no longer passive instruments of other men's will—mere organs for putting power

into the hands of a controlling oligarchy. The electors themselves are becoming the oligarchy.

"Exactly in proportion as the vote of the elector is determined by his own will, and not by that of somebody who is
his master, his position is similar to that of a member of Parliament, and publicity is indispensable. So long as any portion
of the community are unrepresented, the argument of the
Chartists [2] against ballot in conjunction with a restricted suffrage is unassailable. The present electors, and the bulk of
those whom any probable Reform Bill would add to the number, are the middle class, and have as much a class interest,
distinct from the working classes, as landlords or great manufacturers. Were the suffrage extended to all skilled laborers,
even these would, or might, still have a class interest distinct
from the unskilled. Suppose it extended to all men—suppose
that what was formerly called by the misapplied name of
universal suffrage, and now by the silly title of manhood
suffrage, became the law; the voters would still have a class
interest, as distinguished from women. Suppose that there
were a question before the Legislature specially affecting
women, as whether women should be allowed to graduate at
universities; whether the mild penalties inflicted on ruffians
who beat their wives daily almost to death's door should be
exchanged for something more effectual; or suppose that anyone should propose in the British Parliament, what one State
after another in America is enacting, not by a mere law, but
by a provision of their revised Constitutions—that married
women should have a right to their own property. Are not a
man's wife and daughters entitled to know whether he votes
for or against a candidate who will support these propositions?

"It will of course be objected that these arguments derive all

2 [The Chartists were members of a working-class movement which
sought more extensive economic and political reforms than those contained in the Reform Act of 1832 by which the middle class was enfran-
chised. Their objectives were detailed in the "People's Charter" of 1838.
The movement disappeared after 1850. One of the most important ex-
ponents of Chartism was Thomas Carlyle (1795-1881).]

their weight from the supposition of an unjust state of the suffrage; that, if the opinion of the non-electors is likely to make the elector vote more honestly or more beneficially than he would vote if left to himself, they are more fit to be electors than he is and ought to have the franchise; that whoever is fit to influence electors is fit to be an elector; that those to whom voters ought to be responsible should be themselves voters; and being such, should have the safeguard of the ballot to shield them from the undue influence of powerful individuals or classes to whom they ought not to be responsible.

"This argument is specious, and I once thought it conclusive. It now appears to me fallacious. All who are fit to influence electors are not, for that reason, fit to be themselves electors. This last is a much greater power than the former, and those may be ripe for the minor political function who could not as yet be safely trusted with the superior. The opinions and wishes of the poorest and rudest class of laborers may be very useful as one influence among others on the minds of the voters, as well as on those of the Legislature, and yet it might be highly mischievous to give them the preponderant influence by admitting them, in their present state of morals and intelligence, to the full exercise of the suffrage. It is precisely this indirect influence of those who have not the suffrage over those who have which, by its progressive growth, softens the transition to every fresh extension of the franchise, and is the means by which, when the time is ripe, the extension is peacefully brought about. But there is another and a still deeper consideration, which should never be left out of the account in political speculations. The notion is itself unfounded that publicity and the sense of being answerable to the public are of no use unless the public are qualified to form a sound judgment. It is a very superficial view of the utility of public opinion to suppose that it does good only when it succeeds in enforcing a servile conformity to itself. To be under the eyes of others—to have to defend oneself to others—is never more important than to those who act in opposition to the opinion of others, for it obliges them to have sure ground of their own. Nothing has so steadying an influence as working against pressure. Unless when under the temporary sway of passionate excitement, no one will do that which he expects to be greatly blamed for, unless from a preconceived and fixed purpose of his own; which is always evidence of a thoughtful and deliberate character and, except in radically bad men, generally proceeds from sincere and strong personal convictions. Even the bare fact of having to give an account of their conduct is a powerful inducement to adhere to conduct of which at least some decent account can be given. If anyone thinks that the mere obligation of preserving decency is not a very considerable check on the abuse of power, he has never had his attention called to the conduct of those who do not feel under the necessity of observing that restraint. Publicity is inappreciable, even when it does no more than prevent that which can by no possibility be plausibly defended— than compel deliberation and force everyone to determine, before he acts, what he shall say if called to account for his actions.

"But if not now (it may be said), at least hereafter, when all are fit to have votes, and when all men and women are admitted to vote in virtue of their fitness, *then* there can no longer be danger of class legislation; then the electors, being the nation, can have no interest apart from the general interest; even if individuals still vote according to private or class inducements, the majority will have no such inducement; and as there will then be no nonelectors to whom they ought to be responsible, the effect of the ballot, excluding none but the sinister influences, will be wholly beneficial.

"Even in this I do not agree. I cannot think that even if the people were fit for, and had obtained, universal suffrage, the ballot would be desirable. First, because it could not, in such circumstances, be supposed to be needful. Let us only conceive the state of things which the hypothesis implies: a people universally educated, and every grown-up human being possessed of a vote. If, even when only a small proportion are electors and the majority of the population almost uneducated, public opinion is already, as everyone now sees that it is, the ruling power in the last resort, it is a chimera to suppose that over a community who all read, and who all have votes, any power could be exercised by landlords and rich people against their own inclination which it would be at all difficult for them to throw off. But though the protection of secrecy would then be needless, the control of publicity would be as needful as ever. The universal observation of mankind has been very fallacious if the mere fact of being one of the community, and not being in a position of pronounced contrariety of interest to the public at large, is enough to ensure the performance of a public duty, without either the stimulus or the restraint derived from the opinion of our fellow creatures. A man's own particular share of the public interest, even though he may have no private interest drawing him in the opposite direction, is not, as a general rule, found sufficient to make him do his duty to the public without other external inducements. Neither can it be admitted that even if all had votes they would give their votes as honestly in secret as in public. The proposition that the electors when they compose the whole of the community cannot have an interest in voting against the interest of the community will be found on examination to have more sound than meaning in it. Though the community as a whole can have (as the terms imply) no other interest than its collective interest, any or every individual in it may. A man's interest consists of whatever he takes an interest *in*. Everybody has as many different interests as he has feelings, likings or dislikings, either of a selfish or of a better kind. It cannot be said that any of these, taken by itself, constitutes 'his interest'; he is a good man or a bad according as he prefers one class of his interests or another. A man who is a tyrant at home will be apt to sympathize with tyranny (when not exercised over himself): he will be almost certain not to sympathize with resistance to tyranny. An envious man will vote against Aristides because he is called the Just. A selfish man will prefer even a trifling individual benefit to his share of the advantage which his country would derive from a good law; because interests peculiar to himself are those which the habits of his mind both dispose him to dwell on and make him best able to estimate. A great number of the electors will have two sets of preferences—those on private and those on public grounds. The last are the only ones which the elector would like to avow. The best side of their character is that which people are anxious to show, even to those who are no better than themselves. People will give dishonest or mean votes from lucre, from malice, from pique, from personal rivalry, even from the interests or prejudices of class or sect, more readily in secret than in public. And cases exist—they may come to be more frequent—in which almost the only restraint upon a majority of knaves consists in their involuntary respect for the opinion of an honest minority. In such a case as that of the repudiating States of North America, is there not some check to the unprincipled voter in the shame of looking an honest man in the face? Since all this good would be sacrificed by the ballot, even in the circumstances most favorable to it, a much stronger case is requisite than can now be made out for its necessity (and the case is continually becoming still weaker) to make its adoption desirable." [3]

On the other debatable points connected with the mode of voting it is not necessary to expend so many words. The system of personal representation, as organized by Mr. Hare, renders necessary the employment of voting papers. But it appears to me indispensable that the signature of the elector should be affixed to the paper at a public polling place or, if there be no such place conveniently accessible, at some office open to all the world, and in the presence of a responsible public officer. The proposal which has been thrown out of allowing the voting papers to be filled up at the voter's own residence and sent by the post, or called for by a public officer, I should regard as fatal. The act would be done in the absence of the salutary and the presence of all the pernicious influences. The briber might, in the shelter of privacy, behold with

[3] *Thoughts on Parliamentary Reform*, 2nd ed., pp. 32-36.

his own eyes his bargain fulfilled, and the intimidator could see the extorted obedience rendered irrevocably on the spot; while the beneficent counterinfluence of the presence of those who knew the voter's real sentiments, and the inspiring effect of the sympathy of those of his own party or opinion, would be shut out.[4]

The polling places should be so numerous as to be within easy reach of every voter; and no expenses of conveyance, at the cost of the candidate, should be tolerated under any pretext. The infirm, and they only on medical certificate, should

[4] "This expedient has been recommended, both on the score of saving expense and on that of obtaining the votes of many electors who otherwise would not vote, and who are regarded by the advocates of the plan as a particularly desirable class of voters. The scheme has been carried into practice in the election of poor-law guardians, and its success in that instance is appealed to in favor of adopting it in the more important case of voting for a member of the Legislature. But the two cases appear to me to differ in the point on which the benefits of the expedient depend. In a local election for a special kind of administrative business, which consists mainly in the dispensation of a public fund, it is an object to prevent the choice from being exclusively in the hands of those who actively concern themselves about it; for the public interest which attaches to the election being of a limited kind, and in most cases not very great in degree, the disposition to make themselves busy in the matter is apt to be in a great measure confined to persons who hope to turn their activity to their own private advantage; and it may be very desirable to render the intervention of other people as little onerous to them as possible, if only for the purpose of swamping these private interests. But when the matter in hand is the great business of national government, in which everyone must take an interest who cares for anything out of himself, or who cares even for himself intelligently, it is much rather an object to prevent those from voting who are indifferent to the subject than to induce them to vote by any other means than that of awakening their dormant minds. The voter who does not care enough about the election to go to the poll is the very man who, if he can vote without that small trouble, will give his vote to the first person who asks for it, or on the most trifling or frivolous inducement. A man who does not care whether he votes is not likely to care much which way he votes; and he who is in that state of mind has no moral right to vote at all; since, if he does so, a vote which is not the expression of a conviction counts for as much and goes as far in determining the result as one which represents the thoughts and purposes of a life." [*Ibid.*, p. 39.]

have the right of claiming suitable carriage conveyance at the cost of the State or of the locality. Hustings, poll clerks, and all the necessary machinery of elections should be at the public charge. Not only the candidate should not be required, he should not be permitted, to incur any but a limited and trifling expense for his election. Mr. Hare thinks it desirable that a sum of £50 should be required from everyone who places his name on the list of candidates to prevent persons who have no chance of success, and no real intention of attempting it, from becoming candidates in wantonness or from mere love of notoriety, and perhaps carrying off a few votes which are needed for the return of more serious aspirants. There is one expense which a candidate or his supporters cannot help incurring, and which it can hardly be expected that the public should defray for everyone who may choose to demand it—that of making his claims known to the electors by advertisements, placards, and circulars. For all necessary expenses of this kind the £50 proposed by Mr. Hare, if allowed to be drawn upon for these purposes (it might be made £100 if requisite), ought to be sufficient. If the friends of the candidate choose to go to expense for committees and canvassing there are no means of preventing them; but such expenses out of the candidate's own pocket, or any expenses whatever beyond the deposit of £50 (or £100), should be illegal and punishable. If there appeared any likelihood that opinion would refuse to connive at falsehood, a declaration on oath or honor should be required from every member on taking his seat that he had not expended, nor would expend, money or money's worth beyond the £50, directly or indirectly, for the purposes of his election; and if the assertion were proved to be false or the pledge to have been broken, he should be liable to the penalties of perjury. It is probable that those penalties, by showing that the Legislature was in earnest, would turn the course of opinion in the same direction and would hinder it from regarding, as it has hitherto done, this most serious crime against society as a venial peccadillo. When once this effect has been produced, there need be no doubt that the declaration on oath or honor would be considered binding.[5] "Opinion tolerates a false disclaimer only when it already tolerates the thing disclaimed." This is notoriously the case with regard to electoral corruption. There has

[5] Several of the witnesses before the Committee of the House of Commons in 1860, on the operation of the Corrupt Practices Prevention Act, some of them of great practical experience in election matters, were favorable (either absolutely or as a last resort) to the principle of requiring a declaration from members of Parliament; and were of opinion that, if supported by penalties, it would be, to a great degree, effectual. (*Evidence,* pp. 46, 54-57, 67, 123, 198-202, 208.) The Chief Commissioner of the Wakefield Inquiry said (in reference certainly to a different proposal), "If they see that the Legislature is earnest upon the subject, the machinery will work. . . . I am quite sure that if some personal stigma were applied upon conviction of bribery, it would change the current of public opinion" (pp. 26 and 32). A distinguished member of the Committee (and of the present Cabinet) seemed to think it very objectionable to attach the penalties of perjury to a merely promissory as distinguished from an assertory oath; but he was reminded that the oath taken by a witness in a court of justice is a promissory oath; and the rejoinder (that the witness's promise relates to an act to be done at once, while the member's would be a promise for all future time) would only be to the purpose, if it could be supposed that the swearer might forget the obligation he had entered into, or could possibly violate it unawares: contingencies which, in a case like the present, are out of the question.

A more substantial difficulty is that one of the forms most frequently assumed by election expenditure is that of subscriptions to local charities or other local objects; and it would be a strong measure to enact that money should not be given in charity, within a place, by the member for it. When such subscriptions are *bona fide,* the popularity which may be derived from them is an advantage which it seems hardly possible to deny to superior riches. But the greatest part of the mischief consists in the fact that money so contributed is employed in bribery, under the euphemistic name of keeping up the member's interest. To guard against this, it should be part of the member's promissory declaration that all sums expended by him in the place, or for any purpose connected with it or with any of its inhabitants (with the exception perhaps of his own hotel expenses), should pass through the hands of the election auditor, and be by him (and not by the member himself or his friends) applied to its declared purpose.

The principle of making all lawful expenses of elections a charge not upon the candidate, but upon the locality, was upheld by two of the best witnesses (pp. 20, 65-70, 277).

never yet been, among political men, any real and serious attempt to prevent bribery, because there has been no real desire
that elections should not be costly. Their costliness is an advantage to those who can afford the expense, by excluding a multitude of competitors; and anything, however noxious, is cher-
ished as having a conservative tendency if it limits the access
to Parliament to rich men. This is a rooted feeling among
our legislators of both political parties, and is almost the only
point on which I believe them to be really ill-intentioned.
They care comparatively little who votes as long as they feel
assured that none but persons of their own class can be voted
for. They know that they can rely on the fellow-feeling of one
of their class with another, while the subservience of *nou-
veaux enrichis*, who are knocking at the door of the class, is
a still surer reliance; and that nothing very hostile to the class
interests or feelings of the rich need be apprehended under
the most democratic suffrage as long as democratic persons can
be prevented from being elected to Parliament. But, even
from their own point of view, this balancing of evil by evil, instead of combining good with good, is a wretched policy. The
object should be to bring together the best members of both
classes under such a tenure as shall induce them to lay aside
their class preferences and pursue jointly the path traced by
the common interest, instead of allowing the class feelings of
the Many to have full swing in the constituencies, subject to the
impediment of having to act through persons imbued with the
class feelings of the Few.

There is scarcely any mode in which political institutions
are more morally mischievous—work greater evil through their
spirit—than by representing political functions as a favor to
be conferred, a thing which the depositary is to ask for as
desiring it for himself, and even pay for as if it were designed
for his pecuniary benefit. Men are not fond of paying large
sums for leave to perform a laborious duty. Plato had a much
juster view of the conditions of good government when he
asserted that the persons who should be sought out to be invested with political power are those who are personally most

averse to it, and that the only motive which can be relied on for inducing the fittest men to take upon themselves the toils of government is the fear of being governed by worse men. What must an elector think when he sees three or four gentlemen, none of them previously observed to be lavish of their money on projects of disinterested beneficence, vying with one another in the sums they expend to be enabled to write M.P. after their names? Is it likely he will suppose that it is for *his* interest they incur all this cost? And if he forms an uncomplimentary opinion of their part in the affair, what moral obligation is he likely to feel as to his own? Politicians are fond of treating it as the dream of enthusiasts that the electoral body will ever be uncorrupt—truly enough, until they are willing to become so themselves; for the electors, assuredly, will take their moral tone from the candidates. So long as the elected member, in any shape or manner, pays for his seat, all endeavors will fail to make the business of election anything but a selfish bargain on all sides. "So long as the candidate himself, and the customs of the world, seem to regard the function of a member of Parliament less as a duty to be discharged than a personal favor to be solicited, no effort will avail to implant in an ordinary voter the feeling that the election of a member of Parliament is also a matter of duty, and that he is not at liberty to bestow his vote on any other consideration than that of personal fitness."

The same principle which demands that no payment of money for election purposes should be either required or tolerated on the part of the person elected dictates another conclusion, apparently of contrary tendency, but really directed to the same object. It negatives what has often been proposed as a means of rendering Parliament accessible to persons of all ranks and circumstances—the payment of members of Parliament. If, as in some of our colonies, there are scarcely any fit persons who can afford to attend to an unpaid occupation, the payment should be an indemnity for loss of time or money, not a salary. The greater latitude of choice which a salary would give is an illusory advantage. No remuneration which anyone would think of attaching to the post would attract to it those who were seriously engaged in other lucrative professions with a prospect of succeeding in them. The business of a member of Parliament would therefore become an occupation in itself, carried on, like other professions, with a view chiefly to its pecuniary returns, and under the demoralizing influences of an occupation essentially precarious. It would become an object of desire to adventurers of a low class; and 658 persons in possession, with ten or twenty times as many in expectancy, would be incessantly bidding to attract or retain the suffrages of the electors by promising all things, honest or dishonest, possible or impossible, and rivaling each other in pandering to the meanest feelings and most ignorant prejudices of the vulgarest part of the crowd. The auction between Cleon and the sausage-seller in Aristophanes is a fair caricature of what would be always going on.[6] Such an institution would be a perpetual blister applied to the most peccant parts of human nature. It amounts to offering 658 prizes for the most successful flatterer, the most adroit misleader, of a body of his fellow countrymen. Under no despotism has there been such an organized system of tillage for raising a rich crop of vicious courtiership.[7] When, by reason of pre-eminent qualifications (as may at any time happen

6 [Aristophanes (c. 450-c. 385 B.C.), Athenian playwright. Mill's reference is to *The Knights* (425 B.C.), in which Aristophanes attacks Cleon as the typical demagogue.]

7 "As Mr. Lorimer remarks, by creating a pecuniary inducement to persons of the lowest class to devote themselves to public affairs, the calling of the demagogue would be formally inaugurated. Nothing is more to be deprecated than making it the private interest of a number of active persons to urge the form of government in the direction of its natural perversion. The indications which either a multitude or an individual can give, when merely left to their own weaknesses, afford but a faint idea of what those weaknesses would become when played upon by a thousand flatterers. If there were 658 places of certain, however moderate, emolument, to be gained by persuading the multitude that ignorance is as good as knowledge, and better, it is terrible odds that they would believe and act upon the lesson." (Article in *Fraser's Magazine* for April 1859, headed "Recent Writers on Reform.")

to be the case), it is desirable that a person entirely without
independent means, either derived from property or from
a trade or profession, should be brought into Parliament to
render services which no other person accessible can render as
well, there is the resource of a public subscription; he may be
supported while in Parliament, like Andrew Marvel, by the
contributions of his constituents. This mode is unobjectionable, for such an honor will never be paid to mere subserviency; bodies of men do not care so much for the difference between one sycophant and another as to go to the expense of his
maintenance in order to be flattered by that particular individual. Such a support will only be given in consideration of
striking and impressive personal qualities which, though no
absolute proof of fitness to be a national representative, are
some presumption of it and, at all events, some guarantee
for the possession of an independent opinion and will.

CHAPTER XI

OF THE DURATION OF PARLIAMENTS

AFTER how long a term should members of Parliament be
subject to re-election? The principles involved are here
very obvious; the difficulty lies in their application. On
the one hand, the member ought not to have so long a tenure
of his seat as to make him forget his responsibility, take his
duties easily, conduct them with a view to his own personal
advantage, or neglect those free and public conferences with
his constituents which, whether he agrees or differs with them,
are one of the benefits of representative government. On the
other hand, he should have such a term of office to look forward to as will enable him to be judged, not by a single act,
but by his course of action. It is important that he should have
the greatest latitude of individual opinion and discretion compatible with the popular control essential to free government;

and for this purpose it is necessary that the control should be exercised, as in any case it is best exercised, after sufficient time has been given him to show all the qualities he possesses, and to prove that there is some other way than that of a mere obedient voter and advocate of their opinions by which he can render himself in the eyes of his constituents a desirable and creditable representative.

It is impossible to fix, by any universal rule, the boundary between these principles. Where the democratic power in the constitution is weak or overpassive and requires stimulation; where the representative, on leaving his constituents, enters at once into a courtly or aristocratic atmosphere whose influences all tend to deflect his course into a different direction from the popular one, to tone down any democratic feelings which he may have brought with him and make him forget the wishes and grow cool to the interests of those who chose him—the obligation of a frequent return to them for a renewal of his commission is indispensable to keeping his temper and character up to the right mark. Even three years, in such circumstances, are almost too long a period; and any longer term is absolutely inadmissible. Where, on the contrary, democracy is the ascendant power and still tends to increase, requiring rather to be moderated in its exercise than encouraged to any abnormal activity; where unbounded publicity, and an ever-present newspaper press, give the representative assurance that his every act will be immediately known, discussed, and judged by his constituents, and that he is always either gaining or losing ground in their estimation; while by the same means the influence of their sentiments, and all other democratic influences, are kept constantly alive and active in his own mind—less than five years would hardly be a sufficient period to prevent timid subserviency. The change which has taken place in English politics as to all these features explains why annual Parliaments, which forty years ago stood prominently in front of the creed of the more advanced reformers, are so little cared for and so seldom heard of at present. It deserves consideration that, whether the term is

short or long, during the last year of it the members are in
the position in which they would always be if Parliaments
were annual, so that if the term were very brief, there would
virtually be annual Parliaments during a great proportion of
all time. As things now are, the period of seven years, though
of unnecessary length, is hardly worth altering for any benefit
likely to be produced, especially since the possibility, always
impending, of an earlier dissolution keeps the motives for
standing well with constituents always before the member's
eyes.

Whatever may be the term most eligible for the duration of
the mandate, it might seem natural that the individual member should vacate his seat at the expiration of that term from
the day of his election, and that there should be no general
renewal of the whole House. A great deal might be said for
this system if there were any practical object in recommending
it. But it is condemned by much stronger reasons than can be
alleged in its support. One is, that there would be no means
of promptly getting rid of a majority which had pursued a
course offensive to the nation. The certainty of a general election after a limited, which would often be a nearly expired,
period, and the possibility of it at any time when the minister
either desires it for his own sake, or thinks that it would make
him popular with the country, tend to prevent that wide
divergence between the feelings of the assembly and those of
the constituency, which might subsist indefinitely if the majority of the House had always several years of their term still
to run—if it received new infusions drop by drop, which would
be more likely to assume than to modify the qualities of the
mass they were joined to. It is as essential that the general
sense of the House should accord in the main with that of the
nation as it is that distinguished individuals should be able,
without forfeiting their seats, to give free utterance to the most
unpopular sentiments. There is another reason, of much
weight, against the gradual and partial renewal of a representative assembly. It is useful that there should be a periodical general muster of opposing forces, to gauge the state of

the national mind and ascertain, beyond dispute, the relative strength of different parties and opinions. This is not done conclusively by any partial renewal, even where, as in some of the French constitutions, a large fraction, a fifth or a third, go out at once.

The reasons for allowing to the executive the power of dissolution will be considered in a subsequent chapter, relating to the constitution and functions of the Executive in a representative government.

CHAPTER XII

OUGHT PLEDGES TO BE REQUIRED FROM MEMBERS OF PARLIAMENT?

SHOULD a member of the legislature be bound by the instructions of his constituents? Should he be the organ of their sentiments or of his own? their ambassador to a congress, or their professional agent, empowered not only to act for them, but to judge for them what ought to be done? These two theories of the duty of a legislator in a representative government have each its supporters, and each is the recognized doctrine of some representative governments. In the Dutch United Provinces the members of the States General were mere delegates; and to such a length was the doctrine carried that, when any important question arose which had not been provided for in their instructions, they had to refer back to their constituents, exactly as an ambassador does to the government from which he is accredited. In this and most other countries which possess representative constitutions, law and custom warrant a member of Parliament in voting according to his opinion of right, however different from that of his constituents; but there is a floating notion of the opposite kind, which has considerable practical operation on many minds, even of members of Parliament, and often makes them, independently of desire for popularity or concern for their re-election, feel bound in conscience to let their conduct, on questions on which their constituents have a decided opinion, be the expression of that opinion rather than of their own. Abstractedly from positive law, and from the historical traditions of any particular people, which of these notions of the duty of a representative is the true one?

Unlike the questions which we have hitherto treated, this is not a question of constitutional legislation, but of what may more properly be called constitutional morality—the ethics of representative government. It does not so much concern institutions as the temper of mind which the electors ought to bring to the discharge of their functions, the ideas which should prevail as to the moral duties of an elector. For, let the system of representation be what it may, it will be converted into one of mere delegation if the electors so choose. As long as they are free not to vote, and free to vote as they like, they cannot be prevented from making their vote depend on any condition they think fit to annex to it. By refusing to elect anyone who will not pledge himself to all their opinions, and even, if they please, to consult with them before voting on any important subject not foreseen, they can reduce their representative to their mere mouthpiece, or compel him in honor, when no longer willing to act in that capacity, to resign his seat. And since they have the power of doing this, the theory of the Constitution ought to suppose that they will wish to do it, since the very principle of constitutional government requires it to be assumed that political power will be abused to promote the particular purposes of the holder, not because it always is so, but because such is the natural tendency of things, to guard against which is the especial use of free institutions. However wrong, therefore, or however foolish, we may think it in the electors to convert their representative into a delegate, that stretch of the electoral privilege being a natural and not improbable one, the same precautions ought to be taken as if it were certain. We may hope that the electors will not act on this notion of the use of the suffrage; but a representative government needs to be so framed that, even if they do, they shall not be able to effect what ought not to be in the power of any body of persons—class legislation for their own benefit.

When it is said that the question is only one of political morality, this does not extenuate its importance. Questions of constitutional morality are of no less practical moment than those relating to the constitution itself. The very existence of some governments, and all that renders others endurable, rests on the practical observance of doctrines of constitutional morality—traditional notions in the minds of the several constituted authorities, which modify the use that might otherwise be made of their powers. In unbalanced governments—pure monarchy, pure aristocracy, pure democracy—such maxims are the only barrier which restrains the government from the utmost excesses in the direction of its characteristic tendency. In imperfectly balanced governments, where some attempt is made to set constitutional limits to the impulses of the strongest power, but where that power is strong enough to overstep them with at least temporary impunity, it is only by doctrines of constitutional morality, recognized and sustained by opinion, that any regard at all is preserved for the checks and limitations of the constitution. In well-balanced governments, in which the supreme power is divided, and each sharer is protected against the usurpations of the others in the only manner possible—namely, by being armed for defense with weapons as strong as the others can wield for attack—the government can only be carried on by forbearance on all sides to exercise those extreme powers, unless provoked by conduct equally extreme on the part of some other sharer of power; and in this case we may truly say that only by the regard paid to maxims of constitutional morality is the constitution kept in existence. The question of pledges is not one of those which vitally concern the existence of representative governments, but it is very material to their beneficial operation. The laws cannot prescribe to the electors the principles by which they shall direct their choice, but it makes a great practical difference by what principles they think they ought to direct it. And the whole of that great question is involved in the inquiry whether they should make it a condition that the representative shall adhere to certain opinions laid down for him by his constituents.

No reader of this treatise can doubt what conclusion, as to this matter, results from the general principles which it professes. We have from the first affirmed, and unvaryingly kept in view, the coequal importance of two great requisites of government: responsibility to those for whose benefit political power ought to be, and always professes to be, employed; and jointly therewith to obtain, in the greatest measure possible, for the function of government the benefits of superior intellect, trained by long meditation and practical discipline to that special task. If this second purpose is worth attaining, it is worth the necessary price. Superior powers of mind and profound study are of no use if they do not sometimes lead a person to different conclusions from those which are formed by ordinary powers of mind without study: and if it be an object to possess representatives in any intellectual respect superior to average electors, it must be counted upon that the representative will sometimes differ in opinion from the majority of his constituents, and that when he does, his opinion will be the oftenest right of the two. It follows that the electors will not do wisely if they insist on absolute conformity to their opinions as the condition of his retaining his seat.

The principle is, thus far, obvious; but there are real difficulties in its application; and we will begin by stating them in their greatest force. If it is important that the electors should choose a representative more highly instructed than themselves, it is no less necessary that this wiser man should be responsible to them; in other words, they are the judges of the manner in which he fulfills his trust; and how are they to judge, except by the standard of their own opinions? How are they even to select him in the first instance but by the same standard? It will not do to choose by mere brilliancy—by superiority of showy talent. The tests by which an ordinary man can judge beforehand of mere ability are very imperfect: such as they are, they have almost exclusive reference to the arts of expression, and little or none to the worth of what is expressed. The latter cannot be inferred from the former; and if the electors are to put their own opinions in abeyance, what criterion remains to them of the ability to govern well? Neither, if they could ascertain, even infallibly, the ablest man, ought they to allow him altogether to judge for them, without any reference to their own opinions. The ablest candidate may be a Tory and the electors Liberals; or a Liberal and they may be Tories. The political questions of the day may be Church questions, and he may be a High Churchman or a Rationalist, while they may be Dissenters or Evangelicals; and *vice versa*. His abilities, in these cases, might only enable him to go greater lengths, and act with greater effect, in what they may conscientiously believe to be a wrong course; and they may be bound, by their sincere convictions, to think it more important that their representative should be kept, on these points, to what they deem the dictate of duty than that they should be represented by a person of more than average abilities. They may also have to consider, not solely how they can be most ably represented, but how their particular moral position and mental point of view shall be represented at all. The influence of every mode of thinking which is shared by numbers ought to be felt in the legislature; and the constitution being supposed to have made due provision that other and conflicting modes of thinking shall be represented likewise, to secure the proper representation for their own mode may be the most important matter which the electors on the particular occasion have to attend to. In some cases, too, it may be necessary that the representative should have his hands tied to keep him true to their interest, or rather to the public interest as they conceive it. This would not be needful under a political system which assured them an indefinite choice of honest and unprejudiced candidates; but under the existing system, in which the electors are almost always obliged, by the expenses of election and the general circumstances of society, to select their representative from persons of a station in life widely different from theirs and having a different class interest, who will affirm that they ought to abandon themselves to his discretion? Can we blame an elector of the poorer classes, who has only the choice among two or three rich men, for requiring from the one he votes for a pledge to those measures which he considers as a test of emancipation from the class interests of the rich? It moreover always happens to some members of the electoral body to be obliged to accept the representative selected by a majority of their own side. But though a candidate of their own choosing would have no chance, their votes may be necessary to the success of the one chosen for them; and their only means of exerting their share of influence on his subsequent conduct may be to make their support of him dependent on his pledging himself to certain conditions.

These considerations and counterconsiderations are so intimately interwoven with one another; it is so important that the electors should choose as their representatives wiser men than themselves, and should consent to be governed according to that superior wisdom, while it is impossible that conformity to their own opinions, when they have opinions, should not enter largely into their judgment as to who possesses the wisdom, and how far its presumed possessor has verified the presumption by his conduct; that it seems quite impracticable to lay down for the elector any positive rule of duty; and the result will depend less on any exact prescription or authoritative doctrine of political morality than on the general tone of mind of the electoral body, in respect to the important requisite of deference to mental superiority. Individuals, and peoples, who are acutely sensible of the value of superior wisdom are likely to recognize it, where it exists, by other signs than thinking exactly as they do, and even in spite of considerable differences of opinion; and when they have recognized it they will be far too desirous to secure it, at any admissible cost, to be prone to impose their own opinion as a law upon persons whom they look up to as wiser than themselves. On the other hand, there is a character of mind which does not look up to anyone, which thinks no other person's opinion much better than its own, or nearly so good as that of a hundred or a thousand persons like itself. Where this is the turn of mind of the electors, they will elect no one who is not, or at least who does not profess to be, the image of their own sentiments, and will continue him no longer than while he reflects those sentiments in his conduct; and all aspirants to political honors will endeavor, as Plato says in the "Gorgias," to fashion themselves after the model of the demos, and make themselves as like to it as possible. It cannot be denied that a complete democracy has a strong tendency to cast the sentiments of the electors in this mold. Democracy is not favorable to the reverential spirit. That it destroys reverence for mere social position must be counted among the good, not the bad part of its influences, though by doing this it closes the principal *school* of reverence (as to merely human relations) which exists in society. But also democracy, in its very essence, insists so much more forcibly on the things in which all are entitled to be considered equally than on those in which one person is entitled to more consideration than another, that respect for even personal superiority is likely to be below the mark. It is for this, among other reasons, I hold it of so much importance that the institutions of the country should stamp the opinions of persons of a more educated class as entitled to greater weight than those of the less educated; and I should still contend for assigning plurality of votes to authenticated superiority of education, were it only to give the tone to public feeling, irrespective of any direct political consequences.

When there does exist in the electoral body an adequate sense of the extraordinary difference in value between one person and another, they will not lack signs by which to distinguish the persons whose worth for their purposes is the greatest. Actual public services will naturally be the foremost indication: to have filled posts of magnitude and done important

things in them, of which the wisdom has been justified by the
results; to have been the author of measures which appear
from their effects to have been wisely planned; to have made
predictions which have been often verified by the event, seldom
or never falsified by it; to have given advice which when
taken has been followed by good consequences, when neglected, by bad. There is doubtless a large portion of uncer-
tainty in these signs of wisdom; but we are seeking for such as
can be applied by persons of ordinary discernment. They will
do well not to rely much on any one indication, unless corrob-
orated by the rest; and, in their estimation of the success or
merit of any practical effort, to lay great stress on the general
opinion of disinterested persons conversant with the subject
matter. The tests which I have spoken of are only applicable
to tried men; among whom must be reckoned those who,
though untried practically, have been tried speculatively; who,
in public speech or in print, have discussed public affairs in
a manner which proves that they have given serious study to
them. Such persons may, in the mere character of political
thinkers, have exhibited a considerable amount of the same
titles to confidence as those who have been proved in the position of practical statesmen. When it is necessary to choose persons wholly untried, the best criteria are reputation for ability
among those who personally know them, and the confidence
placed and recommendations given by persons already looked
up to. By tests like these, constituencies who sufficiently value
mental ability, and eagerly seek for it, will generally succeed in
obtaining men beyond mediocrity, and often men whom they
can trust to carry on public affairs according to their unfettered judgment; to whom it would be an affront to require
that they should give up that judgment at the behest of their inferiors in knowledge. If such persons, honestly sought, are not
to be found, then indeed the electors are justified in taking other
precautions; for they cannot be expected to postpone their
particular opinions, unless in order that they may be served
by a person of superior knowledge to their own. They would

do well, indeed, even then to remember that when once chosen the representative, if he devotes himself to his duty, has greater opportunities of correcting an original false judgment than fall to the lot of most of his constituents—a consideration which generally ought to prevent them (unless compelled by necessity to choose someone whose impartiality they do not fully trust) from exacting a pledge not to change his opinion or, if he does, to resign his seat. But when an unknown person, not certified in unmistakable terms by some high authority, is elected for the first time, the elector cannot be expected not to make conformity to his own sentiments the primary requisite. It is enough if he does not regard a subsequent change of those sentiments, honestly avowed, with its grounds undisguisedly stated, as a peremptory reason for withdrawing his confidence.

Even supposing the most tried ability and acknowledged eminence of character in the representative, the private opinions of the electors are not to be placed entirely in abeyance. Deference to mental superiority is not to go the length of self-annihilation—abnegation of any personal opinion. But when the difference does not relate to the fundamentals of politics, however decided the elector may be in his own sentiments, he ought to consider that, when an able man differs from him, there is at least a considerable chance of his being in the wrong, and that even if otherwise, it is worth while to give up his opinion in things not absolutely essential for the sake of the inestimable advantage of having an able man to act for him in the many matters in which he himself is not qualified to form a judgment. In such cases he often endeavors to reconcile both wishes by inducing the able man to sacrifice his own opinion on the points of difference; but for the able man to lend himself to this compromise is treason against his especial office, abdication of the peculiar duties of mental superiority, of which it is one of the most sacred not to desert the cause which has the clamor against it, nor to deprive of his services those of his opinions which need them the most. A man of conscience and known ability should insist on full freedom to act as he in his own judgment deems best, and should not consent to serve on any other terms. But the electors are entitled to know how he means to act, what opinions on all things which concern his public duty he intends should guide his conduct. If some of these are unacceptable to them, it is for him to satisfy them that he nevertheless deserves to be their representative; and if they are wise, they will overlook, in favor of his general value, many and great differences between his opinions and their own. There are some differences, however, which they cannot be expected to overlook. Whoever feels the amount of interest in the government of his country which befits a freeman has some convictions on national affairs which are like his lifeblood; which the strength of his belief in their truth, together with the importance he attaches to them, forbid him to make a subject of compromise or postpone to the judgment of any person, however greatly his superior. Such convictions, when they exist in a people, or in any appreciable portion of one, are entitled to influence in virtue of their mere existence, and not solely in that of the probability of their being grounded in truth. A people cannot be well governed in opposition to their primary notions of right, even though these may be in some points erroneous. A correct estimate of the relation which should subsist between governors and governed does not require the electors to consent to be represented by one who intends to govern them in opposition to their fundamental convictions. If they avail themselves of his capacities of useful service in other respects, at a time when the points on which he is vitally at issue with them are not likely to be mooted, they are justified in dismissing him at the first moment when a question arises involving these, and on which there is not so assured a majority for what they deem right as to make the dissenting voice of that particular individual unimportant. Thus (I mention names to illustrate my meaning, not for any personal application) the opinions supposed to be entertained by Mr. Cobden and Mr.

Bright on resistance to foreign aggression might be overlooked during the Crimean War,[1] when there was an overwhelming national feeling on the contrary side, and might yet very properly lead to their rejection by the electors at the time of the Chinese quarrel [2] (though in itself a more doubtful question), because it was then for some time a moot point whether their view of the case might not prevail.

   As the general result of what precedes, we may affirm that actual pledges should not be required unless, from unfavorable social circumstances or faulty institutions, the electors are so narrowed in their choice as to be compelled to fix it on a person presumptively under the influence of partialities hostile to their interest; that they are entitled to a full knowledge of the political opinions and sentiments of the candidate, and not only entitled, but often bound, to reject one who differs from themselves on the few articles which are the foundation of their political belief; that in proportion to the opinion they entertain of the mental superiority of a candidate, they ought to put up with his expressing and acting on opinions different from theirs on any number of things not included in their fundamental articles of belief; that they ought to be unremitting in their search for a representative of such caliber as to be entrusted with full power of obeying the dictates of his own judgment; that they should consider it a duty which they owe to their fellow countrymen, to do their utmost toward placing men of this quality in the legislature; and that it is of much greater importance to themselves to be represented by such a man than by one who professes agreement in a greater number of their opinions; for the benefits of his ability are certain, while the hypothesis of his being wrong

1 [In the Crimean War (1853-56), Britain and France checked Russia's efforts to increase her influence in the Turkish empire preparatory to dismembering it and seizing Constantinople.]
2 [Mill refers to the Opium Wars (1839-44, 1856-60) by which Britain compelled the Chinese to admit British opium traders.]

and their being right on the points of difference is a very doubtful one.

I have discussed this question on the assumption that the electoral system in all that depends on positive institution conforms to the principles laid down in the preceding chapters. Even on this hypothesis, the delegation theory of representation seems to me false, and its practical operation hurtful, though the mischief would in that case be confined within certain bounds. But if the securities by which I have endeavored to guard the representative principle are not recognized by the Constitution; if provision is not made for the representation of minorities, nor any difference admitted in the numerical value of votes, according to some criterion of the amount of education possessed by the voters—in that case no words can exaggerate the importance in principle of leaving an unfettered discretion to the representative, for it would then be the only chance, under universal suffrage, for any other opinions than those of the majority to be heard in Parliament. In that falsely called democracy which is really the exclusive rule of the operative classes, all others being unrepresented and unheard, the only escape from class legislation in its narrowest, and political ignorance in its most dangerous, form, would lie in such disposition as the uneducated might have to choose educated representatives and to defer to their opinions. Some willingness to do this might reasonably be expected, and everything would depend upon cultivating it to the highest point. But once invested with political omnipotence, if the operative classes voluntarily concurred in imposing in this or any other manner any considerable limitation upon their self-opinion and self-will, they would prove themselves wiser than any class possessed of absolute power has shown itself or, we may venture to say, is ever likely to show itself under that corrupting influence.

CHAPTER XIII

OF A SECOND CHAMBER

O F ALL topics relating to the theory of representative government, none has been the subject of more discussion, especially on the Continent, than what is known as the question of the Two Chambers. It has occupied a greater amount of the attention of thinkers than many questions of ten times its importance, and has been regarded as a sort of touchstone which distinguishes the partisans of limited from those of uncontrolled democracy. For my own part, I set little value on any check which a Second Chamber can apply to a democracy otherwise unchecked; and I am inclined to think that, if all other constitutional questions are rightly decided, it is but of secondary importance whether the Parliament consists of two Chambers or only of one.

If there are two Chambers, they may either be of similar or of dissimilar composition. If of similar, both will obey the same influences, and whatever has a majority in one of the Houses will be likely to have it in the other. It is true that the necessity of obtaining the consent of both to the passing of any measure may at times be a material obstacle to improvement, since, assuming both the Houses to be representative and equal in their numbers, a number slightly exceeding a fourth of the entire representation may prevent the passing of a Bill, while, if there is but one House, a Bill is secure of passing if it has a bare majority. But the case supposed is rather abstractedly possible than likely to occur in practice. It will not often happen that of two Houses similarly composed, one will be almost unanimous, and the other nearly equally divided; if a majority in one rejects a measure, there will generally have been a large minority unfavorable to it in the other; any improvement, therefore, which could be thus impeded would in almost all cases be one which had not much

more than a simple majority in the entire body, and the worst
consequence that could ensue would be to delay for a short
time the passing of the measure, or give rise to a fresh appeal
to the electors to ascertain if the small majority in Parliament corresponded to an effective one in the country. The inconvenience of delay, and the advantages of the appeal to
the nation, might be regarded in this case as about equally
balanced.

I attach little weight to the argument oftenest urged for
having two Chambers—to prevent precipitancy and compel
a second deliberation; for it must be a very ill-constituted representative assembly in which the established forms of business
do not require many more than two deliberations. The consideration which tells most, in my judgment, in favor of two
Chambers (and this I do regard as of some moment) is the
evil effect produced upon the mind of any holder of power,
whether an individual or an assembly, by the consciousness
of having only themselves to consult. It is important that no
set of persons should, in great affairs, be able, even temporarily, to make their *sic volo* prevail without asking anyone else
for his consent. A majority in a single assembly, when it has
assumed a permanent character—when composed of the same
persons habitually acting together, and always assured of victory in their own House—easily becomes despotic and over-
weening if released from the necessity of considering whether
its acts will be concurred in by another constituted authority. The same reason which induced the Romans to have two
consuls makes it desirable there should be two Chambers:
that neither of them may be exposed to the corrupting influence of undivided power, even for the space of a single year.
One of the most indispensable requisites in the practical conduct of politics, especially in the management of free institutions, is conciliation—a readiness to compromise, a willingness
to concede something to opponents, and to shape good measures so as to be as little offensive as possible to persons of
opposite views; and of this salutary habit, the mutual give and
take (as it has been called) between two Houses is a perpetual

school, useful as such even now, and its utility would probably be even more felt in a more democratic constitution of
the Legislature.

But the Houses need not both be of the same composition;
they may be intended as a check on one another. One being
supposed democratic, the other will naturally be constituted
with a view to its being some restraint upon the democracy.
But its efficacy in this respect wholly depends on the social
support which it can command outside the House. An assembly which does not rest on the basis of some great power in
the country is ineffectual against one which does. An aristocratic House is only powerful in an aristocratic state of society.
The House of Lords was once the strongest power in our
Constitution, and the Commons only a checking body; but
this was when the barons were almost the only power out of
doors. I cannot believe that, in a really democratic state of
society, the House of Lords would be of any practical value as
a moderator of democracy. When the force on one side is
feeble in comparison with that on the other, the way to give
it effect is not to draw both out in line and muster their
strength in open field over against one another. Such tactics
would ensure the utter defeat of the less powerful. It can
only act to advantage by not holding itself apart, and compelling everyone to declare himself either with or against it,
but taking a position among, rather than in opposition to,
the crowd, and drawing to itself the elements most capable
of allying themselves with it on any given point; not appear-
ing at all as an antagonist body, to provoke a general rally
against it, but working as one of the elements in a mixed
mass, infusing its leaven and often making what would be the
weaker part the stronger by the addition of its influence. The
really moderating power in a democratic constitution must
act in and through the democratic House.

That there should be, in every polity, a center of resistance
to the predominant power in the Constitution—and in a democratic constitution, therefore, a nucleus of resistance to the
democracy—I have already maintained; and I regard it as a

fundamental maxim of government. If any people who possess a democratic representation are, from their historical antecedents, more willing to tolerate such a center of resistance in the form of a Second Chamber or House of Lords than in any other shape, this constitutes a strong reason for having it in that shape. But it does not appear to me the best shape in itself, nor by any means the most efficacious for its object. If there are two Houses, one considered to represent the people, the other to represent only a class or not to be representative at all, I cannot think that where democracy is the ruling power in society the Second House would have any real ability to resist even the aberrations of the first. It might be suffered to exist in deference to habit and association, but not as an effective check. If it exercised an independent will, it would be required to do so in the same general spirit as the other House: to be equally democratic with it, and to content itself with correcting the accidental oversights of the more popular branch of the legislature, or competing with it in popular measures.

The practicability of any real check to the ascendancy of the majority depends henceforth on the distribution of strength in the most popular branch of the governing body; and I have indicated the mode in which, to the best of my judgment, a balance of forces might most advantageously be established there. I have also pointed out that even if the numerical majority were allowed to exercise complete predominance by means of a corresponding majority in Parliament, yet if minorities also are permitted to enjoy the equal right due to them on strictly democratic principles—of being represented proportionally to their numbers—this provision will ensure the perpetual presence in the House, by the same popular title as its other members, of so many of the first intellects in the country that, without being in any way banded apart or invested with any invidious prerogative, this portion of the national representation will have a personal weight much more than in proportion to its numerical strength and will afford, in a most effective form, the moral center of resistance which is needed. A Second Chamber, therefore, is not required for this purpose, and would not contribute to it, but might even, in some conceivable modes, impede its attainment. If, however, for the other reasons already mentioned, the decision were taken that there should be such a Chamber, it is desirable that it should be composed of elements which, without being open to the imputation of class interests adverse to the majority, would incline it to oppose itself to the class interests of the majority, and qualify it to raise its voice with authority against their errors and weaknesses. These conditions evidently are not found in a body constituted in the manner of our House of Lords. So soon as conventional rank and individual riches no longer overawe the democracy, a House of Lords becomes insignificant.

Of all principles on which a wisely conservative body, destined to moderate and regulate democratic ascendancy, could possibly be constructed, the best seems to be that exemplified in the Roman Senate, itself the most consistently prudent and sagacious body that ever administered public affairs. The deficiencies of democratic assembly, which represents the general public, are the deficiencies of the public itself: want of special training and knowledge. The appropriate corrective is to associate with it a body of which special training and knowledge should be the characteristics. If one House represents popular feeling, the other should represent personal merit, tested and guaranteed by actual public service, and fortified by practical experience. If one is the People's Chamber, the other should be the Chamber of Statesmen—a council composed of all living public men who have passed through important political offices or employments. Such a Chamber would be fitted for much more than to be a merely moderating body. It would not be exclusively a check, but also an impelling force. In its hands the power of holding the people back would be vested in those most competent, and who would generally be most inclined to lead them forward in any right course. The council to whom the task would be entrusted of rectifying the people's mistakes would not represent

a class believed to be opposed to their interest, but would
consist of their own natural leaders in the path of progress.
No mode of composition could approach to this in giving
weight and efficacy to their function of moderators. It would
be impossible to cry down a body always foremost in promoting improvements as a mere obstructive body, whatever
amount of mischief it might obstruct.

Were the place vacant in England for such a Senate (I need
scarcely say that this is a mere hypothesis), it might be composed of some such elements as the following. All who were
or had been members of the Legislative Commission described
in a former chapter, and which I regard as an indispensable
ingredient in a well-constituted popular government. All who
were or had been Chief Justices or heads of any of the superior courts of law or equity. All who had for five years filled
the office of puisne judge. All who had held for two years any
Cabinet office; but these should also be eligible to the House
of Commons, and if elected members of it, their peerage or
senatorial office should be held in suspense. The condition of
time is needed to prevent persons from being named Cabinet
Ministers merely to give them a seat in the Senate; and the
period of two years is suggested, that the same term which
qualifies them for a pension might entitle them to a senator-
ship. All who had filled the office of Commander-in-Chief; and
all who, having commanded an army or a fleet, had been
thanked by Parliament for military or naval successes. All
who had held, during ten years, first-class diplomatic appointments. All who had been Governors-General of India or
British America, and all who had held for ten years any Colonial Governorships. The permanent civil service should also
be represented; all should be senators who had filled, during
ten years, the important offices of Under-Secretary to the Treasury, permanent Under-Secretary of State, or any others equally high and responsible. If, along with the persons thus qualified by practical experience in the administration of public
affairs, any representation of the speculative class were to
be included—a thing in itself desirable—it would be worth

consideration whether certain professorships, in certain national institutions, after a tenure of a few years, might confer
a seat in the Senate. Mere scientific and literary eminence
are too indefinite and disputable; they imply a power of selection, whereas the other qualifications speak for themselves; if
the writings by which reputation has been gained are uncon-
nected with politics, they are no evidence of the special qualities required, while, if political, they would enable successive
ministries to deluge the House with party tools.

The historical antecedents of England render it all but
certain that, unless in the improbable case of a violent sub-
version of the existing Constitution, any Second Chamber
which could possibly exist would have to be built on the
foundation of the House of Lords. It is out of the question to
think practically of abolishing that assembly, to replace it by
such a Senate as I have sketched, or by any other; but there
might not be the same insuperable difficulty in aggregating
the classes or categories just spoken of to the existing body, in
the character of Peers for life. An ulterior and perhaps, on
this supposition, a necessary step might be that the hereditary
Peerage should be present in the House by their representatives instead of personally—a practice already established in
the case of the Scotch and Irish Peers, and which the mere
multiplication of the order will probably at some time or
other render inevitable. An easy adaptation of Mr. Hare's plan
would prevent the representative Peers from representing exclusively the party which has the majority in the Peerage. If,
for example, one representative were allowed for every ten
Peers, any ten might be admitted to choose a representative,
and the Peers might be free to group themselves for that purpose as they pleased. The election might be thus conducted:
all Peers who were candidates for the representation of their
order should be required to declare themselves such and enter their names in a list. A day and place should be appointed
at which Peers desirous of voting should be present, either in
person or, in the usual parliamentary manner, by their prox-
ies. The votes should be taken, each Peer voting for only

one. Every candidate who had as many as ten votes should be declared elected. If anyone had more, all but ten should be allowed to withdraw their votes, or ten of the number should be selected by lot. These ten would form his constituency, and the remainder of his voters would be set free to give their votes over again for someone else. This process should be repeated until (so far as possible) every Peer present either personally or by proxy was represented. When a number less than ten remained over, if amounting to five they might still be allowed to agree on a representative; if fewer than five, their votes must be lost or they might be permitted to record them in favor of somebody already elected. With this inconsiderable exception, every representative Peer would represent ten members of the Peerage, all of whom had not only voted for him, but selected him as the one, among all open to their choice, by whom they were most desirous to be represented. As a compensation to the Peers who were not chosen representatives of their order, they should be eligible to the House of Commons—a justice now refused to Scotch Peers and to Irish Peers in their own part of the kingdom, while the representation in the House of Lords of any but the most numerous party in the Peerage is denied equally to both.

The mode of composing a senate which has been here advocated not only seems the best in itself, but is that for which historical precedent, and actual brilliant success, can to the greatest extent be pleaded. It is not, however, the only feasible plan that might be proposed. Another possible mode of forming a Second Chamber would be to have it elected by the First, subject to the restriction that they should not nominate any of their own members. Such an assembly, emanating like the American Senate from popular choice, only once removed, would not be considered to clash with democratic institutions, and would probably acquire considerable popular influence. From the mode of its nomination it would be peculiarly unlikely to excite the jealousy of, or to come into any hostile collision with, the popular House. It would, moreover (due provision being made for the representation of the minority), be almost sure to be well composed and to comprise many of that class of highly capable men who, either from accident or for want of showy qualities, had been unwilling to seek, or unable to obtain, the suffrages of a popular constituency.

The best constitution of a Second Chamber is that which embodies the greatest number of elements from the class interests and prejudices of the majority, but having in themselves nothing offensive to democratic feeling. I repeat, however, that the main reliance for tempering the ascendancy of the majority cannot be placed in a Second Chamber of any kind. The character of a representative government is fixed by the constitution of the popular House. Compared with this, all other questions relating to the form of government are insignificant.

CHAPTER XIV

OF THE EXECUTIVE IN A REPRESENTA-
TIVE GOVERNMENT

IT WOULD be out of place in this treatise to discuss the question into what departments or branches the executive business of government may most conveniently be divided. In this respect the exigencies of different governments are different; and there is little probability that any great mistake will be made in the classification of the duties when men are willing to begin at the beginning and do not hold themselves bound by the series of accidents which, in an old government like ours, has produced the existing division of the public business. It may be sufficient to say that the classification of functionaries should correspond to that of subjects, and that there should not be several departments independent of one another to superintend different parts of the same natural whole, as in our own military administration down to a recent period, and in a less degree even at present. Where the object to be attained is single (such as that of having an efficient army), the authority commissioned to attend to it should be single likewise. The entire aggregate of means provided for one end should be under one and the same control and responsibility. If they are divided among independent authorities, the means, with each of those authorities, become ends, and it is the business of nobody except the head of the Government, who is probably without the appropriate departmental experience to take care of the real end. The different classes of means are not combined and adapted to one another under the guidance of any leading idea; and while every department pushes forward its own requirements, regardless of those of the rest, the purpose of the work is perpetually sacrificed to the work itself.

As a general rule, every executive function, whether superior or subordinate, should be the appointed duty of some given individual. It should be apparent to all the world who did everything, and through whose default anything was left undone. Responsibility is null when nobody knows who is responsible. Nor, even when real, can it be divided without being weakened. To maintain it at its highest there must be one person who receives the whole praise of what is well done, the whole blame of what is ill. There are, however, two modes of sharing responsibility: by one it is only enfeebled, by the other, absolutely destroyed. It is enfeebled when the concurrence of more than one functionary is required to the same act. Each one among them has still a real responsibility; if a wrong has been done, none of them can say he did not do it; he is as much a participant as an accomplice is in an offense; if there has been legal criminality, they may all be punished legally, and their punishment needs not be less severe than if there had been only one person concerned. But it is not so with the penalties, any more than with the rewards, of opinion: these are always diminished by being shared. Where there has been no definite legal offense, no corruption or malversation, only an error or an imprudence, or what may pass for such, every participator has an excuse to himself and to the world in the fact that other persons are jointly involved with him. There is hardly anything, even to pecuniary dishonesty, for which men will not feel themselves almost absolved if those whose duty it was to resist and remonstrate have failed to do it, still more if they have given a formal assent.

In this case, however, though responsibility is weakened, there still is responsibility: every one of those implicated has in his individual capacity assented to, and joined in, the act. Things are much worse when the act itself is only that of a majority—a Board, deliberating with closed doors, nobody knowing or, except in some extreme case, being ever likely to know whether an individual member voted for the act or against it. Responsibility in this case is a mere name. "Boards," it is happily said by Bentham, "are screens." What "the Board" does is the act of nobody; and nobody can be made to answer for it. The Board suffers, even in reputation, only in its collective character; and no individual member feels this further than his disposition leads him to identify his own estimation with that of the body—a feeling often very strong when the body is a permanent one, and he is wedded to it for better for worse; but the fluctuations of a modern official career give no time for the formation of such an *esprit de corps,* which, if it exists at all, exists only in the obscure ranks of the permanent subordinates. Boards, therefore, are not a fit instrument for executive business; and are only admissible in it when, for other reasons, to give full discretionary power to a single minister would be worse.

On the other hand, it is also a maxim of experience that in the multitude of counselors there is wisdom; and that a man seldom judges right, even in his own concerns, still less in those of the public, when he makes habitual use of no knowledge but his own or that of some single adviser. There is no necessary incompatibility between this principle and the other. It is easy to give the effective power and the full responsibility to one, providing him when necessary with advisers, each of whom is responsible only for the opinion he gives.

In general, the head of a department of the executive government is a mere politician. He may be a good politician and a man of merit; and unless this is usually the case, the government is bad. But his general capacity, and the knowledge he ought to possess of the general interests of the country, will not, unless by occasional accident, be accompanied by adequate, and what may be called professional, knowledge of the department over which he is called to preside. Professional advisers must therefore be provided for him. Wherever mere experience and attainments are sufficient—wherever the qualities required in a professional adviser may possibly be united in a single well-selected individual (as in the case, for example, of a law officer), one such person for general purposes, and a staff of clerks to supply knowledge of details, meet the demands of the case. But, more frequently, it is not sufficient that the minister should consult some one competent person and, when himself not conversant with the subject, act implicitly on that person's advice. It is often necessary that he should, not only occasionally but habitually, listen to a variety of opinions and inform his judgment by the discussions among a body of advisers. This, for example, is emphatically necessary in military and naval affairs. The military and naval ministers, therefore, and probably several others, should be provided with a Council composed, at least in those two departments, of able and experienced professional men. As a means of obtaining the best men for the purpose under every change of administration, they ought to be permanent, by which I mean that they ought not, like the Lords of the Admiralty, to be expected to resign with the ministry by whom they were appointed; but it is a good rule that all who hold high appointments to which they have risen by selection, and not by the ordinary course of promotion, should retain their office only for a fixed term, unless reappointed, as is now the rule with staff appointments in the British army. This rule renders appointments somewhat less likely to be jobbed, not being a provision for life, and at the same time affords a means, without affront to anyone, of getting rid of those who are least worth keeping, and bringing in highly qualified persons of younger standing, for whom there might never be room if death vacancies or voluntary resignations were waited for.

The Councils should be consultative merely in this sense, that the ultimate decision should rest undividedly with the minister himself, but neither ought they to be looked upon, or to look upon themselves, as ciphers, or as capable of being reduced to such at his pleasure. The advisers attached to a powerful and perhaps self-willed man ought to be placed under conditions which make it impossible for them, without discredit, not to express an opinion, and impossible for him not to listen to and consider their recommendations, whether he adopts them or not. The relation which ought to exist between a chief and this description of advisers is very accurately hit by the constitution of the Council of the Governor-General and those of the different Presidencies in India. These Councils are composed of persons who have professional knowledge of Indian affairs, which the Governor-General and Governors usually lack, and which it would not be desirable to require of them. As a rule, every member of Council is expected to give an opinion, which is, of course, very often a simple acquiescence; but if there is a difference of sentiment, it is at the option of every member, and is the invariable practice, to record the reasons of his opinion, the Governor-General, or Governor, doing the same. In ordinary cases the decision is according to the sense of the majority; the Council, therefore, has a substantial part in the government; but if the Governor-General, or Governor, thinks fit, he may set aside even their unanimous opinion, recording his reasons. The result is that the chief is individually and effectively responsible for every act of the Government. The members of Council have only the responsibility of advisers; but it is always known, from documents capable of being produced, and which if called for by Parliament or public opinion always are produced, what each has advised, and what reasons he gave for his advice, while, from their dignified position and ostensible participation in all acts of government, they have nearly as strong motives to apply themselves to the public business and to form and express a well-considered opinion on every part of it, as if the whole responsibility rested with themselves.

This mode of conducting the highest class of administrative business is one of the most successful instances of the adaptation of means to ends which political history, not hitherto very prolific in works of skill and contrivance, has yet to show. It is one of the acquisitions with which the art of politics has been enriched by the experience of the East India Company's rule; and, like most of the other wise contrivances by which India has been preserved to this country, and an amount of good government produced which is truly wonderful considering the circumstances and the materials, it is probably destined to perish in the general holocaust which the traditions of Indian government seem fated to undergo, since they have been placed at the mercy of public ignorance and the presumptuous vanity of political men. Already an outcry is raised for abolishing the Councils as a superfluous and expensive clog on the wheels of government, while the clamor has long been urgent, and is daily obtaining more countenance in the highest quarters, for the abrogation of the professional civil service which breeds the men that compose the Councils, and the existence of which is the sole guarantee for their being of any value.

A most important principle of good government in a popular constitution is that no executive functionaries should be appointed by popular election, neither by the votes of the people themselves nor by those of their representatives. The entire business of government is skilled employment; the qualifications for the discharge of it are of that special and professional kind which cannot be properly judged of except by persons who have themselves some share of those qualifications, or some practical experience of them. The business of finding the fittest persons to fill public employments—not merely selecting the best who offer, but looking out for the absolutely best, and taking note of all fit persons who are met with, that they may be found when wanted—is very laborious, and requires a delicate as well as highly conscientious discernment; and as there is no public duty which is in general so badly performed, so there is none for which it is of greater importance to enforce the utmost practicable amount of personal responsibility by imposing it as a special obligation on high functionaries in the several departments. All subordinate public officers who are not appointed by some mode of public competition should be selected on the direct responsibility of the minister under whom they serve. The ministers, all but the chief, will naturally be selected by the chief; and the chief himself, though really designated by Parliament, should be, in a regal government, officially appointed by the Crown. The functionary who appoints should be the sole person empowered to remove any subordinate officer who is liable to removal; which the far greater number ought not to be, except for personal misconduct; since it would be vain to expect that the body of persons by whom the whole detail of the public business is transacted, and whose qualifications are generally of much more importance to the public than those of the minister himself, will devote themselves to their profession and acquire the knowledge and skill on which the minister must often place entire dependence if they are liable at any moment to be turned adrift for no fault, that the minister may gratify himself or promote his political interest by appointing somebody else.

To the principle which condemns the appointment of executive officers by popular suffrage, ought the chief of the executive, in a republican government, to be an exception? Is it a good rule which, in the American Constitution, provides for the election of the President once in every four years by the entire people? The question is not free from difficulty. There is unquestionably some advantage, in a country like America, where no apprehension needs be entertained of a *coup d'état*, in making the chief minister constitutionally independent of the legislative body and rendering the two great branches of the government, while equally popular both in their origin and in their responsibility, an effective check on one another. The plan is in accordance with that sedulous avoidance of the concentration of great masses of power in the same hands, which is a marked characteristic of the American Federal Constitution. But the advantage, in this instance, is purchased at a price above all reasonable estimates of its value. It seems far better that the chief magistrate in a republic should be appointed avowedly, as the chief minister in a constitutional monarchy is virtually, by the representative body. In the first place, he is certain, when thus appointed, to be a more eminent man. The party which has the majority in Parliament would then, as a rule, appoint its own leader, who is always one of the foremost, and often the very foremost person in political life, while the President of the United States, since the last survivor of the founders of the republic disappeared from the scene, is almost always either an obscure man or one who has gained any reputation he may possess in some other field than politics. And this, as I have before observed, is no accident, but the natural effect of the situation. The eminent men of a party, in an election extending to the whole country, are never its most available candidates. All eminent men have made personal enemies or have done something or, at the lowest, professed some opinion obnoxious to some local or other considerable division of the community, and likely to tell with fatal effect upon the number of votes; whereas a man without antecedents, of whom nothing is known but that he professes the creed of the party, is readily voted for by its entire strength. Another important consideration is the great mischief of unintermitted electioneering. When the highest dignity in the State is to be conferred by popular election once in every few years, the whole intervening time is spent in what is virtually a canvass. President, ministers, chiefs of parties, and their followers, are all electioneerers: the whole community is kept intent on the mere personalities of politics, and every public question is discussed

and decided with less reference to its merits than to its expected bearing on the presidential election. If a system had
been devised to make party spirit the ruling principle of action in all public affairs and create an inducement not only
to make every question a party question, but to raise questions for the purpose of founding parties upon them, it would
have been difficult to contrive any means better adapted to the
purpose.

I will not affirm that it would at all times and places be
desirable that the head of the executive should be so completely dependent upon the votes of a representative assembly
as the Prime Minister is in England, and is without inconvenience. If it were thought best to avoid this, he might,
though appointed by Parliament, hold his office for a fixed
period, independent of a parliamentary vote, which would be
the American system, minus the popular election and its evils.[1]
There is another mode of giving the head of the administration as much independence of the legislature as is at all compatible with the essentials of free government. He never could
be unduly dependent on a vote of Parliament if he had, as
the British Prime Minister practically has, the power to dissolve the House and appeal to the people—if, instead of being
turned out of office by a hostile vote, he could only be reduced by it to the alternative of resignation or dissolution.
The power of dissolving Parliament is one which I think it
desirable he should possess, even under the system by which
his own tenure of office is secured to him for a fixed period.
There ought not to be any possibility of that deadlock in
politics which would ensue on a quarrel breaking out between a President and an Assembly, neither of whom, during
an interval which might amount to years, would have any
legal means of ridding itself of the other. To get through such
a period without a *coup d'état* being attempted, on either

---

[1] [The foregoing statement regarding the American system of government is somewhat misleading inasmuch as it does not take into account
its major principle, the division of power—executive, legislature, and judiciary—on a coeval basis.]

THE EXECUTIVE

side or on both, requires such a combination of the love of liberty and the habit of self-restraint as very few nations have yet shown themselves capable of; and though this extremity were avoided, to expect that the two authorities would not paralyze each other's operations is to suppose that the political life of the country will always be pervaded by a spirit of mutual forbearance and compromise, imperturbable by the passions and excitements of the keenest party struggles. Such a spirit may exist, but even where it does there is imprudence in trying it too far.

Other reasons make it desirable that some power in the state (which can only be the executive) should have the liberty of at any time, and at discretion, calling a new Parliament. When there is a real doubt which of two contending parties has the strongest following, it is important that there should exist a constitutional means of immediately testing the point and setting it at rest. No other political topic has a chance of being properly attended to while this is undecided; and such an interval is mostly an interregnum for purposes of legislative or administrative improvement, neither party having sufficient confidence in its strength to attempt things likely to provoke opposition in any quarter that has either direct or indirect influence in the pending struggle.

I have not taken account of the case in which the vast power centralized in the chief magistrate and the insufficient attachment of the mass of the people to free institutions give him a chance of success in an attempt to subvert the Constitution and usurp sovereign power. Where such peril exists, no first magistrate is admissible whom the Parliament cannot, by a single vote, reduce to a private station. In a state of things holding out any encouragement to that most audacious and profligate of all breaches of trust, even this entireness of constitutional dependence is but a weak protection.

Of all officers of government, those in whose appointment any participation of popular suffrage is the most objectionable are judicial officers. While there are no functionaries whose special and professional qualifications the popular judgment is less fitted to estimate, there are none in whose case absolute impartiality and freedom from connection with politicians or sections of politicians are of anything like equal importance. Some thinkers, among others Mr. Bentham, have been of opinion that, although it is better that judges should not be appointed by popular election, the people of their district ought to have the power, after sufficient experience, of removing them from their trust. It cannot be denied that the irremovability of any public officer, to whom great interests are entrusted, is in itself an evil. It is far from desirable that there should be no means of getting rid of a bad or incompetent judge, unless for such misconduct as he can be made to answer for in a criminal court; and that a functionary on whom so much depends should have the feeling of being free from responsibility except to opinion and his own conscience. The question, however, is whether in the peculiar position of a judge, and supposing that all practicable securities have been taken for an honest appointment, irresponsibility, except to his own and the public conscience, has not on the whole less tendency to pervert his conduct than responsibility to the government or to a popular vote. Experience has long decided this point in the affirmative as regards responsibility to the executive; and the case is quite equally strong when the responsibility sought to be enforced is to the suffrages of electors. Among the good qualities of a popular constituency, those peculiarly incumbent upon a judge—calmness and impartiality—are not numbered. Happily, in that intervention of popular suffrage which is essential to freedom they are not the qualities required. Even the quality of justice, though necessary to all human beings, and therefore to all electors, is not the inducement which decides any popular election. Justice and impartiality are as little wanted for electing a member of Parliament as they can be in any transaction of men. The electors have not to award something which either candidate has a right to, nor to pass judgment on the general merits of the competitors, but to declare which of them has most of their personal confidence, or best represents their political convictions. A judge is bound to treat his political friend, or the person best known to him, exactly as he treats other people; but it would be a breach of duty as well as an absurdity if an elector did so. No argument can be grounded on the beneficial effect produced on judges, as on all other functionaries, by the moral jurisdiction of opinion; for even in this respect that which really exercises a useful control over the proceedings of a judge, when fit for the judicial office, is not (except sometimes in political cases) the opinion of the community generally, but that of the only public by whom his conduct or qualifications can be duly estimated—the bar of his own court. I must not be understood to say that the participation of the general public in the administration of justice is of no importance; it is of the greatest; but in what manner? By the actual discharge of a part of the judicial office, in the capacity of jurymen. This is one of the few cases in politics in which it is better that the people should act directly and personally than through their representatives, being almost the only case in which the errors that a person exercising authority may commit can be better borne than the consequences of making him responsible for them. If a judge could be removed from office by a popular vote, whoever was desirous of supplanting him would make capital for that purpose out of all his judicial decisions; would carry all of them, as far as he found practicable, by irregular appeal before a public opinion wholly incompetent, for want of having heard the case, or from having heard it without either the precautions or the impartiality belonging to a judicial hearing; would play upon popular passion and prejudice where they existed, and take pains to arouse them where they did not. And in this, if the case were interesting, and he took sufficient trouble, he would infallibly be successful unless the judge or his friends descended into the arena and made equally powerful appeals on the other side. Judges would end by feeling that they risked their office upon every decision they gave in a case susceptible of general interest, and that it was less essential for them to consider what decision was just than what would be most applauded by the public, or would least admit of insidious mis-representation. The practice introduced by some of the new revised state constitutions in America, of submitting judicial officers to periodical popular re-election, will be found, I apprehend, to be one of the most dangerous errors ever yet committed by democracy; and were it not that the practical good sense, which never totally deserts the people of the United States, is said to be producing a reaction, likely in no long time to lead to the retraction of the error, it might with reason be regarded as the first great downward step in the degeneration of modern democratic government.[2]

With regard to that large and important body which constitutes the permanent strength of the public service, those who do not change with changes of politics, but remain to aid every minister by their experience and traditions, inform him by their knowledge of business, and conduct official details under his general control—those, in short, who form the class of professional public servants, entering their profession as others do while young, in the hope of rising progressively to its higher grades as they advance in life; it is evidently inadmissible that these should be liable to be turned out and deprived of the whole benefit of their previous service, except for positive, proved, and serious misconduct. Not, of course, such delinquency only as makes them amenable to the law, but voluntary neglect of duty or conduct implying untrustworthiness for the purposes for which their trust is given them. Since, therefore, unless in case of personal culpability, there is

2 I have been informed, however, that in the States which have made their judges elective, the choice is not really made by the people but by the leaders of parties; no elector ever thinking of voting for anyone but the party candidate, and that, in consequence, the person elected is usually in effect the same who would have been appointed to the office by the President or by the Governor of the State. Thus one bad practice limits and corrects another; and the habit of voting *en masse* under a party banner, which is so full of evil in all cases in which the function of electing is rightly vested in the people, tends to alleviate a still greater mischief in a case where the officer to be elected is one who *ought* to be chosen not by the people but for them.

no way of getting rid of them except by quartering them on the public as pensioners, it is of the greatest importance that the appointments should be well made in the first instance; and it remains to be considered by what mode of appointment this purpose can best be attained.

In making first appointments, little danger is to be apprehended from want of special skill and knowledge in the choosers, but much from partiality and private or political interest. Being, as a rule, appointed at the commencement of manhood, not as having learned, but in order that they may learn, their profession, the only thing by which the best candidates can be discriminated is proficiency in the ordinary branches of liberal education; and this can be ascertained without difficulty, provided there be the requisite pains and the requisite impartiality in those who are appointed to inquire into it. Neither the one nor the other can reasonably be expected from a minister; who must rely wholly on recommendations and, however disinterested as to his personal wishes, never will be proof against the solicitations of persons who have the power of influencing his own election, or whose political adherence is important to the ministry to which he belongs. These considerations have introduced the practice of submitting all candidates for first appointments to a public examination conducted by persons not engaged in politics, and of the same class and quality with the examiners for honors at the universities. This would probably be the best plan under any system; and under our parliamentary government it is the only one which affords a chance, I do not say of honest appointment, but even of abstinence from such as are manifestly and flagrantly profligate.

It is also absolutely necessary that the examinations should be competitive and the appointments given to those who are most successful. A mere pass examination never, in the long run, does more than exclude absolute dunces. When the question, in the mind of an examiner, lies between blighting the prospects of an individual and neglecting a duty to the public which, in the particular instance, seldom appears of first-rate importance; and when he is sure to be bitterly reproached for doing the first, while in general no one will either know or care whether he has done the latter; the balance, unless he is a man of very unusual stamp, inclines to the side of good nature. A relaxation in one instance establishes a claim to it in others, which every repetition of indulgence makes it more difficult to resist; each of these in succession becomes a precedent for more, until the standard of proficiency sinks gradually to something almost contemptible. Examinations for degrees at the two great universities [3] have generally been as slender in their requirements as those for honors are trying and serious. Where there is no inducement to exceed a certain minimum, the minimum comes to be the maximum; it becomes the general practice not to aim at more, and as in everything there are some who do not attain all they aim at, however low the standard may be pitched, there are always several who fall short of it. When, on the contrary, the appointments are given to those, among a great number of candidates, who most distinguish themselves, and where the successful competitors are classed in order of merit, not only each is stimulated to do his very utmost, but the influence is felt in every place of liberal education throughout the country. It becomes with every schoolmaster an object of ambition, and an avenue to success, to have furnished pupils who have gained a high place in these competitions; and there is hardly any other mode in which the State can do so much to raise the quality of educational institutions throughout the country. Though the principle of competitive examinations for public employment is of such recent introduction in this country, and is still so imperfectly carried out, the Indian service being as yet nearly the only case in which it exists in its completeness, a sensible effect has already begun to be produced on the places of middle-class education, notwithstanding the difficulties which the principle has encountered from the disgracefully low existing state of education in the country, which these very examinations have brought into strong light. So contemptible has the

[3] [Reference is to the universities of Oxford and Cambridge.]

standard of acquirement been found to be among the youths who obtain the nomination from the minister which entitles them to offer themselves as candidates that the competition of such candidates produces almost a poorer result than would be obtained from a mere pass examination; for no one would think of fixing the conditions of a pass examination so low as is actually found sufficient to enable a young man to surpass his fellow candidates. Accordingly, it is said that successive years show on the whole a decline of attainments, less effort being made because the results of former examinations have proved that the exertions then used were greater than would have been sufficient to attain the object. Partly from this decrease of effort, and partly because, even at the examinations which do not require a previous nomination, conscious ignorance reduces the number of competitors to a mere handful, it has so happened that though there have always been a few instances of great proficiency, the lower part of the list of successful candidates represents but a very moderate amount of acquirement; and we have it on the word of the Commissioners that nearly all who have been unsuccessful have owed their failure to ignorance not of the higher branches of instruction, but of its very humblest elements—spelling and arithmetic.

The outcries which continue to be made against these examinations by some of the organs of opinion are often, I regret to say, as little creditable to the good faith as to the good sense of the assailants. They proceed partly by misrepresentation of the kind of ignorance which, as a matter of fact, actually leads to failure in the examinations. They quote with emphasis the most recondite questions [4] which can be shown to have been ever asked, and make it appear as if unexceptionable answers to all these were made the *sine qua non* of

[4] Not always, however, the most recondite; for a late denouncer of competitive examination in the House of Commons had the *naïveté* to produce a set of almost elementary questions in algebra, history, and geography as a proof of the exorbitant amount of high scientific attainment which the Commissioners were so wild as to exact.

success. Yet it has been repeated to satiety that such questions are not put because it is expected of everyone that he should answer them, but in order that whoever is able to do so may have the means of proving and availing himself of that portion of his knowledge. It is not as a ground of rejection, but as an additional means of success, that this opportunity is given. We are then asked whether the kind of knowledge supposed in this, that, or the other question is calculated to be of any use to the candidate after he has attained his object. People differ greatly in opinion as to what knowledge is useful. There are persons in existence, and a late Foreign Secretary of State is one of them, who think English spelling a useless accomplishment in a diplomatic attaché or a clerk in a government office. About one thing the objectors seem to be unanimous, that general mental cultivation is not useful in these employments, whatever else may be so. If, however (as I presume to think), it is useful, or if any education at all is useful, it must be tested by the tests most likely to show whether the candidate possesses it or not. To ascertain whether he has been well educated, he must be interrogated in the things which he is likely to know if he has been well educated, even though not directly pertinent to the work to which he is to be appointed. Will those who object to his being questioned in classics and mathematics, in a country where the only things regularly taught are classics and mathematics, tell us what they would have him questioned in? There seems, however, to be equal objection to examining him in these, and to examining him in anything *but* these. If the Commissioners—anxious to open a door of admission to those who have not gone through the routine of a grammar school, or who make up for the smallness of their knowledge of what is there taught by greater knowledge of something else—allow marks to be gained by proficiency in any other subject of real utility, they are reproached for that, too. Nothing will satisfy the objectors but free admission of total ignorance.

We are triumphantly told that neither Clive nor Wellington could have passed the test which is prescribed for an aspirant to an engineer cadetship. As if, because Clive and Wellington did not do what was not required of them, they could not have done it if it had been required. If it be only meant to inform us that it is possible to be a great general without these things, so it is without many other things which are very useful to great generals. Alexander the Great had never heard of Vauban's rules,[5] nor could Julius Caesar speak French. We are next informed that bookworms, a term which seems to be held applicable to whoever has the smallest tincture of book knowledge, may not be good at bodily exercises, or have the habits of gentlemen. This is a very common line of remark with dunces of condition; but whatever the dunces may think, they have no monopoly of either gentlemanly habits or bodily activity. Wherever these are needed, let them be inquired into and separately provided for, not to the exclusion of mental qualifications, but in addition. Meanwhile, I am credibly informed that in the Military Academy at Woolwich the competition cadets are as superior to those admitted on the old system of nomination in these respects as in all others; that they learn even their drill more quickly, as indeed might be expected, for an intelligent person learns all things sooner than a stupid one; and that in general demeanor they contrast so favorably with their predecessors that the authorities of the institutions are impatient for the day to arrive when the last remains of the old leaven shall have disappeared from the place. If this be so, and it is easy to ascertain whether it is so, it is to be hoped we shall soon have heard for the last time that ignorance is a better qualification than knowledge for the military, and *a fortiori* for every other, profession; or that any one good quality, however little apparently connected with liberal education, is at all likely to be promoted by going without it.

Though the first admission to government employment be decided by competitive examination, it would in most cases be impossible that subsequent promotion should be so de-

5 [Mill here refers to Sebastien Le Prestre de Vauban's (1633-1707) system of building, defending, and attacking fortresses.]

cided; and it seems proper that this should take place, as it usually does at present, on a mixed system of seniority and selection. Those whose duties are of a routine character should rise by seniority to the highest point to which duties merely of that description can carry them, while those to whom functions of particular trust and requiring special capacity are confided should be selected from the body on the discretion of the chief of the office. And this selection will generally be made honestly by him if the original appointments take place by open competition; for under that system his establishment will generally consist of individuals to whom, but for the official connection, he would have been a stranger. If among them there be any in whom he, or his political friends and supporters, take an interest, it will be but occasionally, and only when to this advantage of connection is added, as far as the initiatory examination could test it, at least equality of real merit. And, except when there is a very strong motive to job these appointments, there is always a strong one to appoint the fittest person—being the one who gives to his chief the most useful assistance, saves him most trouble, and helps most to build up that reputation for good management of public business which necessarily and properly redounds to the credit of the minister, however much the qualities to which it is immediately owing may be those of his subordinates.

CHAPTER XV

OF LOCAL REPRESENTATIVE BODIES

I T IS but a small portion of the public business of a country which can be well done, or safely attempted, by the central authorities; and even in our own government, the least centralized in Europe, the legislative portion at least of the governing body busies itself far too much with local affairs, employing the supreme power of the State in cutting small

knots which there ought to be other and better means of un-
tying. The enormous amount of private business which takes
up the time of Parliament, and the thoughts of its individual
members, distracting them from the proper occupations of
the great council of the nation, is felt by all thinkers and observers as a serious evil and, what is worse, an increasing one.

It would not be appropriate to the limited design of this
treatise to discuss at large the great question, in no way
peculiar to representative government, of the proper limits of
governmental action. I have said elsewhere [1] what seemed to
me most essential respecting the principles by which the extent of that action ought to be determined. But after sub-
tracting from the functions performed by most European
governments those which ought not to be undertaken by public authorities at all, there still remains so great and various
an aggregate of duties that, if only on the principle of division
of labor, it is indispensable to share them between central
and local authorities. Not only are separate executive officers required for purely local duties (an amount of separation which
exists under all governments), but the popular control over
those officers can only be advantageously exerted through a
separate organ. Their original appointment, the function of
watching and checking them, the duty of providing, or the discretion of withholding, the supplies necessary for their operations, should rest, not with the national Parliament or the national executive, but with the people of the locality. In some of
the New England States these functions are still exercised directly by the assembled people; it is said, with better results
than might be expected; and those highly educated communities are so well satisfied with this primitive mode of local government that they have no desire to exchange it for the only representative system they are acquainted with, by which all minorities are disfranchised. Such very peculiar circumstances, however, are required to make this arrangement work tolerably in

[1] *On Liberty,* concluding chapter [Liberal Arts Press edition, pp. 114-
141] and, at greater length, in final chapter of *Principles of Political
Economy.*

practice, that recourse must generally be had to the plan of representative sub-Parliaments for local affairs. These exist in England, but very incompletely, and with great irregularity and want of system; in some other countries much less popularly governed their constitution is far more rational. In England there has always been more liberty, but worse organization, while in other countries there is better organization, but less liberty. It is necessary, then, that in addition to the national representation there should be municipal and provincial representations; and the two questions which remain to be resolved are, how the local representative bodies should be constituted, and what should be the extent of their functions.

In considering these questions, two points require an equal degree of our attention: how the local business itself can be best done; and how its transaction can be made most instrumental to the nourishment of public spirit and the development of intelligence. In an earlier part of this inquiry I have dwelt in strong language—hardly any language is strong enough to express the strength of my conviction—on the importance of that portion of the operation of free institutions which may be called the public education of the citizens. Now, of this operation the local administrative institutions are the chief instrument. Except by the part they may take as jurymen in the administration of justice, the mass of the population have very little opportunity of sharing personally in the conduct of the general affairs of the community. Reading newspapers and perhaps writing to them, public meetings and solicitations of different sorts addressed to the political authorities are the extent of the participation of private citizens in general politics during the interval between one parliamentary election and another. Though it is impossible to exaggerate the importance of these various liberties, both as securities for freedom and as means of general cultivation, the practice which they give is more in thinking than in action, and in thinking without the responsibilities of action; which with most people amounts to little more than passively receiving the thoughts of someone else. But in the case of local bodies, besides the function of electing, many citizens in turn have the chance of being elected, and many, either by selection or by rotation, fill one or other of the numerous local executive offices. In these positions they have to act for public interests, as well as to think and to speak, and the thinking cannot all be done by proxy. It may be added that these local functions, not being in general sought by the higher ranks, carry down the important political education which they are the means of conferring to a much lower grade in society. The mental discipline being thus a more important feature in local concerns than in the general affairs of the State, while there are not such vital interests dependent on the quality of the administration, a greater weight may be given to the former consideration, and the latter admits much more frequently of being postponed to it than in matters of general legislation and the conduct of imperial affairs.

The proper constitution of local representative bodies does not present much difficulty. The principles which apply to it do not differ in any respect from those applicable to the national representation. The same obligation exists, as in the case of the more important function, for making the bodies elective; and the same reasons operate as in that case, but with still greater force, for giving them a widely democratic basis: the dangers being less, and the advantages, in point of popular education and cultivation, in some respects even greater. As the principal duty of the local bodies consists of the imposition and expenditure of local taxation, the electoral franchise should vest in all who contribute to the local rates, to the exclusion of all who do not. I assume that there is no indirect taxation, no *octroi* duties, or that if there are, they are supplementary only; those on whom their burden falls being also rated to a direct assessment. The representation of minorities should be provided for in the same manner as in the national Parliament, and there are the same strong reasons for plurality of votes. Only there is not so decisive an objection, in the inferior as in the higher body, to making the plural voting depend (as in some of the local elections of our own

country) on a mere money qualification; for the honest and
frugal dispensation of money forms so much larger a part of
the business of the local than of the national body that there is
more justice as well as policy in allowing a greater proportional influence to those who have a larger money interest at stake.

In the most recently established of our local representative institutions, the Boards of Guardians,[2] the justices of
peace of the district sit *ex officio* along with the elected members, in number limited by law to a third of the whole. In the
peculiar constitution of English society I have no doubt of the
beneficial effect of this provision. It secures the presence, in
these bodies, of a more educated class than it would perhaps
be practicable to attract thither on any other terms; and while
the limitation in number of the *ex officio* members precludes
them from acquiring predominance by mere numerical
strength, they as a virtual representation of another class, having sometimes a different interest from the rest, are a check
upon the class interests of the farmers or petty shopkeepers,
who form the bulk of the elected Guardians. A similar commendation cannot be given to the constitution of the only
provincial boards we possess, the Quarter Sessions, consisting
of the justices of peace alone; on whom, over and above their
judicial duties, some of the most important parts of the administrative business of the country depend for their performance.
The mode of formation of these bodies is most anomalous,
they being neither elected nor, in any proper sense of the
term, nominated, but holding their important functions, like
the feudal lords to whom they succeeded, virtually by right of
their acres; the appointment vested in the Crown (or, speaking practically, in one of themselves, the Lord Lieutenant)
being made use of only as a means of excluding anyone who
it is thought would do discredit to the body, or, now and
then, one who is on the wrong side in politics. The institution is the most aristocratic in principle which now remains
in England, far more so than the House of Lords, for it grants

2 [An elective body which supervised the execution of the Poor Law in
England and Wales.]

public money and disposes of important public interests, not in conjunction with a popular assembly, but alone. It is clung to with proportionate tenacity by our aristocratic classes, but is obviously at variance with all the principles which are the foundation of representative government. In a County Board there is not the same justification as in Boards of Guardians for even an admixture of *ex officio* with elected members; since the business of a county being on a sufficiently large scale to be an object of interest and attraction to country gentlemen, they would have no more difficulty in getting themselves elected to the Board than they have in being returned to Parliament as county members.

In regard to the proper circumscription of the constituencies which elect the local representative bodies, the principle which, when applied as an exclusive and unbending rule to parliamentary representation, is inappropriate, namely, community of local interests, is here the only just and applicable one. The very object of having a local representation is in order that those who have any interest in common, which they do not share with the general body of their countrymen, may manage that joint interest by themselves; and the purpose is contradicted if the distribution of the local representation follows any other rule than the grouping of those joint interests. There are local interests peculiar to every town, whether great or small, and common to all its inhabitants; every town, therefore, without distinction of size, ought to have its municipal council. It is equally obvious that every town ought to have but one. The different quarters of the same town have seldom or never any material diversities of local interest; they all require to have the same things done, the same expenses incurred; and, except as to their churches, which it is probably desirable to leave under simply parochial management, the same arrangements may be made to serve for all. Paving, lighting, water supply, drainage, port and market regulations cannot without great waste and inconvenience be different for different quarters of the same town. The subdivision of London into six or seven independent dis-

REPRESENTATIVE GOVERNMENT

tricts, each with its separate arrangements for local business (several of them without unity of administration even within themselves), prevents the possibility of consecutive or well-regulated co-operation for common objects, precludes any uniform principle for the discharge of local duties, compels the general government to take things upon itself which would be best left to local authorities if there were any whose authority extended to the entire metropolis and answers no purpose but to keep up the fantastical trappings of that union of modern jobbing and antiquated foppery, the Corporation of the City of London.

Another equally important principle is that in each local circumscription there should be but one elected body for all local business, not different bodies for different parts of it. Division of labor does not mean cutting up every business into minute fractions; it means the union of such operations as are fit to be performed by the same persons, and the separation of such as can be better performed by different persons. The executive duties of the locality do indeed require to be divided into departments, for the same reason as those of the State; because they are of diverse kinds, each requiring knowledge peculiar to itself, and needing for its due performance the undivided attention of a specially qualified functionary. But the reasons for subdivision which apply to the execution do not apply to the control. The business of the elective body is not to do the work, but to see that it is properly done, and that nothing necessary is left undone. This function can be fulfilled for all departments by the same superintending body; and by a collective and comprehensive far better than by a minute and microscopic view. It is as absurd in public affairs as it would be in private that every workman should be looked after by a superintendent to himself. The Government of the Crown consists of many departments, and there are many ministers to conduct them, but those ministers have not a Parliament apiece to keep them to their duty. The local, like the national, Parliament has for its proper business to consider the interest of the locality as a whole, composed of parts all of which must be adapted to one another, and attended to in the order and ratio of their importance. There is another very weighty reason for uniting the control of all the business of a locality under one body. The greatest imperfection of popular local institutions, and the chief cause of the failure which so often attends them, is the low caliber of the men by whom they are almost always carried on. That these should be of a very miscellaneous character is, indeed, part of the usefulness of the institution; it is that circumstance chiefly which renders it a school of political capacity and general intelligence. But a school supposes teachers as well as scholars; the utility of the instruction greatly depends on its bringing inferior minds into contact with superior, a contact which in the ordinary course of life is altogether exceptional, and the want of which contributes more than anything else to keep the generality of mankind on one level of contented ignorance. The school, moreover, is worthless, and a school of evil instead of good, if through the want of due surveillance, and of the presence within itself of a higher order of characters, the action of the body is allowed, as it so often is, to degenerate into an equally unscrupulous and stupid pursuit of the self-interest of its members. Now it is quite hopeless to induce persons of a high class, either socially or intellectually, to take a share of local administration in a corner by piecemeal, as members of a Paving Board or a Drainage Commission. The entire local business of their town is not more than a sufficient object to induce men whose tastes incline them and whose knowledge qualifies them for national affairs to become members of a mere local body and devote to it the time and study which are necessary to render their presence anything more than a screen for the jobbing of inferior persons under the shelter of their responsibility. A mere Board of Works, though it comprehend the entire metropolis, is sure to be composed of the same class of persons as the vestries of the London parishes; nor is it practicable, or even desirable, that such should not form the majority; but it is important for every purpose which local bodies are designed to serve, whether it be the enlightened and honest performance of their special duties, or the cultivation of the political intelligence of the nation, that every such body should contain a portion of the very best minds of the locality, who are thus brought into perpetual contact, of the most useful kind, with minds of a lower grade, receiving from them what local or professional knowledge they have to give, and in return inspiring them with a portion of their own more enlarged ideas, and higher and more enlightened purposes.

A mere village has no claim to a municipal representation. By a village, I mean a place whose inhabitants are not markedly distinguished by occupation or social relations from those of the rural districts adjoining, and for whose local wants the arrangements made for the surrounding territory will suffice. Such small places have rarely a sufficient public to furnish a tolerable municipal council; if they contain any talent or knowledge applicable to public business, it is apt to be all concentrated in some one man, who thereby becomes the dominator of the place. It is better that such places should be merged in a larger circumscription. The local representation of rural districts will naturally be determined by geographical considerations; with due regard to those sympathies of feeling by which human beings are so much aided to act in concert, and which partly follow historical boundaries, such as those of counties or provinces, and partly community of interest and occupation, as in agricultural, maritime, manufacturing, or mining districts. Different kinds of local business may require different areas of representation. The Unions of parishes have been fixed on as the most appropriate basis for the representative bodies which superintend the relief of indigence, while for the proper regulation of highways, or prisons, or police a large extent, like that of an average county, is not more than sufficient. In these large districts, therefore, the maxim that an elective body constituted in any locality should have authority over all the local concerns common to the locality requires modification from another principle—as well as from the competing consideration of the importance of obtaining for the discharge of the local duties the highest qualifications possible. For example, if it be necessary (as I believe it to be) for the proper administration of the Poor Laws that the area of rating should not be more extensive than most of the present Unions, a principle which requires a Board of Guardians for each Union—yet, as a much more highly qualified class of persons is likely to be obtainable for a County Board than those who compose an average Board of Guardians, it may on that ground be expedient to reserve for the County Boards some higher descriptions of local business, which might otherwise have been conveniently managed within itself by each separate Union.

Besides the controlling Council, or local sub-Parliament, local business has its executive department. With respect to this, the same questions arise as with respect to the executive authorities in the State; and they may, for the most part, be answered in the same manner. The principles applicable to all public trusts are in substance the same. In the first place, each executive officer should be single, and singly responsible for the whole of the duty committed to his charge. In the next place, he should be nominated, not elected. It is ridiculous that a surveyor, or a health officer, or even a collector of rates should be appointed by popular suffrage. The popular choice usually depends on interest with a few local leaders, who, as they are not supposed to make the appointment, are not responsible for it, or on an appeal to sympathy, founded on having twelve children and having been a ratepayer in the parish for thirty years. If in cases of this description election by the population is a farce, appointment by the local representative body is little less objectionable. Such bodies have a perpetual tendency to become joint-stock associations for carrying into effect the private jobs of their various members. Appointments should be made on the individual responsibility of the chairman of the body, let him be called Mayor, Chairman of Quarter Sessions, or by whatever other title. He occupies in the locality a position analogous to that of the prime minister in the State, and under a well-organized system the appointment and watching of the local officers would be the most important part of his duty, he himself being appointed by the Council from its own number, subject either to annual re-election or to removal by a vote of the body.

From the constitution of the local bodies I now pass to the e-qually important and more difficult subject of their proper attri-butions. This question divides itself into two parts: what should be their duties, and whether they should have full authority within the sphere of those duties or should be liable to any, and what, interference on the part of the central government.

It is obvious, to begin with, that all business purely local— all which concerns only a single locality—should devolve upon the local authorities. The paving, lighting, and cleansing of the streets of a town, and in ordinary circumstances the drain-ing of its houses, are of little consequence to any but its in-habitants. The nation at large is interested in them in no other way than that in which it is interested in the private well-being of all its individual citizens. But among the duties classed as local, or performed by local functionaries, there are many which might with equal propriety be termed national, being the share, belonging to the locality, of some branch of the public administration in the efficiency of which the whole nation is alike interested: the gaols, for instance, most of which in this country are under county management; the local police; the local administration of justice, much of which, especially in corporate towns, is performed by officers elected by the locality and paid from local funds. None of these can be said to be matters of local, as distinguished from national, importance. It would not be a matter personally indifferent to the rest of the country if any part of it became a nest of rob-bers or a focus of demoralization, owing to the maladministra-tion of its police; or if, through the bad regulations of its gaol, the punishment which the courts of justice intended to inflict on the criminals confined therein (who might have come from, or committed their offenses in, any other district) might be doubled in intensity, or lowered to practical impunity. The points, moreover, which constitute good management of these things are the same everywhere; there is no good reason why police, or gaols, or the administration of justice should be differently managed in one part of the kingdom and in another; while there is great peril that in things so important, and to which the most instructed minds available to the State are not more than adequate, the lower average of capacities which alone can be counted on for the service of the localities might commit errors of such magnitude as to be a serious blot upon the general administration of the country. Security of person and property and equal justice between individuals are the first needs of society and the primary ends of government; if these things can be left to any responsibility below the highest, there is nothing, except war and treaties, which requires a general government at all. Whatever are the best arrangements for securing these primary objects should be made universally obligatory and, to secure their enforcement, should be placed under central superintendence. It is often useful, and with the institutions of our own country even necessary, from the scarcity, in the localities, of officers representing the general government, that the execution of duties imposed by the central authority should be entrusted to functionaries appointed for local purposes by the locality. But experience is daily forcing upon the public a conviction of the necessity of having at least inspectors appointed by the general government to see that the local officers do their duty. If prisons are under local management, the central government appoints inspectors of prisons to take care that the rules laid down by Parliament are observed, and to suggest others if the state of the gaols shows them to be requisite; as there are inspectors of factories, and inspectors of schools, to watch over the observance of the acts of Parliament relating to the first, and the fulfillment of the conditions on which State assistance is granted to the latter.

But if the administration of justice, police and gaols included, is both so universal a concern, and so much a matter of general science independent of local peculiarities, that it may be, and ought to be, uniformly regulated throughout the country, and its regulation enforced by more trained and skillful hands than those of purely local authorities—there is also business, such as the administration of the poor laws, sanitary regulation, and others, which, while really interesting to the whole country, cannot consistently with the very purposes of local administration be managed otherwise than by the localities. In regard to such duties the question arises how far the local authorities ought to be trusted with discretionary power, free from any superintendence or control of the State.

To decide this question it is essential to consider what is the comparative position of the central and the local authorities as to capacity for the work, and security against negligence or abuse. In the first place, the local representative bodies and their officers are almost certain to be of a much lower grade of intelligence and knowledge than Parliament and the national executive. Secondly, besides being themselves of inferior qualifications, they are watched by, and accountable to, an inferior public opinion. The public under whose eyes they act, and by whom they are criticized, is both more limited in extent and generally far less enlightened than that which surrounds and admonishes the highest authorities at the capital, while the comparative smallness of the interests involved causes even that inferior public to direct its thoughts to the subject less intently, and with less solicitude. Far less interference is exercised by the press and by public discussion, and that which is exercised may with much more impunity be disregarded in the proceedings of local than in those of national authorities. Thus far the advantage seems wholly on the side of management by the central government. But, when we look more closely, these motives of preference are found to be balanced by others fully as substantial. If the local authorities and public are inferior to the central ones in knowledge of the principles of administration, they have the compensating advantage of a far more direct interest in the result. A man's neighbors or his landlord may be much cleverer than himself, and not without an indirect interest in his

prosperity, but for all that his interests will be better attended
to in his own keeping than in theirs. It is further to be remembered that, even supposing the central government to administer through its own officers, its officers do not act at the
center, but in the locality; and however inferior the local
public may be to the central, it is the local public alone which
has any opportunity of watching them, and it is the local
opinion alone which either acts directly upon their own conduct or calls the attention of the government to the points in
which they may require correction. It is but in extreme cases
that the general opinion of the country is brought to bear at
all upon details of local administration, and still more rarely
has it the means of deciding upon them with any just appreciation of the case. Now, the local opinion necessarily acts far
more forcibly upon purely local administrators. They, in the
natural course of things, are permanent residents, not expect-
ing to be withdrawn from the place when they cease to exercise authority in it; and their authority itself depends, by
supposition, on the will of the local public. I need not dwell
on the deficiencies of the central authority in detailed knowledge of local persons and things, and the too great engross-
ment of its time and thoughts by other concerns, to admit of
its acquiring the quantity and quality of local knowledge
necessary even for deciding on complaints and enforcing responsibility from so great a number of local agents. In the
details of management, therefore, the local bodies will generally have the advantage; but in comprehension of the principles even of purely local management, the superiority of the
central government, when rightly constituted, ought to be
prodigious, not only by reason of the probably great personal superiority of the individuals composing it, and the multitude of thinkers and writers who are at all times engaged in
pressing useful ideas upon their notice, but also because the
knowledge and experience of any local authority is but local
knowledge and experience, confined to their own part of the
country and its modes of management, whereas the central

government has the means of knowing all that is to be learned from the united experience of the whole kingdom, with the addition of easy access to that of foreign countries.

The practical conclusion from these premises is not diffi- cult to draw. The authority which is most conversant with principles should be supreme over principles, while that which is most competent in details should have the details left to it. The principal business of the central authority should be to give instruction, of the local authority to apply it. Power may be localized, but knowledge, to be most useful, must be centralized; there must be somewhere a focus at which all its scattered rays are collected, that the broken and colored lights which exist elsewhere may find there what is necessary to com- plete and purify them. To every branch of local administra- tion which affects the general interest there should be a corres- ponding central organ, either a minister or some specially ap- pointed functionary under him; even if that functionary does no more than collect information from all quarters and bring the experience acquired in one locality to the knowledge of another where it is wanted. But there is also something more than this for the central authority to do. It ought to keep open a perpetual communication with the localities: informing it- self by their experience, and them by its own; giving advice freely when asked, volunteering it when seen to be required; compelling publicity and recordation of proceedings, and en- forcing obedience to every general law which the legislature has laid down on the subject of local management. That some such laws ought to be laid down few are likely to deny. The localities may be allowed to mismanage their own interests, but not to prejudice those of others, nor violate those princi- ples of justice between one person and another of which it is the duty of the State to maintain the rigid observance. If the local majority attempts to oppress the minority, or one class another, the State is bound to interpose. For example, all local rates ought to be voted exclusively by the local represent- ative body; but that body, though elected solely by ratepayers, may raise its revenues by imposts of such a kind, or assess them in such a manner, as to throw an unjust share of the burden on the poor, the rich, or some particular class of the population; it is the duty, therefore, of the legislature, while leaving the mere amount of the local taxes to the discretion of the local body, to lay down authoritatively the modes of taxation and rules of assessment which alone the localities shall be permitted to use. Again, in the administration of public charity the industry and morality of the whole laboring population depend, to a most serious extent, upon adherence to certain fixed principles in awarding relief. Though it belongs essentially to the local functionaries to determine who, according to those principles, is entitled to be relieved, the national Parliament is the proper authority to prescribe the principles themselves; and it would neglect a most important part of its duty if it did not, in a matter of such grave national concern, lay down imperative rules, and make effectual provision that those rules should not be departed from. What power of actual interference with the local administrators it may be necessary to retain, for the due enforcement of the laws, is a question of detail into which it would be useless to enter. The laws themselves will naturally define the penalties and fix the mode of their enforcement. It may be requisite, to meet extreme cases, that the power of the central authority should extend to dissolving the local representative council or dismissing the local executive, but not to making new appointments or suspending the local institutions. Where Parliament has not interfered, neither ought any branch of the executive to interfere with authority; but as an adviser and critic, an enforcer of the laws, and a denouncer to Parliament or the local constituencies of conduct which it deems condemnable, the functions of the executive are of the greatest possible value.

Some may think that, however much the central authority surpasses the local in knowledge of the principles of administration, the great object which has been so much insisted on, the social and political education of the citizens, requires that they should be left to manage these matters by their own, however imperfect, lights. To this it might be answered that the education of the citizens is not the only thing to be considered; government and administration do not exist for that alone, great as its importance is. But the objection shows a very imperfect understanding of the function of popular institutions as a means of political instruction. It is but a poor education that associates ignorance with ignorance and leaves them, if they care for knowledge, to grope their way to it without help, and to do without it if they do not. What is wanted is the means of making ignorance aware of itself and able to profit by knowledge, accustoming minds which know only routine to act upon and feel the value of principles, teaching them to compare different modes of action and learn by the use of their reason to distinguish the best. When we desire to have a good school, we do not eliminate the teacher. The old remark, "as the schoolmaster is, so will be the school," is as true of the indirect schooling of grown people by public business as of the schooling of youth in academies and colleges. A government which attempts to do everything is aptly compared by M. Charles de Rémusat to a schoolmaster who does all the pupils' tasks for them; he may be very popular with the pupils, but he will teach them little. A government, on the other hand, which neither does anything itself that can possibly be done by anyone else, nor shows anyone else how to do anything, is like a school in which there is no schoolmaster, but only pupil teachers who have never themselves been taught.

CHAPTER XVI

OF NATIONALITY, AS CONNECTED WITH REPRESENTATIVE GOVERNMENT

A PORTION of mankind may be said to constitute a nationality if they are united among themselves by common sympathies which do not exist between them and any others—which make them co-operate with each other more willingly than with other people, desire to be under the same government, and desire that it should be government by themselves or a portion of themselves exclusively. This feeling of nationality may have been generated by various causes. Sometimes it is the effect of identity of race and descent. Community of language and community of religion greatly contribute to it. Geographical limits are one of its causes. But the strongest of all is identity of political antecedents: the possession of a national history, and consequent community of recollections; collective pride and humiliation, pleasure and regret, connected with the same incidents in the past. None of these circumstances, however, are either indispensable or necessarily sufficient by themselves. Switzerland has a strong sentiment of nationality, though the cantons are of different races, different languages, and different religions. Sicily has, throughout history, felt itself quite distinct in nationality from Naples, notwithstanding identity of religion, almost identity of language, and a considerable amount of common historical antecedents. The Flemish and the Walloon provinces of Belgium, notwithstanding diversity of race and language, have a much greater feeling of common nationality than the former have with Holland, or the latter with France. Yet in general the national feeling is proportionally weakened by the failure of any of the causes which contribute to it. Identity of language, literature, and, to some extent, of race and recollections have maintained the feeling of nationality in considerable strength among the different portions of the German name, though they have at no time been really united under the same government; but the feeling has never reached to making the separate states desire to get rid of their autonomy. Among Italians an identity, far from complete, of language and literature, combined with a geographical position which separates them by a distinct line from other countries, and, perhaps more than everything else, the possession of a common name, which makes them all glory in the past achievements in arts, arms, politics, religious primacy, science, and literature, of any who share the same designation, give rise to an amount of national feeling in the population which, though still imperfect, has been sufficient to produce the great events now passing before us,[1] notwithstanding a great mixture of races, and although they have never, in either ancient or modern history, been under the same government except while that government extended or was extending itself over the greater part of the known world.[2]

Where the sentiment of nationality exists in any force, there is a *prima facie* case for uniting all the members of the nationality under the same government, and a government to themselves apart. This is merely saying that the question of government ought to be decided by the governed. One hardly knows what any division of the human race should be free to do if not to determine with which of the various collective bodies of human beings they choose to associate themselves. But when a people are ripe for free institutions, there is a still more vital consideration. Free institutions are next to impossible in a country made up of different nationalities. Among a people without fellow-feeling, especially if they read and speak different languages, the united public opinion, necessary to the working of representative government, cannot exist. The influences which form opinions and decide political acts are different in the different sections of the country. An alto-

1 [Reference is to the Italian struggle for unification. See note 2, p. 11.]
2 [The Roman Empire.]

gether different set of leaders have the confidence of one part
of the country and of another. The same books, newspapers,
pamphlets, speeches do not reach them. One section does not
know what opinions or what instigations are circulating in another. The same incidents, the same acts, the same system of
government affect them in different ways; and each fears
more injury to itself from the other nationalities than from
the common arbiter, the state. Their mutual antipathies are
generally much stronger than jealousy of the government.
That any one of them feels aggrieved by the policy of the common ruler is sufficient to determine another to support that
policy. Even if all are aggrieved, none feel that they can rely
on the others for fidelity in a joint resistance; the strength of
none is sufficient to resist alone, and each may reasonably
think that it consults its own advantage most by bidding for
the favor of the government against the rest. Above all, the
grand and only effectual security in the last resort against the
despotism of the government is in that case wanting: the sympathy of the army with the people. The military are the part
of every community in whom, from the nature of the case, the
distinction between their fellow countrymen and foreigners is
the deepest and strongest. To the rest of the people foreigners
are merely strangers; to the soldier, they are men against whom
he may be called, at a week's notice, to fight for life or death.
The difference to him is that between friends and foes—we
may almost say between fellow men and another kind of animals; for as respects the enemy, the only law is that of force,
and the only mitigation the same as in the case of other animals—that of simple humanity. Soldiers to whose feelings half
or three-fourths of the subjects of the same government are
foreigners will have no more scruple in mowing them down,
and no more desire to ask the reason why, than they would
have in doing the same thing against declared enemies. An
army composed of various nationalities has no other patriotism than devotion to the flag. Such armies have been the exe-
cutioners of liberty through the whole duration of modern
history. The sole bond which holds them together is their

officers and the government which they serve; and their only idea, if they have any, of public duty is obedience to orders. A government thus supported—by keeping its Hungarian regiments in Italy and its Italian in Hungary—can long continue to rule in both places with the iron rod of foreign conquerors.

If it be said that so broadly marked a distinction between what is due to a fellow countryman and what is due merely to a human creature is more worthy of savages than of civilized beings, and ought, with the utmost energy, to be contended against, no one holds that opinion more strongly than myself. But this object, one of the worthiest to which human endeavor can be directed, can never, in the present state of civilization, be promoted by keeping different nationalities of anything like equivalent strength under the same government. In a barbarous state of society the case is sometimes different. The government may then be interested in softening the antipathies of the races that peace may be preserved and the country more easily governed. But when there are either free institutions or a desire for them, in any of the peoples artificially tied together, the interest of the government lies in an exactly opposite direction. It is then interested in keeping up and envenoming their antipathies that they may be prevented from coalescing, and it may be enabled to use some of them as tools for the enslavement of others. The Austrian court has now for a whole generation made these tactics its principal means of government, with what fatal success, at the time of the Vienna insurrection and the Hungarian contest, the world knows too well.[3] Happily there are now signs that improvement is too far advanced to permit this policy to be any longer successful.

For the preceding reasons, it is in general a necessary condition of free institutions that the boundaries of governments

[3] [The Vienna insurrection in 1848 was inspired by the news of the revolution in Paris, which had also prompted the Hungarian people, under the leadership of Lajos Kossuth, to revolt against the Hapsburg rule and to proclaim an independent republic. The Hapsburgs suppressed this movement, however, with the help of Russian troops, one year later.]

should coincide in the main with those of nationalities. But several considerations are liable to conflict in practice with this general principle. In the first place, its application is often precluded by geographical hindrances. There are parts even of Europe in which different nationalities are so locally intermingled that it is not practicable for them to be under separate governments. The population of Hungary is composed of Magyars, Slovaks, Croats, Serbs, Romanians, and in some districts Germans, so mixed up as to be incapable of local separation; and there is no course open to them but to make a virtue of necessity and reconcile themselves to living together under equal rights and laws. The community of servitude, which dates only from the destruction of Hungarian independence in 1849, seems to be ripening and disposing them for such an equal union. The German colony of East Prussia is cut off from Germany by part of the ancient Poland and, being too weak to maintain separate independence, must, if geographical continuity is to be maintained, be either under a non-German government or the intervening Polish territory must be under a German one. Another considerable region in which the dominant element of the population is German, the provinces of Kurland, Estonia, and Livonia, is condemned by its local situation to form part of a Slavonian state. In Eastern Germany itself there is a large Slavonic population: Bohemia is principally Slavonic, Silesia and other districts partially so. The most united country in Europe, France, is far from being homogeneous: independently of the fragments of foreign nationalities at its remote extremities, it consists, as language and history prove, of two portions, one occupied almost exclusively by a Gallo-Roman population, while in the other the Frankish, Burgundian, and other Teutonic races form a considerable ingredient.

When proper allowance has been made for geographical exigencies, another more purely moral and social consideration offers itself. Experience proves that it is possible for one nationality to merge and be absorbed in another; and when it was originally an inferior and more backward portion of the human race the absorption is greatly to its advantage. Nobody can suppose that it is not more beneficial to a Breton, or a Basque of French Navarre, to be brought into the current of the ideas and feelings of a highly civilized and cultivated people—to be a member of the French nationality, admitted on equal terms to all privileges of French citizenship, sharing the advantages of French protection and the dignity and prestige of French power—than to sulk on his own rocks, the half-savage relic of past times, revolving in his own little mental orbit, without participation or interest in the general movement of the world. The same remark applies to the Welshman or the Scottish Highlander as members of the British nation.

Whatever really tends to the admixture of nationalities and the blending of their attributes and peculiarities in a common union is a benefit to the human race. Not by extinguishing types, of which, in these cases, sufficient examples are sure to remain, but by softening their extreme forms and filling up the intervals between them. The united people, like a crossed breed of animals (but in a still greater degree, because the influences in operation are moral as well as physical), inherits the special aptitudes and excellences of all its progenitors, protected by the admixture from being exaggerated into the neighboring vices. But to render this admixture possible, there must be peculiar conditions. The combinations of circumstances which occur, and which affect the result, are various.

The nationalities brought together under the same government may be about equal in numbers and strength, or they may be very unequal. If unequal, the least numerous of the two may either be the superior in civilization, or the inferior. Supposing it to be superior, it may either, through that superiority, be able to acquire ascendancy over the other, or it may be overcome by brute strength and reduced to subjection. This last is a sheer mischief to the human race and one which civilized humanity with one accord should rise in arms to prevent. The absorption of Greece by Macedonia was one of the greatest misfortunes which ever happened to the world; that of any of the principal countries of Europe by Russia would be a similar one.

If the smaller nationality, supposed to be the more advanced in improvement, is able to overcome the greater, as the Macedonians, reinforced by the Greeks, did Asia, and the English India, there is often a gain to civilization; but the conquerors and the conquered cannot in this case live together under the same free institutions. The absorption of the conquerors in the less advanced people would be an evil; these must be governed as subjects, and the state of things is either a benefit or a misfortune, according as the subjugated people have or have not reached the state in which it is an injury not to be under a free government, and according as the conquerors do or do not use their superiority in a manner calculated to fit the conquered for a higher stage of improvement. This topic will be particularly treated of in a subsequent chapter.

When the nationality which succeeds in overpowering the other is both the most numerous and the most improved, and especially if the subdued nationality is small and has no hope of reasserting its independence, then, if it is governed with any tolerable justice and if the members of the more powerful nationality are not made odious by being invested with exclusive privileges, the smaller nationality is gradually reconciled to its position and becomes amalgamated with the larger. No Bas-Breton, nor even any Alsatian, has the smallest wish at the present day to be separated from France. If all Irishmen have not yet arrived at the same disposition toward England, it is partly because they are sufficiently numerous to be capable of constituting a respectable nationality by themselves; but principally because, until of late years, they had been so atrociously governed that all their best feelings combined with their bad ones in rousing bitter resentment against the Saxon rule. This disgrace to England, and calamity to the whole empire, has, it may be truly said, completely ceased for nearly a generation. No Irishman is now less free

than an Anglo-Saxon, nor has a less share of every benefit
either to his country or to his individual fortunes than if he
were sprung from any other portion of the British dominions.
The only remaining real grievance of Ireland, that of the
State Church, is one which half, or nearly half, the people
of the larger island have in common with them. There is now
next to nothing, except the memory of the past and the difference in the predominant religion, to keep apart two races, perhaps the most fitted of any two in the world to be the completing counterpart of one another. The consciousness of being
at last treated not only with equal justice but with equal
consideration is making such rapid way in the Irish nation as
to be wearing off all feelings that could make them insensible
to the benefits which the less numerous and less wealthy people
must necessarily derive from being fellow citizens instead of
foreigners to those who are not only their nearest neighbors,
but the wealthiest and one of the freest as well as most civilized and powerful nations of the earth.

The cases in which the greatest practical obstacles exist to
the blending of nationalities are when the nationalities which
have been bound together are nearly equal in numbers and in
the other elements of power. In such cases each, confiding in
its strength and feeling itself capable of maintaining an equal
struggle with any of the others, is unwilling to be merged in it;
each cultivates with party obstinacy its distinctive peculiarities; obsolete customs, and even declining languages, are revived to deepen the separation; each deems itself tyrannized
over if any authority is exercised within itself by functionaries
of a rival race; and whatever is given to one of the conflicting
nationalities is considered to be taken from all the rest. When
nations thus divided are under a despotic government which
is a stranger to all of them, or which, though sprung from one,
yet feeling greater interest in its own power than in any sympathies of nationality, assigns no privilege to either nation and
chooses its instruments indifferently from all, in the course of
a few generations identity of situation often produces harmony of feeling and the different races come to feel toward

each other as fellow countrymen, particularly if they are dispersed over the same tract of country. But if the era of aspiration to free government arrives before this fusion has been effected, the opportunity has gone by for effecting it. From that time, if the unreconciled nationalities are geographically separate, and especially if their local position is such that there is no natural fitness or convenience in their being under the same government (as in the case of an Italian province under a French or German yoke), there is not only an obvious propriety, but, if either freedom or concord is cared for, a necessity, for breaking the connection altogether. There may be cases in which the provinces, after separation, might usefully remain united by a federal tie; but it generally happens that if they are willing to forego complete independence and become members of a federation, each of them has other neighbors with whom it would prefer to connect itself, having more sympathies in common if not also greater community of interest.

CHAPTER XVII

OF FEDERAL REPRESENTATIVE GOVERNMENTS

PORTIONS of mankind who are not fitted, or not disposed, to live under the same internal government may often with advantage be federally united as to their relations with foreigners: both to prevent wars among themselves and for the sake of more effectual protection against the aggression of powerful states.

To render a federation advisable, several conditions are necessary. The first is that there should be a sufficient amount of mutual sympathy among the populations. The federation binds them always to fight on the same side; and if they have such feelings toward one another, or such diversity of feeling

toward their neighbors, that they would generally prefer to
fight on opposite sides, the federal tie is neither likely to be
of long duration nor to be well observed while it subsists.
The sympathies available for the purpose are those of race,
language, religion, and, above all, of political institutions, as
conducing most to a feeling of identity of political interest.
When a few free states, separately insufficient for their own defense, are hemmed in on all sides by military or feudal monarchs, who hate and despise freedom even in a neighbor, those
states have no chance for preserving liberty and its blessings
but by a federal union. The common interest arising from this
cause has in Switzerland, for several centuries, been found
adequate to maintain efficiently the federal bond, in spite
not only of difference of religion when religion was the grand
source of irreconcilable political enmity throughout Europe,
but also in spite of great weakness in the constitution of the
federation itself. In America, where all the conditions for the
maintenance of union existed at the highest point, with the
sole drawback of difference of institutions in the single but
most important article of slavery, this one difference has
gone so far in alienating from each other's sympathies the two
divisions of the Union that the maintenance or disruption of
a tie of so much value to them both depends on the issue of
an obstinate civil war.

A second condition of the stability of a federal government
is that the separate states be not so powerful as to be able to
rely, for protection against foreign encroachment, on their
individual strength. If they are, they will be apt to think that
they do not gain by union with others the equivalent of what
they sacrifice in their own liberty of action; and, consequently,
whenever the policy of the confederation, in things reserved to
its cognizance, is different from that which any one of its
members would separately pursue, the internal and sectional
breach will, through absence of sufficient anxiety to preserve
the union, be in danger of going so far as to dissolve it.

A third condition, not less important than the two others,
is that there be not a very marked inequality of strength

among the several contracting states. They cannot, indeed, be exactly equal in resources; in all federations there will be a gradation of power among the members; some will be more populous, rich, and civilized than others. There is a wide difference in wealth and population between New York and Rhode Island; between Bern and Zug or Glarus. The essential is that there should not be any one State so much more powerful than the rest as to be capable of vying in strength with many of them combined. If there be such a one, and only one, it will insist on being master of the joint deliberations; if there be two, they will be irresistible when they agree; and whenever they differ everything will be decided by a struggle for ascendancy between the rivals. This cause is alone enough to reduce the German Bund to almost a nullity, independently of its wretched internal constitution.[1] It effects none of the real purposes of a confederation. It has never bestowed on Germany a uniform system of customs, nor so much as a uniform coinage; and has served only to give Austria and Prussia a legal right of pouring in their troops to assist the local sovereigns in keeping their subjects obedient to despotism, while in regard to external concerns the Bund would make all Germany a dependency of Prussia if there were no Austria, and of Austria if there were no Prussia; and in the meantime each petty prince has little choice but to be a partisan of one or the other, or to intrigue with foreign governments against both.

There are two different modes of organizing a federal union. The federal authorities may represent the governments solely, and their acts may be obligatory only on the governments as such, or they may have the power of enacting laws and issuing orders which are binding directly on individual citizens. The former is the plan of the German so-called Confederation, and of the Swiss Constitution previous to 1847.

1 [Reference is to the German confederation, the loose organization of German states, including Austria, created at the Congress of Vienna in 1815. The rivalry between Prussia and Austria for the leadership of the confederation prevented its developing into an effective national polity. The confederation was terminated in 1866 when Prussia defeated Austria and united the northern German states under Prussian hegemony.]

It was tried in America for a few years immediately following the War of Independence. The other principle is that of the existing Constitution of the United States, and has been adopted within the last dozen years by the Swiss Confederacy. The Federal Congress of the American Union is a substantive part of the government of every individual State. Within the limits of its attributions, it makes laws which are obeyed by every citizen individually, executes them through its own officers, and enforces them by its own tribunals. This is the only principle which has been found, or which is ever likely, to produce an effective federal government. A union between the governments only is a mere alliance, and subject to all the contingencies which render alliances precarious. If the acts of the President and of Congress were binding solely on the governments of New York, Virginia, or Pennsylvania, and could only be carried into effect through orders issued by those governments to officers appointed by them, under responsibility to their own courts of justice, no mandates of the Federal Government which were disagreeable to a local majority would ever be executed. Requisitions issued to a government have no other sanction, or means of enforcement, than war; and a federal army would have to be always in readiness to enforce the decrees of the federation against any recalcitrant state; subject to the probability that other states, sympathizing with the recusant, and perhaps sharing its sentiments on the particular point in dispute, would withhold their contingents, if not send them to fight in the ranks of the disobedient state. Such a federation is more likely to be a cause than a preventive of internal wars; and if such was not its effect in Switzerland until the events of the years immediately preceding 1847, it was only because the Federal Government felt its weakness so strongly that it hardly ever attempted to exercise any real authority. In America, the experiment of a federation on this principle broke down in the first few years of its existence—happily while the men of enlarged knowledge and acquired ascendancy, who founded the independence of the Republic, were still alive to guide it through the difficult transition. The *Federalist,* a collection of papers by three of these eminent men,[2] written in explanation and defense of the new federal Constitution while still awaiting the national acceptance, is even now the most instructive treatise we possess on federal government.[3] In Germany, the more imperfect kind of federation, as all know, has not even answered the purpose of maintaining an alliance. It has never, in any European war, prevented single members of the Confederation from allying themselves with foreign powers against the rest. Yet this is the only federation which seems possible among monarchical states. A king, who holds his power by inheritance, not by delegation, and who cannot be deprived of it, nor made responsible to anyone for its use, is not likely to renounce having a separate army or to brook the exercise of sovereign authority over his own subjects, not through him but directly by another power. To enable two or more countries under kingly government to be joined together in an effectual confederation it seems necessary that they should all be under the same king. England and Scotland were a federation of this description during the interval of about a century between the union of the Crowns and that of the Parliaments. Even this was effective, not through federal institutions, for none existed, but because the regal power in both Constitutions was during the greater part of that time so nearly absolute as to enable the foreign policy of both to be shaped according to a single will.

Under the more perfect mode of federation, where every citizen of each particular State owes obedience to two governments, that of his own state and that of the federation, it is evidently necessary not only that the constitutional limits of the authority of each should be precisely and clearly defined, but that the power to decide between them in any case of dis-

2 [Alexander Hamilton, James Madison, and John Jay.]

3 Mr. Freeman's *History of Federal Governments,* of which only the first volume has yet appeared, is already an accession to the literature of the subject, equally valuable by its enlightened principles and its mastery of historical details.

pute should not reside in either of the governments, or in
any functionary subject to it, but in an umpire independent
of both. There must be a Supreme Court of Justice, and a
system of subordinate courts in every State of the Union, before whom such questions shall be carried, and whose judgment on them, in the last stage of appeal, shall be final. Every
State of the Union, and the federal Government itself, as well
as every functionary of each, must be liable to be sued in those
courts for exceeding their powers, or for nonperformance of
their federal duties, and must in general be obliged to employ
those courts as the instrument for enforcing their federal
rights. This involves the remarkable consequence, actually
realized in the United States, that a Court of Justice, the highest
federal tribunal, is supreme over the various governments,
both state and federal; having the right to declare that any
law made, or act done by them, exceeds the powers assigned
to them by the federal Constitution and, in consequence, has
no legal validity. It was natural to feel strong doubts, before
trial had been made, how such a provision would work—whether the tribunal would have the courage to exercise its constitutional power; if it did, whether it would exercise it wisely
and whether the governments would consent to submit peace-
ably to its decision. The discussions on the American Constitution, before its final adoption, give evidence that these natural
apprehensions were strongly felt; but they are now entirely
quieted, since, during the two generations and more which
have subsequently elapsed, nothing has occurred to verify
them, though there have at times been disputes of considerable acrimony, and which became the badges of parties, respecting the limits of the authority of the federal and state
governments. The eminently beneficial working of so singular
a provision is probably, as M. de Tocqueville remarks, in a
great measure attributable to the peculiarity inherent in a
Court of Justice acting as such—namely, that it does not declare the law *eo nomine* and in the abstract, but waits until a
case between man and man is brought before it judicially involving the point in dispute; from which arises the happy

effect that its declarations are not made in a very early stage of the controversy, that much popular discussion usually precedes them; that the Court decides after hearing the point fully argued on both sides by lawyers of reputation; decides only as much of the question at a time as is required by the case before it, and its decision, instead of being volunteered for political purposes, is drawn from it by the duty which it cannot refuse to fulfill, of dispensing justice impartially between adverse litigants. Even these grounds of confidence would not have sufficed to produce the respectful submission with which all authorities have yielded to the decisions of the Supreme Court on the interpretation of the Constitution were it not that complete reliance has been felt, not only on the intellectual pre-eminence of the judges composing that exalted tribunal, but on their entire superiority over either private or sectional partialities. This reliance has been in the main justified; but there is nothing which more vitally imports the American people than to guard with the most watchful solicitude against everything which has the remotest tendency to produce deterioration in the quality of this great national institution. The confidence on which depends the stability of federal institutions was for the first time impaired by the judgment declaring slavery to be of common right and, consequently, lawful in the Territories while not yet constituted as States, even against the will of a majority of their inhabitants. This memorable decision has probably done more than anything else to bring the sectional division to the crisis which has issued in civil war. The main pillar of the American Constitution is scarcely strong enough to bear many more such shocks.

The tribunals which act as umpires between the federal and the state governments naturally also decide all disputes between two states or between a citizen of one state and the government of another. The usual remedies between nations, war and diplomacy, being precluded by the federal union, it is necessary that a judicial remedy should supply their place. The Supreme Court of the federation dispenses inter-

national law, and is the first great example of what is now
one of the most prominent wants of civilized society, a real
international tribunal.

The powers of a federal government naturally extend not
only to peace and war, and all questions which arise between
the country and foreign governments, but to making any
other arrangements which are, in the opinion of the states,
necessary to their enjoyment of the full benefits of union. For
example, it is a great advantage to them that their mutual
commerce should be free, without the impediment of frontier
duties and customhouses. But this internal freedom cannot
exist if each State has the power of fixing the duties on inter-
change of commodities between itself and foreign countries,
since every foreign product let in by one State would be let
into all the rest. And hence all custom duties and trade regulations in the United States are made or repealed by the
Federal Government exclusively. Again, it is a great convenience to the States to have but one coinage and but one system of weights and measures, which can only be ensured if
the regulation of these matters is entrusted to the Federal
Government. The certainty and celerity of Post Office communication is impeded, and its expense increased, if a letter
has to pass through half a dozen sets of public offices, subject
to different supreme authorities; it is convenient, therefore,
that all post offices should be under the federal government.
But on such questions the feelings of different communities
are liable to be different. One of the American states, under
the guidance of a man who has displayed powers as a speculative political thinker superior to any who has appeared in
American politics since the authors of the *Federalist*,[4] claimed
a veto for each state on the custom laws of the Federal Congress: and that statesman, in a posthumous work of great
ability which has been printed and widely circulated by the
legislature of South Carolina, vindicated this pretension on
the general principle of limiting the tyranny of the majority

---

4 [Reference is here to John Calhoun, senator and vice president of the
United States, and to his celebrated essay, *A Disquisition on Government*.]

and protecting minorities by admitting them to a substantial participation in political power. One of the most disputed topics in American politics, during the early part of this century, was whether the power of the Federal Government ought to extend, and whether by the Constitution it did extend, to making roads and canals at the cost of the Union. It is only in transactions with foreign powers that the authority of the Federal Government is of necessity complete. On every other subject, the question depends on how closely the people in general wish to draw the federal tie, what portion of their local freedom of action they are willing to surrender in order to enjoy more fully the benefit of being one nation.

Respecting the fitting constitution of a federal government within itself much need not be said. It of course consists of a legislative branch and an executive, and the constitution of each is amenable to the same principles as that of representative governments generally. As regards the mode of adapting these general principles to a federal government, the provision of the American Constitution seems exceedingly judicious, that Congress should consist of two Houses, and that while one of them is constituted according to population, each state being entitled to representatives in the ratio of the number of its inhabitants, the other should represent not the citizens, but the state governments, and every state, whether large or small, should be represented in it by the same number of members. This provision precludes any undue power from being exercised by the more powerful states over the rest, and guarantees the reserved rights of the state governments by making it impossible, as far as the mode of representation can prevent, that any measure should pass Congress unless approved not only by a majority of the citizens, but by a majority of the states. I have before adverted to the further incidental advantage obtained of raising the standard of qualifications in one of the Houses. Being nominated by select bodies, the legislatures of the various states, whose choice, for reasons already indicated, is more likely to fall on eminent men than any popular election—who have not only the power of electing such, but a strong motive to do so, because the influence of their state in the general deliberations must be materially affected by the personal weight and abilities of its representatives; the Senate of the United States, thus chosen, has always contained nearly all the political men of established and high reputation in the Union, while the Lower House of Congress has, in the opinion of competent observers, been generally as remarkable for the absence of conspicuous personal merit as the Upper House for its presence.

When the conditions exist for the formation of efficient and durable federal unions, the multiplication of them is always a benefit to the world. It has the same salutary effect as any other extension of the practice of co-operation through which the weak, by uniting, can meet on equal terms with the strong. By diminishing the number of those petty states which are not equal to their own defense, it weakens the temptations to an aggressive policy, whether working directly by arms or through the prestige of superior power. It of course puts an end to war and diplomatic quarrels, and usually also to restrictions on commerce, between the states composing the union, while, in reference to neighboring nations, the increased military strength conferred by it is of a kind to be almost exclusively available for defensive, scarcely at all for aggressive, purposes. A federal government has not a sufficiently concentrated authority to conduct with much efficiency any war but one of self-defense, in which it can rely on the voluntary co-operation of every citizen, nor is there anything very flattering to national vanity or ambition in acquiring, by a successful war, not subjects, nor even fellow citizens, but only new, and perhaps troublesome, independent members of the confederation. The warlike proceedings of the Americans in Mexico were purely exceptional, having been carried on principally by volunteers, under the influence of the migratory propensity which prompts individual Americans to possess themselves of unoccupied land, and stimulated, if by any public motive, not by that of national aggrandizement, but by the purely sectional purpose of extending slavery. There are few signs in the proceedings of Americans, nationally or individually, that the desire of territorial acquisition for their country as such has any considerable power over them. Their hankering after Cuba is, in the same manner, merely sectional, and the northern States, those opposed to slavery, have never in any way favored it.

The question may present itself (as in Italy at its present uprising) whether a country which is determined to be united should form a complete or a merely federal union. The point is sometimes necessarily decided by the mere territorial magnitude of the united whole. There is a limit to the extent of country which can advantageously be governed, or even whose government can be conveniently superintended, from a single center. There are vast countries so governed; but they, or at least their distant provinces, are in general deplorably ill administered, and it is only when the inhabitants are almost savages that they could not manage their affairs better separately. This obstacle does not exist in the case of Italy, the size of which does not come up to that of several very efficiently governed single states in past and present times. The question then is whether the different parts of the nation require to be governed in a way so essentially different that it is not probable the same legislature and the same ministry or administrative body will give satisfaction to them all. Unless this be the case, which is a question of fact, it is better for them to be completely united. That a totally different system of laws and very different administrative institutions may exist in two portions of a country without being any obstacle to legislative unity is proved by the case of England and Scotland. Perhaps, however, this undisturbed coexistence of two legal systems under one united legislature, making different laws for the two sections of the country in adaptation to the previous differences, might not be so well preserved, or the same confidence might not be felt in its preservation, in a country whose legislators were more possessed (as is apt to be the case on the Continent) with the mania for uniformity. A people having that unbounded toleration which is characteristic of this country for every description of anomaly, so long as those whose interests it concerns do not feel aggrieved by it, afforded an exceptionally advantageous field for trying this difficult experiment. In most countries, if it was an object to retain different systems of law, it might probably be necessary to retain distinct legislatures as guardians of them; which is perfectly compatible with a national parliament and king, or a national parliament without a king, supreme over the external relations of all the members of the body.

Whenever it is not deemed necessary to maintain permanently, in the different provinces, different systems of jurisprudence, and fundamental institutions grounded on different principles, it is always practicable to reconcile minor diversities with the maintenance of unity of government. All that is needful is to give a sufficiently large sphere of action to the local authorities. Under one and the same central government there may be local governors and provincial assemblies for local purposes. It may happen, for instance, that the people of different provinces may have preferences in favor of different modes of taxation. If the general legislature could not be depended on for being guided by the members for each province in modifying the general system of taxation to suit that province, the constitution might provide that as many of the expenses of the government as could by any possibility be made local should be defrayed by local rates imposed by the provincial assemblies, and that those which must of necessity be general, such as the support of an army and navy, should, in the estimates for the year, be apportioned among the different provinces according to some general estimate of their resources, the amount assigned to each being levied by the local assembly on the principles most acceptable to the locality, and paid *en bloc* into the national treasury. A practice approaching to this existed even in the old French monarchy, so far as regarded the *pays d'états*; each of which, having consented or been required to furnish a fixed sum, was left to assess it upon the inhabitants by its own officers, thus escaping

the grinding despotism of the royal *intendants* and *subdélé-
gués;* and this privilege is always mentioned as one of the advantages which mainly contributed to render them, as some
of them were, the most flourishing provinces of France.

Identity of central government is compatible with many
different degrees of centralization, not only administrative, but
even legislative. A people may have the desire, and the capacity, for a closer union than one merely federal, while yet their
local peculiarities and antecedents render considerable diversities desirable in the details of their government. But if there is
a real desire on all hands to make the experiment successful,
there needs seldom be any difficulty in not only preserving
these diversities, but giving them the guarantee of a constitutional provision against any attempt at assimilation, except by
the voluntary act of those who would be affected by the change.

CHAPTER XVIII

OF THE GOVERNMENT OF DEPENDENCIES
BY A FREE STATE

F REE STATES, like all others, may possess dependencies, acquired either by conquest or by colonization; and our
own is the greatest instance of the kind in modern history.
It is a most important question how such dependencies ought
to be governed.

It is unnecessary to discuss the case of small posts, like
Gibraltar, Aden, or Helgoland, which are held only as naval
or military positions. The military or naval object is in this
case paramount, and the inhabitants cannot, consistently with
it, be admitted to the government of the place; though they
ought to be allowed all liberties and privileges compatible
with that restriction, including the free management of municipal affairs; and as a compensation for being locally sacri-

ficed to the convenience of the governing state should be admitted to equal rights with its native subjects in all other
parts of the empire.

Outlying territories of some size and population, which are
held as dependencies, that is, which are subject, more or less,
to acts of sovereign power on the part of the paramount
country without being equally represented (if represented at
all) in its legislature, may be divided into two classes. Some
are composed of people of similar civilization to the ruling
country, capable of, and ripe for, representative government:
such as the British possessions in America and Australia.
Others, like India, are still at a great distance from that
state.

In the case of dependencies of the former class, this country
has at length realized, in rare completeness, the true principle
of government. England has always felt under a certain degree
of obligation to bestow on such of her outlying populations
as were of her own blood and language, and on some who were
not, representative institutions formed in imitation of her
own; but until the present generation she has been on the
same bad level with other countries as to the amount of self-
government which she allowed them to exercise through the
representative institutions that she conceded to them. She
claimed to be the supreme arbiter even of their purely internal concerns, according to her own, not their, ideas of how
those concerns could be best regulated. This practice was a
natural corollary from the vicious theory of colonial policy—
once common to all Europe, and not yet completely relinquished by any other people—which regarded colonies as valuable by affording markets for our commodities that could be
kept entirely to ourselves—a privilege we valued so highly
that we thought it worth purchasing by allowing to the colonies the same monopoly of our market for their own produc-
tions which we claimed for our commodities in theirs. This notable plan for enriching them and ourselves by making each
pay enormous sums to the other, dropping the greatest part by

the way, has been for some time abandoned. But the bad habit of meddling in the internal government of the colonies did not at once terminate when we relinquished the idea of making any profit by it. We continued to torment them, not for any benefit to ourselves, but for that of a section or faction among the colonists: and this persistence in domineering cost us a Canadian rebellion before we had the happy thought of giving it up. England was like an ill-brought-up elder brother, who persists in tyrannizing over the younger ones from mere habit, till one of them, by a spirited resistance, though with unequal strength, gives him notice to desist. We were wise enough not to require a second warning. A new era in the colonial policy of nations began with Lord Durham's Report; the imperishable memorial of that nobleman's courage, patriotism, and enlightened liberality, and of the intellect and practical sagacity of its joint authors, Mr. Wakefield and the lamented Charles Buller.[1]

It is now a fixed principle of the policy of Great Britain, professed in theory and faithfully adhered to in practice, that her colonies of European race, equally with the parent country, possess the fullest measure of internal self-government. They have been allowed to make their own free representative constitutions by altering in any manner they thought fit the already very popular constitutions which we had given them. Each is governed by its own legislature and executive, constituted on highly democratic principles. The veto of the Crown and of Parliament, though nominally reserved, is only exercised (and that very rarely) on questions which concern

[1] I am speaking here of the *adoption* of this improved policy, not, of course, of its original suggestion. The honor of having been its earliest champion belongs unquestionably to Mr. Roebuck. [Reference here is to the "Report on the Affairs of British North America," which the Earl of Durham (1792-1840) presented to parliament in 1839 as a justification of his colonial policy in Canada. The opposition to this policy in England had led him to resign his post of special commissioner in Canada. Edward Gibbon Wakefield (1796-1862) and Charles Buller (1806-1848) were his assistants and probably coauthors of his "Report."]

the empire, and not solely the particular colony. How liberal a construction has been given to the distinction between imperial and colonial questions is shown by the fact that the whole of the unappropriated lands in the regions behind our American and Australian colonies have been given up to the uncontrolled disposal of the colonial communities, though they might, without injustice, have been kept in the hands of the Imperial Government, to be administered for the greatest advantage of future emigrants from all parts of the empire. Every colony has thus as full power over its own affairs as it could have if it were a member of even the loosest federation; and much fuller than would belong to it under the Constitution of the United States, being free even to tax at its pleasure the commodities imported from the mother country. Their union with Great Britain is the slightest kind of federal union; but not a strictly equal federation, the mother country retaining to itself the powers of a federal government, though reduced in practice to their very narrowest limits. This inequality is, of course, as far as it goes, a disadvantage to the dependencies, which have no voice in foreign policy, but are bound by the decisions of the superior country. They are compelled to join England in war without being in any way consulted previous to engaging in it.

Those (now happily not a few) who think that justice is as binding on communities as it is on individuals, and that men are not warranted in doing to other countries, for the supposed benefit of their own country, what they would not be justified in doing to other men for their own benefit—feel even this limited amount of constitutional subordination on the part of the colonies to be a violation of principle and have often occupied themselves in looking out for means by which it may be avoided. With this view it has been proposed by some that the colonies should return representatives to the British legislature; and by others, that the powers of our own, as well as of their Parliaments, should be confined to internal policy, and that there should be another representative body for foreign and imperial concerns in which last the dependencies of Great Britain should be represented in the same manner, and with the same completeness, as Great Britain itself. On this system there would be a perfectly equal federation between the mother country and her colonies, then no longer dependencies.

The feelings of equity, and conceptions of public morality, from which these suggestions emanate are worthy of all praise; but the suggestions themselves are so inconsistent with rational principles of government that it is doubtful if they have been seriously accepted as a possibility by any reasonable thinker. Countries separated by half the globe do not present the natural conditions for being under one government, or even members of one federation. If they had sufficiently the same interests, they have not, and never can have, a sufficient habit of taking counsel together. They are not part of the same public; they do not discuss and deliberate in the same arena, but apart, and have only a most imperfect knowledge of what passes in the minds of one another. They neither know each other's objects, nor have confidence in each other's principles of conduct. Let any Englishman ask himself how he should like his destinies to depend on an assembly of which one-third was British American, and another third South African and Australian. Yet to this it must come if there were anything like fair or equal representation; and would not everyone feel that the representatives of Canada and Australia, even in matters of an imperial character, could not know, or feel any sufficient concern for, the interests, opinions, or wishes of English, Irish, and Scotch? Even for strictly federative purposes the conditions do not exist which we have seen to be essential to a federation. England is sufficient for her own protection without the colonies, and would be in a much stronger, as well as more dignified, position if separated from them than when reduced to be a single member of an American, African, and Australian confederation. Over and above the commerce which she might equally enjoy after separation, England derives little advantage, except in prestige, from her dependencies; and the little she does derive is quite outweighed by the expense they cost her, and the dissemination they necessitate of her naval and military force, which in case of war, or any real apprehension of it, requires to be double or treble what would be needed for the defense of this country alone.

But though Great Britain could do perfectly well without her colonies, and though on every principle of morality and justice she ought to consent to their separation should the time come when, after full trial of the best form of union, they deliberately desire to be dissevered—there are strong reasons for maintaining the present slight bond of connection so long as not disagreeable to the feelings of either party. It is a step, as far as it goes, toward universal peace and general friendly co-operation among nations. It renders war impossible among a large number of otherwise independent communities, and, moreover, hinders any of them from being absorbed into a foreign state, and becoming a source of additional aggressive strength to some rival power, either more despotic or closer at hand, which might not always be so unambitious or so pacific as Great Britain. It at least keeps the markets of the different countries open to one another and prevents that mutual exclusion by hostile tariffs which none of the great communities of mankind, except England, have yet completely outgrown. And in the case of the British possessions it has the advantage, especially valuable at the present time, of adding to the moral influence and weight in the councils of the world, of the power which, of all in existence, best understands liberty —and whatever may have been its errors in the past has attained to more of conscience and moral principle in its dealings with foreigners than any other great nation seems either to conceive as possible or recognize as desirable. Since, then, the union can only continue, while it does continue, on the footing of an unequal federation, it is important to consider by what means this small amount of inequality can be prevented from being either onerous or humiliating to the communities occupying the less exalted position.

The only inferiority necessarily inherent in the case is that the mother country decides, both for the colonies and for herself, on questions of peace and war. They gain, in return, the obligation on the mother country to repel aggressions directed against them; but, except when the minor community is so weak that the protection of a stronger power is indispensable to it, reciprocity of obligation is not a full equivalent for nonadmission to a voice in the deliberations. It is essential, therefore, that in all wars, save those which, like the Kaffir or New Zealand wars, are incurred for the sake of the particular colony, the colonists should not (without their own voluntary request) be called on to contribute anything to the expense, except what may be required for the specific local defense of their own ports, shores, and frontiers against invasion. Moreover, as the mother country claims the privilege, at her sole discretion, of taking measures or pursuing a policy which may expose them to attack, it is just that she should undertake a considerable portion of the cost of their military defense even in time of peace; the whole of it, so far as it depends upon a standing army.

But there is a means, still more effectual than these, by which, and in general by which alone, a full equivalent can be given to a smaller community for sinking its individuality as a substantive power among nations in the greater individuality of a wide and powerful empire. This one indispensable and, at the same time, sufficient expedient, which meets at once the demands of justice and the growing exigencies of policy, is to open the service of Government in all its departments, and in every part of the empire, on perfectly equal terms to the inhabitants of the colonies. Why does no one ever hear a breath of disloyalty from the Islands in the British Channel? By race, religion, and geographical position they belong less to England than to France. But while they enjoy, like Canada and New South Wales, complete control over their internal affairs and their taxation, every office or dignity in the gift of the Crown is freely open to the native of Guernsey or Jersey. Generals, admirals, peers of the United Kingdom are made, and there is nothing which hinders prime ministers to be made, from those insignificant islands. The same system was commenced in reference to the colonies generally by an enlightened Colonial Secretary, too early lost, Sir William Molesworth, when he appointed Mr. Hinckes, a leading Canadian politician, to a West Indian government. It is a very shallow view of the springs of political action in a community which thinks such things unimportant because the number of those in a position actually to profit by the concession might not be very considerable. That limited number would be composed precisely of those who have most moral power over the rest; and men are not so destitute of the sense of collective degradation as not to feel the withholding of an advantage from even one person because of a circumstance which they all have in common with him, an affront to all. If we prevent the leading men of a community from standing forth to the world as its chiefs and representatives in the general councils of mankind, we owe it both to their legitimate ambition, and to the just pride of the community, to give them in return an equal chance of occupying the same prominent position in a nation of greater power and importance.

Thus far of the dependencies whose population is in a sufficiently advanced state to be fitted for representative government. But there are others which have not attained that state, and which, if held at all, must be governed by the dominant country or by persons delegated for that purpose by it. This mode of government is as legitimate as any other if it is the one which in the existing state of civilization of the subject people most facilitates their transition to a higher stage of improvement. There are, as we have already seen, conditions of society in which a vigorous despotism is in itself the best mode of government for training the people in what is specifically wanting to render them capable of a higher civilization. There are others in which the mere fact of despotism has indeed no beneficial effect, the lessons which it teaches having already been only too completely learned; but in which, there being no spring of spontaneous improvement in the people themselves, their almost only hope of making any steps in advance depends on the chances of a good despot. Under a native despotism, a good despot is a rare and transitory accident; but when the dominion they are under is that of a more civilized people, that people ought to be able to supply it constantly. The ruling country ought to be able to do for its subjects all that could be done by a succession of absolute monarchs, guaranteed by irresistible force against the precariousness of tenure attendant on barbarous despotisms, and qualified by their genius to anticipate all that experience has taught to the more advanced nation. Such is the ideal rule of a free people over a barbarous or semi-barbarous one. We need not expect to see that ideal realized; but unless some approach to it is, the rulers are guilty of a dereliction of the highest moral trust which can devolve upon a nation; and if they do not even aim at it, they are selfish usurpers, on a par in criminality with any of those whose ambition and rapacity have sported from age to age with the destiny of masses of mankind.

As it is already a common, and is rapidly tending to become the universal, condition of the more backward populations to be either held in direct subjection by the more advanced or to be under their complete political ascendancy, there are in this age of the world few more important problems than how to organize this rule so as to make it a good instead of an evil to the subject people, providing them with the best attainable present government and with the conditions most favorable to future permanent improvement. But the mode of fitting the government for this purpose is by no means so well understood as the conditions of good government in a people capable of governing themselves. We may even say that it is not understood at all.

The thing appears perfectly easy to superficial observers. If India (for example) is not fit to govern itself, all that seems to them required is that there should be a minister to govern it; and that this minister, like all other British ministers, should be responsible to the British Parliament. Unfortunately this, though the simplest mode of attempting to govern a dependency, is about the worst and betrays in its advocates a total want of comprehension of the conditions of good government. To govern a country under responsibility to the people of that country and to govern one country under responsibility to the people of another are two very different things. What makes the excellence of the first is that freedom is preferable to despotism; but the last *is* despotism. The only choice the case admits is a choice of despotisms; and it is not certain that the despotism of twenty millions is necessarily better than that of a few, or of one. But it is quite certain that the despotism of those who neither hear, nor see, nor know anything about their subjects has many chances of being worse than that of those who do. It is not usually thought that the immediate agents of authority govern better because they govern in the name of an absent master, and of one who has a thousand more pressing interests to attend to. The master may hold them to a strict responsibility, enforced by heavy penalties; but it is very questionable if those penalties will often fall in the right place.

It is always under great difficulties, and very imperfectly, that a country can be governed by foreigners, even when there is no extreme disparity in habits and ideas between the rulers and the ruled. Foreigners do not feel with the people. They cannot judge, by the light in which a thing appears to their own minds, or the manner in which it affects their feelings, how it will affect the feelings or appear to the minds of the subject population. What a native of the country, of average practical ability, knows as it were by instinct, they have to learn slowly, and after all imperfectly, by study and experience. The laws, the customs, the social relations for which they have to legislate, instead of being familiar to them from childhood, are all strange to them. For most of their detailed knowledge they must depend on the information of natives; and it is difficult for them to know whom to trust. They are feared, suspected, probably disliked by the population; seldom sought by them except for interested purposes; and they are prone to think that the servilely submissive are the trustworthy. Their danger is of despising the natives; that of the natives is of disbelieving that anything the strangers do can be intended for their good. These are but a part of the difficulties that any rulers have to struggle with who honestly attempt to govern well a country in which they are foreigners. To overcome these difficulties in any degree will always be a work of much labor, requiring a very superior degree of capacity in the chief administrators, and a high average among the subordinates; and the best organization of such a government is that which will best ensure the labor, develop the capacity, and place the highest specimens of it in the situations of greatest trust. Responsibility to an authority which has gone through none of the labor, acquired none of the capacity, and for the most part is not even aware that either, in any peculiar degree, is required, cannot be regarded as a very effectual expedient for accomplishing these ends.

The government of a people by itself has a meaning and a reality; but such a thing as government of one people by another does not and cannot exist. One people may keep another as a warren or preserve for its own use, a place to make money in, a human cattle farm to be worked for the profit of its own inhabitants. But if the good of the governed is the proper business of a government, it is utterly impossible that a people should directly attend to it. The utmost they can do is to give some of their best men a commission to look after it; to whom the opinion of their own country can neither be much of a guide in the performance of their duty, nor a competent judge of the mode in which it has been performed. Let anyone consider how the English themselves would be governed if they knew and cared no more about their own affairs than they know and care about the affairs of the Hindus. Even this comparison gives no adequate idea of the state of the case: for a people thus indifferent to politics altogether would probably be simply acquiescent and let the government alone, whereas in the case of India, a politically active people like the English, amidst habitual acquiescence, are every now and then interfering, and almost always in the wrong place. The real causes which determine the prosperity or wretchedness, the improvement or deterioration of the Hindus are too far off to be within their ken. They have not the knowledge necessary for suspecting the existence of those causes, much less for judging of their operation. The most essential interests of the country may be well administered without obtaining any of their approbation, or mismanaged to almost any excess without attracting their notice. The purposes for which they are principally tempted to interfere and control the proceedings of their delegates are of two kinds. One is to force English ideas down the throats of the natives—for instance, by measures of proselytism, or acts intentionally or unintentionally offensive to the religious feelings of the people. This misdirection of opinion in the ruling country is instructively exemplified (the more so, because nothing is meant but justice and fairness, and as much impartiality as can be expected from persons really convinced) by the demand now so general in England for having the Bible taught, at the option of pupils or of their parents, in the Government schools. From the European point of view nothing can wear a fairer aspect, or seem less open to objection on the score of religious freedom. To Asiatic eyes it is quite another thing. No Asiatic people ever believes that a government puts its paid officers and official machinery into motion unless it is bent upon an object; and when bent on an object, no Asiatic believes that any government, except a feeble and contemptible one, pursues it by halves. If Government schools and schoolmasters taught Christianity, whatever pledges might be given of teaching it only to those who spontaneously sought it, no amount of evidence would ever persuade the parents that improper means were not used to make their children Christians, or at all events, outcasts from Hinduism. If they could, in the end, be convinced of the contrary, it would only be by the entire failure of the schools, so conducted, to make any converts. If the teaching had the smallest effect in promoting its object it would compromise not only the utility and even existence of the government education, but perhaps the safety of the government itself. An English Protestant would not be easily induced, by disclaimers of proselytism, to place his children in a Roman Catholic seminary; Irish Catholics will not send their children to schools in which they can be made Protestants; and we expect that Hindus, who believe that the privileges of Hinduism can be forfeited by a merely physical act, will expose theirs to the danger of being made Christians!

Such is one of the modes in which the opinion of the dominant country tends to act more injuriously than beneficially on the conduct of its deputed governors. In other respects, its interference is likely to be oftenest exercised where it will be most pertinaciously demanded, and that is on behalf of some interest of the English settlers. English settlers have friends at home, have organs, have access to the public; they have a common language and common ideas with their countrymen; any complaint by an Englishman is more sympathetically heard, even if no unjust preference is intentionally accorded to it. Now, if there be a fact to which all experience testifies, it is that when a country holds another in subjection, the individuals of the ruling people who resort to the foreign country to make their fortunes are of all others those who most need to be held under powerful restraint. They are always one of the chief difficulties of the government. Armed with the prestige and filled with the scornful overbearingness of the conquering nation, they have the feelings inspired by absolute power without its sense of responsibility. Among a people like that of India the utmost efforts of the public authorities are not enough for the effectual protection of the weak against the strong; and of all the strong, the European settlers are the strongest. Wherever the demoralizing effect of the situation is not in a most remarkable degree corrected by the personal character of the individual, they think the people of the country mere dirt under their feet; it seems to them monstrous that any rights of the natives should stand in the way of their smallest pretensions; the simplest act of protection to the in-

habitants against any act of power on their part which they
may consider useful to their commercial objects, they de-
nounce, and sincerely regard, as an injury. So natural is this
state of feeling in a situation like theirs that even under the
discouragement which it has hitherto met with from the ruling
authorities it is impossible that more or less of the spirit
should not perpetually break out. The Government, itself
free from this spirit, is never able sufficiently to keep it down
in the young and raw even of its own civil and military officers,
over whom it has so much more control than over the independent residents. As it is with the English in India, so, according to trustworthy testimony, it is with the French in Al-
giers; so with the Americans in the countries conquered from
Mexico; so it seems to be with the Europeans in China, and
already even in Japan: there is no necessity to recall how it
was with the Spaniards in South America. In all these cases,
the government to which these private adventurers are subject
is better than they, and does the most it can to protect the
natives against them. Even the Spanish Government did this,
sincerely and earnestly, though ineffectually, as is known to
every reader of Mr. Helps' instructive history. Had the Spanish Government been directly accountable to Spanish opinion
we may question if it would have made the attempt: for the
Spaniards, doubtless, would have taken part with their Christian friends and relations rather than with pagans. The settlers, not the natives, have the ear of the public at home; it is
they whose representations are likely to pass for truth, because they alone have both the means and the motive to press
them perseveringly upon the inattentive and uninterested public mind. The distrustful criticism with which Englishmen,
more than any other people, are in the habit of scanning the
conduct of their country toward foreigners, they usually reserve for the proceedings of the public authorities. In all questions between a government and an individual the presumption in every Englishman's mind is that the government is in
the wrong. And when the resident English bring the batteries
of English political action to bear upon any of the bulwarks

erected to protect the natives against their encroachments, the executive, with their real but faint velleities of something better, generally find it safer to their parliamentary interest, and at any rate less troublesome, to give up the disputed position than to defend it.

What makes matters worse is that when the public mind is invoked (as, to its credit, the English mind is extremely open to be) in the name of justice and philanthropy, in behalf of the subject community or race, there is the same probability of its missing the mark. For in the subject community also there are oppressors and oppressed; powerful individuals or classes, and slaves prostrate before them; and it is the former, not the latter, who have the means of access to the English public. A tyrant or sensualist who has been deprived of the power he had abused and, instead of punishment, is supported in as great wealth and splendor as he ever enjoyed; a knot of privileged landholders, who demand that the State should relinquish to them its reserved right to a rent from their lands, or who resent as a wrong any attempt to protect the masses from their extortion; these have no difficulty in procuring interested or sentimental advocacy in the British Parliament and press. The silent myriads obtain none.

The preceding observations exemplify the operation of a principle—which might be called an obvious one were it not that scarcely anybody seems to be aware of it—that, while responsibility to the governed is the greatest of all securities for good government, responsibility to somebody else not only has no such tendency, but is as likely to produce evil as good. The responsibility of the British rulers of India to the British nation is chiefly useful because, when any acts of the government are called in question, it ensures publicity and discussion; the utility of which does not require that the public at large should comprehend the point at issue, provided there are any individuals among them who do; for, a merely moral responsibility not being responsibility to the collective people, but to every separate person among them who forms a judgment, opinions may be weighed as well as counted, and the approbation or disapprobation of one person well versed in the subject may outweigh that of thousands who know nothing about it at all. It is doubtless a useful restraint upon the immediate rulers that they can be put upon their defense, and that one or two of the jury will form an opinion worth having about their conduct, though that of the remainder will probably be several degrees worse than none. Such as it is, this is the amount of benefit to India from the control exercised over the Indian government by the British Parliament and people.

It is not by attempting to rule directly a country like India, but by giving it good rulers, that the English people can do their duty to that country; and they can scarcely give it a worse one than an English Cabinet Minister, who is thinking of English, not Indian politics; who seldom remains long enough in office to acquire an intelligent interest in so complicated a subject; upon whom the factitious public opinion got up in Parliament, consisting of two or three fluent speakers, acts with as much force as if it were genuine, while he is under none of the influences of training and position which would lead or qualify him to form an honest opinion of his own. A free country which attempts to govern a distant dependency, inhabited by a dissimilar people, by means of a branch of its own executive will almost inevitably fail. The only mode which has any chance of tolerable success is to govern through a delegated body of a comparatively permanent character, allowing only a right of inspection and a negative voice to the changeable Administration of the State. Such a body did exist in the case of India; and I fear that both India and England will pay a severe penalty for the shortsighted policy by which this intermediate instrument of government was done away with.

It is of no avail to say that such a delegated body cannot have all the requisites of good government; above all, cannot have that complete and ever-operative identity of interest with the governed which it is so difficult to obtain even where the people to be ruled are in some degree qualified to look after their own affairs. Real good government is not compatible with the conditions of the case. There is but a choice of imperfections. The problem is so to construct the governing body that, under the difficulties of the position, it shall have as much interest as possible in good government, and as little in bad. Now these conditions are best found in an intermediate body. A delegated administration has always this advantage over a direct one, that it has, at all events, no duty to perform except to the governed. It has no interests to consider except theirs. Its own power of deriving profit from misgovernment may be reduced—in the latest constitution of the East India Company it was reduced—to a singularly small amount: and it can be kept entirely clear of bias from the individual or class interests of anyone else. When the home government and Parliament are swayed by those partial influences in the exercise of the power reserved to them in the last resort, the intermediate body is the certain advocate and champion of the dependency before the imperial tribunal. The intermediate body, moreover, is, in the natural course of things, chiefly composed of persons who have acquired professional knowledge of this part of their country's concerns; who have been trained to it in the place itself and have made its administration the main occupation of their lives. Furnished with these qualifications, and not being liable to lose their office from the accidents of home politics, they identify their character and consideration with their special trust and have a much more permanent interest in the success of their administration and in the prosperity of the country which they administer than a member of a Cabinet under a representative constitution can possibly have in the good government of any country except the one which he serves. So far as the choice of those who carry on the management on the spot devolves upon this body, the appointments are kept out of the vortex of party and parliamentary jobbing, and freed from the influence of those motives to the abuse of patronage for the reward of adherents, or to buy off those who would otherwise be opponents, which are always stronger with statesmen of average honesty than a conscientious sense of the duty of appointing the fittest man. To put this one class of appointments as far as possible out of harm's way is of more consequence than the worst which can happen to all other offices in the state; for in every other department, if the officer is unqualified, the general opinion of the community directs him in a certain degree what to do; but in the position of the administrators of a dependency where the people are not fit to have the control in their own hands, the character of the government entirely depends on the qualifications, moral and intellectual, of the individual functionaries.

It cannot be too often repeated that in a country like India everything depends on the personal qualities and capacities of the agents of government. This truth is the cardinal principle of Indian administration. The day when it comes to be thought that the appointment of persons to situations of trust from motives of convenience, already so criminal in England, can be practiced with impunity in India will be the beginning of the decline and fall of our empire there. Even with a sincere intention of preferring the best candidate, it will not do to rely on chance for supplying fit persons. The system must be calculated to form them. It has done this hitherto; and because it has done so, our rule in India has lasted, and been one of constant, if not very rapid, improvement in prosperity and good administration. As much bitterness is now manifested against this system, and as much eagerness displayed to overthrow it, as if educating and training the officers of government for their work were a thing utterly unreasonable and indefensible, an unjustifiable interference with the rights of ignorance and inexperience. There is a tacit conspiracy between those who would like to job in first-rate Indian offices for their connections here, and those who, being already in India, claim to be promoted from the indigo factory or the attorney's office to administer justice or fix the payments due to government from millions of people. The "monopoly" of the Civil Service, so much inveighed against, is like the monopoly of judicial offices by the bar; and its abolition would be like opening the bench in Westminister Hall to the first comer whose friends certify that he has now and then looked into Blackstone.[2] Were the course ever adopted of sending men from this country or encouraging them in going out, to get themselves put into high appointments without having learned their business by passing through the lower ones, the most important offices would be thrown to Scotch cousins [3] and adventurers, connected by no professional feeling with the country or the work, held to no previous knowledge, and eager only to make money rapidly and return home. The safety of the country is that those by whom it is administered be sent out in youth, as candidates only, to begin at the bottom of the ladder, and ascend higher or not, as, after a proper interval, they are proved qualified. The defect of the East India Company's system was that though the best men were carefully sought out for the most important posts, yet if an officer remained in the service, promotion, though it might be delayed, came at last in some shape or other to the least as well as to the most competent. Even the inferior in qualifications, among such a corps of functionaries, consisted, it must be remembered, of men who had been brought up to their duties, and had fulfilled them for many years, at lowest without disgrace, under the eye and authority of a superior. But though this diminished the evil, it was nevertheless considerable. A man who never becomes fit for more than an assistant's duty should remain an assistant all his life, and his juniors should be promoted over him. With this exception, I am not aware of any real defect in the old system of Indian appointments. It had already received the greatest other improvement it was susceptible of, the choice of the original candidates by competitive examination, which, besides the advantage of recruiting from a higher grade of industry and capacity, has the recommendation that under it, unless by accident, there are no per-

2 [William Blackstone (1723-1780), famous English jurist. His *Commentaries on the Laws of England* (4 vols., 1765-69) exerted a strong influence on British and American jurisprudence.]

3 [Scotch cousin—a distant relative.]

sonal ties between the candidates for offices and those who have a voice in conferring them.

It is in no way unjust that public officers thus selected and trained should be exclusively eligible to offices which require specially Indian knowledge and experience. If any door to the higher appointments, without passing through the lower, be opened even for occasional use, there will be such incessant knocking at it by persons of influence that it will be impossible ever to keep it closed. The only excepted appointment should be the highest one of all. The Viceroy of British India should be a person selected from all Englishmen for his great general capacity for government. If he have this, he will be able to distinguish in others and turn to his own use that special knowledge and judgment in local affairs which he has not himself had the opportunity of acquiring. There are good reasons why (saving exceptional cases) the Viceroy should not be a member of the regular service. All services have, more or less, their class prejudices, from which the supreme ruler ought to be exempt. Neither are men, however able and experienced, who have passed their lives in Asia, so likely to possess the most advanced European ideas in general statesmanship; which the chief ruler should carry out with him and blend with the results of Indian experience. Again, being of a different class, and especially if chosen by a different authority, he will seldom have any personal partialities to warp his appointments to office. This great security for honest bestowal of patronage existed in rare perfection under the mixed government of the Crown and the East India Company. The supreme dispensers of office, the Governor-General and Governors, were appointed, in fact though not formally, by the Crown, that is, by the general Government, not by the intermediate body; and a great officer of the Crown probably had not a single personal or political connection in the local service, while the delegated body, most of whom had themselves served in the country, had and were likely to have such connections. This guarantee for impartiality would be much impaired if the civil servants of Government, even though sent

out in boyhood as mere candidates for employment, should
come to be furnished, in any considerable proportion, by the
class of society which supplies Viceroys and Governors. Even
the initiatory competitive examination would then be an insufficient security. It would exclude mere ignorance and incapacity; it would compel youths of family to start in the race
with the same amount of instruction and ability as other people; the stupidest son could not be put into the Indian service as
he can be into the Church; but there would be nothing to
prevent undue preference afterwards. No longer all equally
unknown and unheard of by the arbiter of their lot, a portion of the service would be personally, and a still greater
number politically, in close relation with him. Members of
certain families, and of the higher classes and influential connections generally, would rise more rapidly than their competitors, and be often kept in situations for which they were
unfit or placed in those for which others were fitter. The same
influences would be brought into play which affect promotions
in the army; and those alone, if such miracles of simplicity
there be, who believe that these are impartial, would expect
impartiality in those of India. This evil is, I fear, irremediable
by any general measures which can be taken under the present
system. No such will afford a degree of security comparable to
that which once flowed spontaneously from the so-called double government.

What is accounted so great an advantage in the case of the
English system of government at home has been its misfortune in India—that it grew up of itself, not from preconceived
design, but by successive expedients and by the adaptation of
machinery originally created for a different purpose. As the
country on which its maintenance depended was not the one
out of whose necessities it grew, its practical benefits did not
come home to the mind of that country, and it would have
required theoretic recommendations to render it acceptable.
Unfortunately, these were exactly what it seemed to be destitute of; and undoubtedly the common theories of government did not furnish it with such, framed as those theories

have been for states of circumstances differing in all the most important features from the case concerned. But in government, as in other departments of human agency, almost all principles which have been durable were first suggested by observation of some particular case in which the general laws of nature acted in some new or previously unnoticed combination of circumstances. The institutions of Great Britain, and those of the United States, have had the distinction of suggesting most of the theories of government which, through good and evil fortune, are now, in the course of generations, reawakening political life in the nations of Europe. It has been the destiny of the government of the East India Company to suggest the true theory of the government of a semi-barbarous dependency by a civilized country and, after having done this, to perish. It would be a singular fortune if, at the end of two or three more generations, this speculative result should be the only remaining fruit of our ascendancy in India; if posterity should say of us that, having stumbled accidentally upon better arrangements than our wisdom would ever have devised, the first use we made of our awakened reason was to destroy them, and allow the good which had been in course of being realized to fall through and be lost, from ignorance of the principles on which it depended. *Di meliora;* but if a fate so disgraceful to England and to civilization can be averted, it must be through far wider political conceptions than merely English or European practice can supply, and through a much more profound study of Indian experience and of the conditions of Indian government than either English politicians, or those who supply the English public with opinions, have hitherto shown any willingness to undertake.

THE END

BIOGRAPHICAL INDEX

ALCIBIADES (*c.* 450-404 B.C.), Athenian general and statesman. He was brought up by his guardian Pericles and became a close friend of Socrates. He participated in the Sicilian expedition of 415-413.

ALEXANDER THE GREAT (356-323 B.C.), son of Philip of Macedon. Educated by Aristotle, he proved himself the greatest military commander of the age, conquering all the known world as far as India in the eleven years between his succession to the throne and his death at 33.

ARANDA, PEDRO PABLO ABARCA DE BOLEA ARANDA, COUNT OF (1719-1798), Spanish statesman and general. Under Charles III he expelled the Jesuits from Spain and Spanish South America.

ARISTIDES (*c.* 520-468 B.C.), Athenian statesman and soldier. He opposed Themistocles' naval policy and was ostracized but later recalled to assist in the defense of Athens against the Persians. His death, reputedly in poverty, was popularly believed to confirm his reputation for honesty.

ARISTOPHANES (*c.* 450-*c.* 385 B.C.), the greatest and best-known Greek writer of comedies. Eleven of his plays are extant.

BAILEY, SAMUEL (1791-1870), English philosopher and economist.

BENEDICT XIV (1675-1758), pope (1740-58), reflected the spirit of the Enlightenment in his conduct of church affairs and patronage of art and literature.

BENTHAM, JEREMY (1748-1832), English philosopher and jurist. A close friend of James Mill, he greatly influenced the philosophical thinking of the younger Mill.

BLACKSTONE, WILLIAM (1723-1780), jurist and author of the famous *Commentaries on the Laws of England* (4 vols., 1765-69).

BRIGHT, JOHN (1811-1889), British statesman and reformer.

BULLER, CHARLES (1806-1848), British colonial statesman, collaborator in the preparation of the Durham Report with Edward Gibbon Wakefield.

CAESAR, GAIUS JULIUS (*c.* 100-44 B.C.), Roman general, statesman, dictator, and author, the outstanding figure in Roman history not only for the diversity of his genius but especially for his role in the transition from the republican to the imperial regime inaugurated by his heir Augustus.

CAPET, HUGH (*c.* 940-996), became king of France in 987, thus founding the Capetian dynasty which survived, in its collateral lines, to the 19th century.

CATHERINE II (1729-1796), the Great, Empress of Russia (1762-96). She affected the spirit of the Enlightenment, gained large territories by conquest, but did nothing to alleviate the increasing misery of her subjects.

CHARLEMAGNE (c. 742-814), king of the Franks (768-814) and Emperor of the West (800-814). He was a wise ruler who expertly organized and administered his vast empire, founded schools, and furthered Christianity.

CHATHAM: see PITT.

CLEMENT XIV (1705-1774), pope (1769-74) who in 1773 suppressed the Jesuit order to pacify the Catholic rulers of Europe.

CLEON (d. 422 B.C.), Athenian statesman and general, successor of Pericles as leader of the popular party.

CLIVE, ROBERT, BARON CLIVE OF PLASSEY (1725-1774), British general and statesman, founder of the empire of British India.

COLBERT, JEAN BAPTISTE (1619-1683), French statesman who brought order into the chaotic financial administration of France. Most notable were his improvements in industry and commerce. He was the most important representative of French mercantilism, also known as Colbertism.

COLERIDGE, SAMUEL TAYLOR (1772-1834), English poet, critic,

and philosopher. He was an intimate friend of William Wordsworth.

DEMOSTHENES (384-322 B.C.), the greatest orator of ancient Athens. He roused the Athenians to the danger of Philip of Macedon and devoted most of his life to fighting the Macedonians in his orations. After the defeat of the Greek army by Antipater he poisoned himself in order to avoid capture.

DISRAELI, BENJAMIN, EARL OF BEACONSFIELD (1804-1881), British prime minister under Queen Victoria whose special confidence he enjoyed. Under his leadership the Tory party championed a program of domestic reform and imperial expansion.

DURHAM, JOHN GEORGE LAMBTON, EARL OF (1792-1840), English statesman and special commissioner in Canada. He wrote his "Report on the Affairs of British North America" to justify his much-criticized colonial policy.

EDWARD II (1284-1327), king of England (1307-27). Defeated in Scotland and dominated by his powerful barons, Edward was finally imprisoned, forced to abdicate, and murdered.

ELIZABETH I (1533-1603), queen of England (1558-1603). Though religious controversy and the question of her legitimacy at first endangered her throne, she succeeded in establishing her authority firmly. Her reign saw a brilliant flowering of English civilization.

FREDERICK II (1712-1786), the Great, king of Prussia (1740-86). The greatest soldier of his age, he was also the leading representative of "enlightened despotism." Military requirements compelled him to impose a relatively efficient, highly centralized, and thoroughly honest administration on his kingdom.

GANGANELLI: see CLEMENT XIV.

GUSTAVUS II (GUSTAVUS ADOLPHUS, 1594-1632), king of Sweden (1611-32). A great soldier, he carried Swedish power into the heart of Europe, championing the Protestant cause in the Thirty Years' War. He was killed at the battle of Lützen.

HENRY III (1207-1272), king of England (1216-72). Various factions during his reign strove for control of the kingdom. In 1258 the barons made him accept the Provisions of Oxford, a number of reforms which curtailed the king's power.

HENRY IV (1553-1610), king of France (1589-1610), first of the Bourbon line. Brought up as a Protestant, he became a Catholic in 1593 to secure his throne. By the Edict of Nantes (1598) he granted partial religious toleration to Protestants. He was assassinated by a religious fanatic.

HILL, SIR ROWLAND (1795-1879), English administrator and educationist, reformer of the postal system.

HYPERBOLUS (d. 411 B.C.), Athenian demagogue who became the leader of the war party after the death of Cleon. He was ostracized in 417 and later murdered.

THOMAS JEFFERSON (1743-1826), third president of the United States (1801-09) and the leading interpreter of the democratic and humanitarian ideals of the new republic.

JOHN (1167?-1216), king of England (1199-1216) whose reign was beset by three struggles: with Philip Augustus of France, which resulted in John's defeat and the French conquest of Normandy; with Pope Innocent III, from which he emerged as the Pope's vassal; and with his barons, which ended in John's signing of Magna Carta in 1215.

JOSEPH II (1741-1790), Holy Roman Emperor (1765-90), coregent with his mother, Maria Theresa (1765-80), and ruler of the Hapsburg dominions (1780-90). One of the "enlightened despots," he published an edict of religious toleration (1781) and restricted the rule of the Catholic Church.

LEOPOLD II (1747-1792), Grand Duke of Tuscany (1765-1790), ruler of the Hapsburg dominions and Holy Roman Emperor (1790-92). His administration of Tuscany placed him among the enlightened reformers of the century; he was less successful as emperor, in which office he succeeded his brother, Joseph II.

LOUIS XIV (1638-1715), king of France (1643-1715), built up a thoroughly personal and absolute system of government. In 1685 he revoked the Edict of Nantes which led to the emigration of French Protestants. Under his reign French court life reached an unsurpassed splendor and became the model for all the courts of Europe.

LUTHER, MARTIN (1483-1546), German religious reformer. An Augustinian monk, his posting of the famous 95 theses on the cathedral door in Wittenberg in 1517 marked the beginning of the Protestant Reformation.

NICIAS (c. 470-413 B.C.), Athenian politician and general, political opponent of Cleon and Alcibiades. A leader of the Sicilian expedition of 415-413, he was captured by the Syracusans and executed.

PEEL, SIR ROBERT (1788-1850), British prime minister (1834-35, 1841-46) who achieved notable reforms, particularly in the areas of civil liberty, financial administration, and regulation of foreign commerce.

PERICLES (c. 495-429 B.C.), leading Athenian statesman in the years of Athens' greatest preeminence as a center of culture and a military power.

PETER I (1672-1725), the Great, Tsar of Russia (1682-1725) noted for his strenuous efforts to westernize his backward country.

PITT, WILLIAM, EARL OF CHATHAM (1708-1778), "the Elder," British prime minister during the Seven Years War in which Britain wrested much of her colonial empire from France.

PITT, WILLIAM (1759-1806), "the Younger," British prime minister at 25, became Napoleon's most resolute enemy, organizing and supporting with subsidies three European coalitions against France.

PITTACUS (c. 650-570 B.C.) of Mytilene in Lesbos, statesman and sage. He instituted important popular social reforms.

POMBAL, SEBASTIÃO JOSÉ DE CARVALHO, E MELLO, MARQUESS OF (1699-1782), Portuguese statesman whose conduct of the country's economic and imperial affairs was typical of the statecraft of the Enlightenment.

RÉMUSAT, CHARLES FRANÇOIS MARIE, COMTE DE (1797-1875), French politician and writer.

RICHELIEU, ARMAND JEAN DU PLESSIS, DUC DE (1585-1642), French statesman and cardinal. Chief minister to Louis XIII, he firmly established the royal power over feudal and religious factions. In the Thirty Years' War he fought with the Protestant powers against France's inveterate enemy, the Hapsburgs.

ROEBUCK, JOHN ARTHUR (1801-1879), British politician.

RUSSELL, JOHN, 1ST EARL RUSSELL (1792-1878), British statesman, prime minister 1846-52.

SAINT-SIMON, CLAUDE HENRI DE ROUVROY, COMTE DE (1760-1825), French social philosopher. He envisioned a hierarchical industrial state in which every man was placed and rewarded according to his productivity.

SOLON (c. 640-560 B.C.), Athenian statesman. He accomplished important social and legal reforms. His exemplary statesmanship has made the name of Solon a synonym for lawgiver.

SULLY, MAXIMILIEN DE BÉTHUNE, DUC DE (1560-1641), French statesman, finance minister under Henry IV, who replenished the treasury after many years of civil war and promoted commerce and agriculture.

THEMISTOCLES (c. 528-c. 462 B.C.), Athenian statesman and general. He persuaded the Athenians to build a powerful fleet which he commanded in the victory over the Persians at Salamis (480 B.C.).

THERAMENES (b. c. 455 B.C.), Athenian statesman and general.

TOCQUEVILLE, ALEXIS DE (1805-1859), French writer and statesman, author of La Démocratie en Amérique (2 vols., 1835, 1840), one of the most penetrating studies of the American political system by a foreign writer.

VAUBAN, SÉBASTIEN LE PRESTRE, MARQUIS DE (1633-1707), French military engineer noted for his system of fortifications.

WAKEFIELD, EDWARD GIBBON (1796-1862), British colonial statesman, coauthor, with Charles Buller, of the Durham Report.

WASHINGTON, GEORGE (1732-1799), first president of the United States (1789-97).

WELLESLEY, ARTHUR, 1ST DUKE OF WELLINGTON (1769-1852), British general who, together with the Prussian army under General Blücher, defeated Napoleon in the Waterloo campaign (1815).

WILLIAM I (1533-1584), "the Silent," Prince of Orange, led the Dutch rebellion against Spain and became first stadholder of the new republic.

WILLIAM III (1650-1702), Prince of Orange and joint British sovereign with Mary II (1689-1702), who led the European coalition against Louis XIV.